T·H·E
Chicago Sports
Barroom Analyst
FOR THE ULTIMATE FANATIC

T · H · E
Chicago Sports Barroom Analyst
FOR THE ULTIMATE FANATIC

BOB LOGAN

CB
CONTEMPORARY
BOOKS
CHICAGO · NEW YORK

Published by Contemporary Books, Inc.
180 North Michigan Avenue, Chicago, Illinois 60601
Manufactured in the United States of America
International Standard Book Number: 0-8092-4720-8

Published simultaneously in Canada by Beaverbooks, Ltd.
195 Allstate Parkway, Valleywood Business Park
Markham, Ontario L3R 4T8 Canada

This book is for Larry Donald, publisher of *Basketball Times* and *Baseball Bulletin*; Joe Gilmartin, sports editor of the *Phoenix Gazette*; Bill Halls of the *Detroit News*; and the late Dick Mackey of the *Kansas City Star* and George Cunningham of the *Atlanta Constitution*. All of them would have been great Chicago newspaper guys. It's also for Dave Moylan of the *Los Angeles Times*, who was a great Chicago editor, and Shari Lesser Wenk of Contemporary Books, who is a great Chicago editor.

CONTENTS

CONTENTS

PREFACE

When I came to Chicago in 1961, it was a four-newspaper town. Newspapers are the best reflection of a city and its personality. As soon as I read the *Tribune, Sun-Times, Daily News,* and *Chicago's American* (later *Chicago Today*) for the first time, I knew this was the right place for me.

Now that I've rounded the quarter-century bend, heading for the 30-year pole as a *Tribune* sportswriter, I still get the same kick out of Chicago's people, sports, politics, controversies, beauty, and ugliness. If you can't get excited about something going on here every day, lie down—you're dead.

This book is one man's reflections on the Chicago sporting scene, not an all-encompassing picture. I know you long-suffering fans love to argue about your teams, so if I happen to wander into your friendly neighborhood saloon, include me in. I'll even buy the first round.

—Bob Logan

ONE

CHICAGO—HOW SWEETNESS IT IS

The Superstars

Maybe Chicago lacks a hall closet where we stash our Stanley Cups, World Series rings, and similar hardware. So what? This city has almost everything else, especially the ability to bounce back from disappointment and to keep hoping. It comes from years of practice.

What we do have is a galaxy of superstars, from Cap Anson in the 1870s to Michael Jordan in the 1980s. These larger-than-life heroes have given Chicago fans enough thrills to atone, at least somewhat, for those pennant race foldups, playoff chokeups, and countless other twists of fate.

Still Payton the Town Red

"Payton shakes off another tackler!" Wayne Larrivee shrieks. "He's in the open!" The 10, the 5—touchdown, Walter! The Bears are in Super Bowl XXIII!"

Fantasy? Wishful thinking? Probably. Walter Payton has gained his 17,358th and last yard for the Bears and scored the last of his touchdowns in regular-season and playoff games. Sweetness is a memory of his 13 years of power and grace gone with the icy wind off Lake Michigan. Or is it?

1

"If the Bears needed help and I knew I could, I'd go back," Walter said.

Sure, it's a longshot. Physically, Payton could go back to Platteville with the zest of a rookie and maybe even regain his starting job. It was the mental pain of knowing he's a step slower that made Payton cry in the middle of his last season, and it will make him think hard before trying one more time to rekindle the old flame.

Anyway, running back Payton shouldn't have to. Mogul Payton, now on the Bears' Board of Directors, or even future NFL owner Payton, belongs in the spotlight now. How much can one man give one team and one city? Besides, Walter already has colors picked out for his NFL franchise: navy, light blue, and white.

"Here's the best football player ever," said his coach, Mike Ditka. Elsewhere in Chicago, short-memoried fans were snarling, "So what's Payton done for us lately? He's washed up."

The bitter disappointment of failing to make it back to the Super Bowl for the second straight time was tough for the Bears to handle. For their fans, it was even tougher. How tough?

Well, some of them even criticized Walter Payton. True, Sweetness made the critical goal-line fumble that opened the floodgates for the Washington Redskins' 27–13 upset over the Bears in their 1987 first-round NFL playoff game. It was Payton's sixth fumble in his last seven games, but this one was the heartbreaker that turned Bearmania into un-bearable defeat.

Even so, the sound of Bear fans rapping Walter Payton was as shocking as the thought of a Chicago alderman criti-cizing the late Mayor Richard J. Daley. Payton, stunned by the uproar, fell out of character by complaining that his blockers "let the Redskin defense get to me almost as soon as the ball did." Then came the rumors, and before long, both Payton and his wife, Connie, were angrily denying that they had separated. In 13 record-shattering Bear seasons, this was the first time that Walter Payton had been on the griddle.

The whole unhappy aftermath of those two shattering

Bear fans won't forget Walter Payton's high stepping strut into the end zone. Sweetness does it again for a Soldier Field touchdown against the Cleveland Browns.

playoff losses was, in some strange fashion, a kind of tribute to Payton. Only a superstar of his stature could have drawn that kind of angry response from fans who had idolized him—and still do. Walter's brief spell as designated scapegoat ended quickly, and Bear fans resumed tracking the records set on every carry by this incredible running back.

That's as it should be. Of all the thousands of athletes who have played on Chicago's pro teams, nobody symbolizes Chicago more than Walter Payton.

"When people tell me it's a shame I didn't get to go to the Super Bowl every other year with the Steelers or the Cowboys, I don't agree," Payton said. "I'm a Chicago Bear and I always will be."

Even when the Bears were mired in mediocrity during his first decade, Payton was a Bear in the mold of Gale Sayers, Red Grange, Bronko Nagurski, George McAfee, Beattie Feathers, Willie Galimore, and Rick Casares. Now that he's eclipsed them all, Payton and Chicago are linked as naturally as Payton and the Bears. His feats have made him, without question, the greatest athlete in Chicago sports history. Despite the way the word "great" has been twisted into meaninglessness by TV sports shills, Payton is great no matter how you measure him, even at the end of his career.

It's all the more remarkable that 12 years of Chicago stardom passed before Payton drew a measurable amount of criticism. Keeping his image untarnished for so long is a remarkable tribute, especially to a man who lists his hobby as "privacy." Even Payton's petulance about not scoring a touchdown in the Bears' 46–10 Super Bowl romp over New England didn't seem to bother most fans. A rare postgame glimpse of Sweetness scowling in victory merely added a gossipy footnote to the general jubilation.

The 5'11", 205-pound superstar from Columbia, Mississippi, has done it by sticking his neck out in Chicago. We've all watched Walter fretting quietly on the sidelines in the closing minutes, champing at the bit to get back in the game and rack up more yardage. He didn't become the NFL's all-time leading ground gainer by being reluctant to tuck the football under his arm and take off. Somehow, Payton avoided the Big Hit and the career-threatening injuries, perhaps because all three of his Bear coaches—Jack Pardee, Neill Armstrong, and Mike Ditka—shared the sensible notion that their indispensable man should be yanked out of harm's way whenever possible.

Payton still grumbled when Ditka gave him the hook to protect his aging legs. The big difference was that since No. 34 broke Jim Brown's career rushing record of 12,312 yards in 1984, all eyes were on him all the time. Payton had gained the kind of nationwide fame and adulation few Southern black kids could have dreamed about before Sweetness made it happen.

And how he did it: by scoring 110 touchdowns rushing and 15 on passes in 190 regular season games, seven playoff games, and one Super Bowl. His all-time ground-gaining record stands at 16,726 yards. Total career yardage: 21,933.

Loss of privacy is part of the price tag for Payton's $10 million annuity, guaranteeing him $240,000 a year until 2027, when he'll be 73 years old. That new contract, signed in 1984, ended Payton's half-hearted flirtation with the United States Football League. He got another million-plus bundle in 1987. For once, the notoriously nickel-nursing Bears paid up, learning a lesson from the disaster that hit the Blackhawks after they let Bobby Hull get away by refusing to give him a well-earned $250,000 yearly paycheck.

You didn't hear anyone in Chicago complaining about Payton's payday. "I didn't realize how much people loved Walter until we went to a concert a few years ago," said Connie Payton. "They introduced him, and the place went crazy. People kept jumping up all night to take pictures of him."

Payton prefers not to talk about those things, or about the other side of the coin. He would rather be home in Barrington, the northwest suburb where he built a $2 million showplace for Connie, their son, Jarrett, and their daughter, Brittney. He won't comment on the persistent rumor that an exclusive golf club blackballed his bid for membership.

Payton has a defense mechanism that shields him from such controversy: a wicked sense of humor that kept teammates loose and disarmed would-be interrogators.

Whenever a loud noise rumbled through the corridors of Halas Hall in Lake Forest, Walter was the chief suspect. He once figured out how to delay the boom from one of his government surplus M-80 antirodent bombs long enough to make a clean getaway. By the time it went off, Payton was sitting in a meeting room, wearing a look of innocence.

"If Walter's not planting one of those things in somebody's locker, he's goosing you or coating the doughnuts with paraffin," said defensive back Gary Fencik.

Such antics enabled Payton to stay within himself, where he's most comfortable, while providing an outlet for his restless energy. Mapping Walter's daily travels through the Bears' Halas Hall headquarters provides an insight into that astonishing energy level. His first love is drumming, and the beat goes on in constant motion.

If a sportswriter reached for a beer in the downstairs pressroom, Payton would pop his head in the door to say, "Diet soda's not fattening," and was gone before his victim could turn around. If the telephone operator took a break, Payton manned the headset to field calls: "Payton? Not here yet. Those so-called superstars are always late."

Onlookers chuckled while Walter slipped away to plot his next caper. Somehow, he still found time to run his private hill, bench-press close to 400 pounds, and start every game, ready to gain the big yards when the Bears needed them. After adding a few more entries to the record book, he shrugged off a new batch of "living legend" queries from the media mob, then hung it up to await his berth in the Pro Football Hall of Fame and become an NFL owner. Why not? He already owns Chicago.

Ryno's Charging to Cooperstown

Ryne Sandberg emerged from obscurity to superstardom by dragging the Cubs by the scruff of the neck from mediocrity to respect in the National League. Ryno obviously wasn't the only reason the Cubs emerged from the NL's nether region in 1984 after lurking there for 40-odd years. But he was certainly one of the major—and most enjoyable—causes of this phenomenon.

While Sandberg showed star potential in his struggling debut with the Cubs, few imagined that he could become a superstar like the Cubs' Ernie Banks, Billy Williams, and Fergie Jenkins. But they do now. In Sandberg, the Cubs have come up with someone to match the Banks and Williams blend of Hall of Fame talent, coupled with class, dignity, and fan appeal.

Dallas Green craftily pried Ryno from Philadelphia, allegedly as a throw-in, in the 1982 deal that sent Larry Bowa to the Cubs in exchange for Ivan DeJesus. That triggered the transformation from unknown Ryne Sandberg, a Phillies' farmhand who might stick around as a utility infielder, to Ryno, the clutch artist who now ranks as one of the National League's best all-around players. Maybe it seems like something that simply had to happen, especially if you're a Cub fan.

But nobody figured it was going to happen when Sandberg came to the Cubs on January 27, 1982—not even Sandberg. "All I wanted was a chance to make it in the majors," Ryno said. "Dallas Green told me I'd get a good look at third

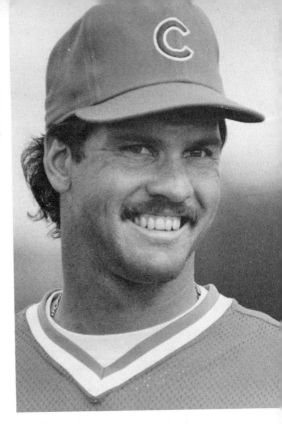

Ryne Sandberg's superstar status was confirmed by the uproar when he grew a moustache. It didn't take long for him to shave it off.

base in spring training. That was better than the situation in Philadelphia. If the Phillies thought I could be a regular, they wouldn't have traded me."

The Phillies were eager to squeeze another NL pennant out of Steve Carlton's aging arm and Mike Schmidt's still-potent bat, to go with the one that manager Dallas Green had won in 1980. With Schmidt a fixture at third base, and up-and-coming Juan Samuel at second, there was no room for Sandberg in the Philadelphia master plan. Scout Bobby Wine already had reported that Sandberg couldn't replace Larry Bowa at shortstop, a judgment that later cost Wine a chance to manage the Phillies.

Green wanted Bowa to steady the Cub infield while the new general manager tried to make his "new Tradition" more than an empty slogan. He also knew that the Phils coveted his shortstop, DeJesus. Sandberg was a fringe player in both the Cub-Phillie trade negotiations and the long-range outlook in Chicago.

"I was hoping Ryne could plug a gap in center field for us," Green said. "He could run, but nobody knew he could hit and field that consistently, until he got into the Cubs' lineup and just kept doing it."

Sandberg survived a rocky start as a rookie in 1982. He fielded everything hit his way at third base, but a 1-for-32 slump to open the season made it appear the overanxious 21-year-old wasn't ready.

The credit for coming back from that poor start belongs to Sandberg. Most rookies soon would have let that lack of base hits punch holes in their gloves. A few errors to speed up the loss of confidence and they would have been on the way out of the lineup and down to the minors, never to be heard from again. Does anyone recall Joe Strain, 1981 Cub pretender at second base? He was just one of many to strain fans' patience until Sandberg took permanent possession of the position.

"I knew the hits would begin falling in if I didn't give up," Sandberg recalls of his rough Cub debut. Ryno stuck it out with the same kind of quiet confidence that had caught the eye of Cub manager Lee Elia in spring training. If only because there was nobody else, Elia stayed with Sandberg until the rookie's bat thawed out. It didn't take long, and Sandberg has been on the upswing ever since, even after a 1987 ankle injury that could have been disastrous.

How good is Sandberg? The answer covers more ground than just his impressive statistics—even more ground than Sandberg covers in Wrigley Field. For openers, the Cubs would not have won their first National League East title in 1984 without Ryno's Gold Glove and booming bat.

It was a superhuman Sandberg showing on national television in 1984 that tuned America into the Cubs. Back-to-back homers off St. Louis relief ace Bruce Sutter capped a 5-for-6, 7-RBI day that brought the Cubs back from the dead to an incredible 12–11 triumph. The young second baseman was an overnight sensation, but he stepped into the fast lane with the same low-key stability that had brought him steadily up the ladder. Ryno, the same modest and polite kid as a hot product that he had been as a rookie, knew how to handle himself, on and off the field.

This smooth, graceful newcomer, who had turned down a scholarship to play quarterback at Washington State to gamble on a baseball career, got Cub fans excited, and the rest of the baseball world soon discovered what a burglary the Cubs had pulled on Philadelphia. Sandberg's rising star turned into a rocket, boosting the Cubs to their 97–65 1984 season. Just like 1969, the year turned from magic to tragic at the end, but heartbroken Cub fans couldn't pin the blame on Sandberg. They knew he was the major reason the ex-Flubs had snapped a 39-year stretch of North Side futility.

Sandberg's skills might yet lead to that elusive NL pennant. Along with Andre Dawson, and Rick Sutcliffe, he gives Cub boss Jim Frey a nucleus to build on, with young sluggers like Rafael Palmiero and Mark Grace.

One more intriguing spin-off accompanied Ryno's rise to fame and fortune. The handsome superstar found himself cast in the unaccustomed role of sex symbol. It was a trifle embarrassing for Sandberg, a family man who had married his Spokane, Washington, high school sweetheart, Cindy White. Still, Ryno handled it with the composure that had brought him to the top. He signed autographs and pictures, made commercials and public appearances, and even posed for a poster, short-lived mustache and all.

When the time comes for an acceptance speech at his inauguration into baseball's Hall of Fame, Ryno will deliver it with style, too. That kind of class doesn't wear out.

Bulls Fly On Air Jordan

Michael Jordan is not a one-man team—he's a one-man league. Working mini-miracles with Air Jordan's limitless talent and coach Doug Collins' bottomless desire, the Bulls actually look like contenders at times.

Unfortunately, that fantasy self-destructs when the Bulls are unmasked by a real contender. Jordan has been burning his candle at both ends of the court yearly to get them into the playoffs, but once there, he's a bull's-eye target for Bull opponents. Superhuman feats or not, he's only human. So it's just as well that Michael got a taste of triumph on his own turf, first by winning the slam jammin' jamboree in the 1988 Chicago Stadium NBA All-Star show with 40 points and MVP laurels for leading the East to a no-sweat 138–133 nod over the West.

Jordan Can't Walk on Water

After watching Michael Jordan defy the law of gravity, Bull fans figure their superstar could stroll across Lake Michigan. Although he's an avid golfer and all-around athlete, Jordan freely admits that water sports are not his bag.

"The only water I go in is where I can touch bottom," he said.

Yep, the slam dunk duke was a typical Chicago election. Atlanta's Dominique Wilkins had actually outslammed Jordan, but so what? The judges merely saved their own skins from severe gouging by outraged Bull fans. Air Jordan earned that free flight by keeping the Chicago franchise aloft all by himself.

If the National Basketball Association worked from a script, Michael Jordan would have been crated and shipped directly to the New York Knicks. There never was more of a natural for the Big Apple, the bright lights of Broadway, and the unrelenting glare of the New York media. It wouldn't even have mattered if the Knicks won or lost with Jordan. New York operates on the star system, and as a rookie in 1984–85, he rewrote the definition of superstar.

Fortunately, the Bulls had enough sense to draft the 6'6" Olympic hero and All-American from North Carolina. It was a rare coup for the Bulls, a blundering NBA franchise that has specialized in turning mismanagement into an art form. Unleashing a winner like Michael Jordan on this losing operation was more than instant help. It was overkill.

Surrounded by a collection of turkey teammates, Jordan still managed to light up dreary old Chicago Stadium with his brand of fireworks. The 1985 Rookie of the Year scored 2,313 points, and Chicago had a new hero.

Jordan has done nothing since then to dim the luster of his pro debut. On the contrary, when Michael rebounded from his injury-marred sophomore campaign with a record-shattering playoff blast of 63 points in Boston Garden on April 20, 1986, it made him an instant legend. Until then, knowl-

Michael Jordan is airborne again for one of those wham-bam-slams that brings down the Chicago Stadium roof. Air Jordan flights take off for the stratosphere in every Bulls game.

edgeable fans had been willing to compare Air Jordan with Dr. J, Julius Erving, only in classy demeanor. Let this kid do it for 10 years, they said, and he'll belong.

After that show, No. 23's place was secure. Soaring dunk shots, unstoppable moves, and basketball instinct, blended with a burning desire to win, kept his reputation growing. Not even a broken left foot, limiting him to 18 games in a depressing 1985–86 season, could quench Jordan's competitive fire. In a way, it was a shame he played at all: if he had accepted being held out for the full season, the Bulls would not have been in the playoffs, and therefore would have made the "Lucky 7" NBA draft lottery.

But Jordan simply refused to accept that verdict, blasting the Bulls "for not wanting to win" by limiting his playing time. He's the franchise, so owner Jerry Reinsdorf gave in, holding his breath every time Jordan put weight on that left foot. It held up, so the Bulls were unable to draft the center they needed so badly. With the burden on his shoulders again, Jordan responded with a record-shattering 3,041 points in 1986–87, a 37.1 average and his first NBA scoring crown.

In between spells of gaping at Michael's magic, Bulls fans had to wonder how long he could keep up the one-man barrage.

They hadn't seen anyone in a Chicago uniform playing basketball with Jordan's kind of intensity since Jerry Sloan and Norm Van Lier in the '70s. Long used to their team being mugged by such superstars as Larry Bird, Kareem Abdul-Jabbar, John Havlicek, Wilt Chamberlain, Magic Johnson, Oscar Robertson, and Jerry West, they couldn't believe their eyes. Here was a man in a Bull uniform defying gravity, galloping from baseline to baseline, making plays that seemed impossible, and turning up the decibel level by turning on the fans. Before his rookie season, such sustained electricity had been absent from the Stadium since the end of the Dick Motta era (1968–76).

Under firebrand Coach Motta, the Bulls were the bullies of the NBA, making the playoffs six straight times. Even more fun was the way Motta's Bulls made their own breaks by scrapping, clawing, and snarling for 48 minutes. On big game nights at the Stadium, when the bulldog Bulls battled against Abdul-Jabbar and the Milwaukee Bucks or Chamberlain and the Los Angeles Lakers, tension hung over the place like a blanket of fog. Win or lose, the battling Bulls sent their fans home hoarse, limp as dishrags, and almost as emotionally spent as the players.

It was a heady, if short-lived, era of sports frenzy in Chicago. Things deteriorated fast. Despite flashes of excitement, notably the sensational 1976 playoff duel won by Bill Walton and the Portland Trail Blazers over Artis Gilmore and the Bulls, it seemed the Bulls never would be able to relive those days. Less than a decade later, Michael Jordan brought the good times back.

Jordan lights up the Bulls' scene, not only at home but all over the NBA. It's hard to recall more than a half-dozen players who put the same look of anticipation on spectators' faces that Jordan does. Naturally, Chamberlain was one, along with Bill Russell and Havlicek of the Boston Celtics, plus Abdul-Jabbar, Julius Erving, Oscar Robertson, Jerry West, and the late Pete Maravich. It takes talent and showmanship to step into the NBA and join that elite company. Jordan has a surplus of both.

When it comes to all-around class, sheer magnetism, and the ability to handle the crushing burden of superstardom while presenting a positive role model to hero-worshiping kids, only Erving and Havlicek are in Jordan's league. What Air Jordan means to pro sports in general and the NBA in particular should be measured by more than the megabucks he generates in sold-out arenas, TV ratings, commercials, and other money-making ventures.

None of Chicago's superstars ever gained quicker or more complete fan acceptance than Jordan, a modest youngster from a solid, middle-class upbringing in Wilmington, North Carolina. A sensation from his first pro shot, Jordan credited his TV exposure during the 1984 Olympic Games for the fans' reaction to him. He added that playing for the Gold Medal-winning U.S. team "enabled me to display my skills better because I came to the Bulls' training camp in shape."

The fact is, staying in shape isn't a problem for Jordan. Lots of golf and a few pickup games in Chapel Hill with other ex-Carolina stars like James Worthy and Sam Perkins keep the acrobatic guard tuned up through the summer.

The real pitfall could have been the bushel baskets of cash showered on Jordan for endorsing his personal Air Jordan shoes by Nike, as well as Chevy, McDonald's, Coca-Cola, Wilson sporting goods, and a flock of other sponsors. That kind of easy money has ruined some young stars. Not Jordan. Somehow, he stayed on an even keel while the price of Air Jordan shoes soared from $64.95 into the stratosphere, because Nike couldn't keep up with demand. "Every time Michael smiles, the cash register rings," says Dick Vitale, the TV guru of America's basketball junkies. The difference is that Jordan's smile is just as genuine now that he's a multi-millionaire.

"This kid is as genuine as they come," said David Rosengard, then the Bulls' marketing director, after watching the 21-year-old rookie charm awestruck kids; sign his name (but not his phone number) for swooning women, not all of them young; deal with ad-agency types and sponsors; then cap it by playing above the rim all night for the Bulls. "He's a winner, on the court or off."

McMahon Needs His Space, Man

McMahon's McFans refuse to believe the McMiracle is over. But the trust is, the McMagic McMan failed to make the Washington Redskins disappear from the top of the Bears' hit list in the 1988 playoffs.

The biggest shock was punky QB Jim McMahon letting a quick 14–0 lead get away, then throwing two fourth-quarter interceptions in the humiliating 21–17 defeat. The only other time he saw playoff action, he took the Bears to Super Bowl XX, where they made Little McMacs out of the New England Patriots 46–10. This time, the Skins peeled off the Bears' confidence and the McMyth of McMahon's invincibility, exposing raw, bleeding egos close to the surface.

Kevin Lamb of the *Sun-Times* had the best description of what happened in the game's waning minutes, when McMahon had so often turned into Superman: "This time, he was Blooperman."

A loyal majority of Bear fans pointed out that their main McMahon was playing hurt. Others think McMahon's outside deals with Taco Bell, movie contracts, and other en-

Heeeeere's Jimmy, hamming it up with Johnny Carson on the Tonight show. Bear quarterback Jim McMahon was so hot that some fans asked "Who's that guy with McMahon?"

dorsements made football just a backdrop for the punky QB image. As always, McMahon bamboozled the media by accepting the blame for the playoff mugging ("I didn't get it done") and hinting that constant injuries would shorten his career ("Living with pain is no fun, man"). That was as close to the real McMahon as he's ever come in public.

Is he a rebel with a cause or just a talented flake? Who or what is Jim McMahon?

Everybody knows he's a superb quarterback. As good as the 1985 Bears were, they could have knocked off the Patriots in Super Bowl XX without McMahon in the lineup. But the final score would not have resembled that record-shattering 46–10, and without McMahon, the Bears wouldn't have been there, anyway.

Sure, the Bears' defense was good, and still is. But it was McMahon who finally convinced the Bears they could beat any team in the National Football League.

If there was a magic moment when that notion grabbed the Bears' collective psyche, it was in Minneapolis on September 19, 1985. The Bears were trailing the Vikings in the

Metrodome, with the whole country tuned to a Thursday edition of "Monday Night Football" on ABC. McMahon, whose string of injuries alone could have supported his doctors, was out again, this time with a balky back.

His back-up, Steve Fuller, was bottled up and the Bears trailed 17–9, midway through the third quarter when McMahon strode up to Ditka on the sidelines and told him, "It's time to make a change." A man who knows something about playing in pain himself, Ditka couldn't resist that kind of spunk.

So in came McMahon and off went the roof of Minnesota's Rollerdome. Boom! McMahon dodged a Minnesota blitz on his first play, mainly because Walter Payton stayed home to throw a saving block, and hit speedster Willie Gault with a 70-yard touchdown pass. Boom! Boom! As soon as the Bears got the ball back on an interception, McMahon's second pass was on target to Dennis McKinnon for a 25-yard scoring strike. Boom! Boom! Boom! The Bears' defensive players watched their miracle worker walk on water twice in two plays and promptly began stomping on the Vikings, too. They forced a punt, and McMahon coolly orchestrated another TD march, capping it with a 43-yard bull's-eye to McKinnon. From that moment on, the Bears were that season's team of the decade. McMahon had already been accepted as the leader of the offense, but this 33–24 triumph made him The Leader, period.

The rest of the team was the supporting cast of the Jim McMahon Show, and all the Bears knew it, including McMahon. The Bears stumbled only once after that, a 38–24 Monday night loss at Miami, which just made them madder. The confidence instilled by McMahon's Minneapolis Massacre turned the Bears from a mob with overripe potential to a team ready to bear up against any opponent.

"Jim has a unique blend of cockiness, confidence, and ability," said defensive back Gary Fencik, who saw a denful of would-be Bear quarterbacks fail in his NFL decade. "I don't know how he does it, but he's another one of the guys off the field and the boss as soon as the game starts."

Ditka resisted the urge to grab credit for McMahon's blitzkrieg, a temptation many coaches would have succumbed to. The coach's innate honesty made him confess that

McMahon was just one of those special guys who comes along maybe every 20 years or so. "I can't explain what Jim sees out there, or how he sees it," shrugged Ditka.

Even the punky QB was a trifle astonished by the way his barrage riddled the Viking defense. Now that the legend of Jim McMahon has grown larger than life, he seems incapable of awe. Not so that night. "I can't recall ever throwing three TD passes in a row, just like that," McMahon confessed. "I must have been blessed or just plain lucky."

So much for humility. That night was as much a turning point for McMahon as it was for the rest of the Bears. Goggle-eyed fans, gazing at TV screens all over Chicago, suddenly saw the superstar quarterback they'd been pining for ever since the late '40s, when George Halas let George Blanda and Bobby Layne get away after Sid Luckman and Johnny Lujack had retired. For one brief, shining moment, the Bears had future Hall of Fame quarterbacks Luckman, Layne, and Blanda grappling with Notre Dame immortal Lujack for playing time. That interlude was followed by 32 years of mediocrity at quarterback, until McMahon became the Bears' top pick and the fifth player tapped in the first round of the 1982 NFL draft.

McMahon's reputation as a flake preceded him from Brigham Young University, where he alternately broke Marc Wilson's passing records, and raised the ire of straight-laced Mormons all over Utah. Coach LaVelle Edwards used to throw McMahon out of BYU practices for cussing out 250-pound tackles or smuggling a six-pack into his locker, but Edwards had a keen eye for talent. "This guy will take some team to the Super Bowl," Edwards predicted.

That forecast wasn't based on the quarterback's physical assets, even though McMahon set 71 passing marks at Brigham Young. Scouts noted that the BYU hotshot was only 6'1", less than ideal for an NFL quarterback; that his arm was not outstanding; that he had stuck a fork in his eye as a kid and impaired his vision. Most of all, they warned, beware of his attitude.

But the new Bear coach, Mike Ditka, knew what he wanted for his first draft in 1982. Ditka had seen enough of journeymen Vince Evans, Bob Avellini, and the like. He wanted a game-breaker, and in Jim McMahon he got one who also could turn into a hell-raiser.

For openers, McMahon raised hell about his first Bear contract, complaining bitterly that he had been "coerced" into signing it before a deadline imposed by the NFL. That pact hiked McMahon's $100,000 rookie salary to $190,000 in 1984, but before long, Chicago's new sensation was in an escalating pay bracket.

Agent Steve Zucker and ill-fated Bear general manager Jerry Vainisi hammered out a contract that will keep Mad Mac in wraparound shades and six-packs for life, even if he doesn't reprise that Super Bowl XX triumph. McMahon had to settle for the paltry $190,000 in 1984, but a $500,000 signing bonus eased the pain. After that, through the 1989 season, McMahon will pull down an average of $800,000 a year.

The whole package was worth close to $5 million, with no deferred money. It's not quite up there with the $13 million-plus deals worked out for quarterbacks Dan Marino and Vinnie Testaverde a few years later, but with groups lining up to plunk $10,000 in his palm for a one-hour rap session, plus commercials, endorsements, and movie deals, he won't starve.

McMahon gave the Bears their money's worth with sensational exploits, despite leading the Blue Cross league in injuries. Because he made things happen, McMahon started 13 of 14 games in 1983, but then things began happening to him. Over the next three seasons, a broken hand, plus assorted back, kidney, buttock, and shoulder wounds benched him for 20 of 48 games.

A lacerated kidney finished McMahon in 1984, and when the Packers' Charles Martin dribbled him off the Soldier Field turf with a cheap-shot late hit on November 23, 1986, the Bear battler's career was in jeopardy. McMahon's refusal to run away from such behemoths was interpreted by some amateur shrinks as the same kind of death wish stunt-car drivers display daily. True or false, you might question his judgment, but not his guts.

It took a major-league effort by Dr. Frank Jobe, the savior of many pitchers' arms, to patch up McMahon's wrecked right shoulder. A few hours later, the impatient patient was awake and ready to take on the world again, predicting he'd be back to boogie the Bears toward more "Super Bowl Shuffles."

Once Doug Flutie was gone to New England and most of the scabs were out of the picture, the Bears attempted to put the 1987 strike behind them. And even though they never did make it to San Diego for the Super Bowl, McMahon showed that his shoulder wasn't going to hold them back. In the October 25 game against Tampa Bay, replacing Mike Tomczak in the third quarter, he completed 7 of 10 passes to come from behind for a 27–26 victory. The Punky QB was back.

"Battle Cry Sox-Cess: Harold! Harold!"

White Sox fans know Harold Baines will live up to his superstar billing soon. They're also confident that the Sox will win a World Series soon. If those events happen, chances are they'll take place in the same year.

But if only one of these longed for scenarios takes place, Baines is the odds-on favorite. After all, Pale Hose faithful have been waiting since 1917 for another World Championship banner to flutter from the Comiskey Park flagpole. Even the remnant of that hard corps of Sox Maniacs who danced in the left-field bleacher aisles through the '70s and early '80s is beginning to melt away. At first, they gyrated to the tune of Comiskey Park organist Nancy Faust's "Na-Na-Hey-Hey-Goodbye," or to the abrasive music of the spellbinding broadcast team of Harry Caray and Jimmy Piersall.

But after 15 years of adulation for Dick Allen, Oscar Gamble, Richie Zisk, Carlton Fisk, Bull Luzinski, Ron Kittle, Greg Walker, and Harold Baines, the signs draped over the outfield walls are disappearing. No more "O-O-Oh for the Long One" or "Please Deposit Baseball Here" or "Pitch at Risk to Zisk" (later changed to "Fisk"). The only chant other than prayer in Comiskey Park is the ever hopeful "Harold! Harold!" when the slender rightfielder steps to the plate with runners on base.

A horrible start to the 1987 season convinced everyone that the White Sox were not the same team that had rebounded from adversity four years earlier to stage a certified miracle on 35th Street. The Sox drooped without Baines, who sat out the first 24 games to recover from a knee injury. By then they were battling for last place in the weak American League West, with little help in sight. His knee swelled when he tried to play regularly, so Baines was relegated to designated hitter, and the Sox were designated for residency in the basement until the late-season surge that pulled them up to a fifth place finish.

Baines will never be known as Hollerin' Harold. If he had charisma to match his talent, the modest clutch hitter could probably spellbind the Chicago media and anesthetize suffering Sox fans long enough for manager Jim Fregosi to pick up the pieces. It's just that doing it is Harold's way, not talking about doing it.

And does he do it: the *Elias Baseball Analyst* cites Barnes as the only player to hit over .280 with 20 or more homers for four straight years, 1983–87. Also during those years, he was alone in batting over .320 with runners on base.

"I don't let outside influences distract my performance," Baines said while he and the rest of the Sox were preparing to start another Chicago fire on the South Side with their blazing 1983 stretch run. "As long as the owners and the manager are satisfied with my play, that's all the recognition I need. It's not my style to get all emotional and start arguing with the umpires or jumping around."

After Baines saw how Julio Cruz turned on the Comiskey crowds with a minimum of talent and a maximum of hot-doggery in the division-winning season of '83, he started to come out of his shell a little. The media swarm around his locker escalated daily as reporters jostled for a perch close enough to tune in on Harold's soft voice, describing his struggling start in life.

"My father, Lynwood Baines, worked six days a week to support us, and he kept working with a bleeding ulcer," Baines recalled. "He's my idol. Our family never was rich, but he saw to it that we got food and clothing. He taught me there are always people worse off, so it doesn't do any good to look back and wish you could change things. That's why I just let things happen and go out there every day to do what I can for the club. I don't try to hit home runs, and I couldn't teach anybody else to do it. Some people are outspoken, but I'm quiet, the way I always have been."

Harold Baines rockets another shot into the Comiskey Park bleachers. Even though their Quiet Man has yet to deliver on his superstar promise, Sox fans still bellow "Harold! Harold!"

Baines learned early that his bat could talk a language everybody understood. When Bill Veeck was living in Maryland, before he bought the White Sox for the second time, a Little League coach tipped him about a scrawny 12-year-old whose batting stroke spoke like thunder. Veeck went to see the kid and stood goggle-eyed while the left-handed swinger whacked a 400-foot homer.

Not surprisingly, Baines, instead of Paul Molitor, was Veeck's first pick in the 1977 amateur draft. He moved steadily through the minors until he came to Chicago for good in three short years. Sox fans have believed ever since that Baines would become their designated superstar, not just their designated hitter, and they have their fingers crossed for that injured knee. Can it be possible that Harold will be 28 years old in 1988, entering his ninth big-league season? More important, will he start demolishing the Comiskey Park fences before wrecking balls move in to do the job on the monument of the Old Roman, Charles A. Comiskey?

The Hull Show on Ice

It's been 16 years since Bobby Hull skated away from Chicago, and the Blackhawks have been on thin ice ever since. Even now, a mention of that magic name sends electricity flowing through the fans who remember Hull.

For a man gone so long, Hull's hold on the affection of Hawk fans is astonishing. Only a phenomenal, charismatic performer could carve such a secure niche in the hearts of Chicago's sporting buffs. Robert Marvin Hull was all that and more. He was the one and only Golden Jet.

From 1957 through 1972, Hull was the symbol of the Blackhawks, the most explosive force in the National Hockey League, and Chicago's reigning superstar. One glimpse of his blond head on the stairway leading to the rink, followed by the broad-shouldered left winger's No. 9 jersey, touched off pandemonium in the balcony.

The atmosphere on hockey nights during the Hull era was indescribable. It was mainly a sense of anticipation, because everyone knew Hull would make something happen. It was

Honest, Blackhawk fans, they really did win an NHL championship—in 1966-67. Bobby Hull (left) displays the evidence with Mayor Richard J. Daley, while Hawk owner Arthur Wirtz counts the house.

not because the Hawks were guaranteed winners. Far from it. They won just one Stanley Cup during Hull's stay.

The payoff came in 1960–61, after they fashioned a so-so 29–24–17 record during the regular season to finish third in the six-team NHL. But the Hawks came through in the playoffs, upsetting the Montreal Canadiens in a six-game semifinal, then knocking off the Detroit Red Wings, 4–2, in the Stanley showdown. This was in the days before expansion diluted the talent. Now the 21-team NHL wades through an 80-game schedule just to weed out its worst five entries from the playoff scramble.

Stan the Man for Hawk Fans

Stan Mikita, one of the best-liked Chicago athletes of his era, also was one of the most durable. For 22 years, the Czech-born center was the glue man of the Blackhawks, holding the team together through good times and bad. They won just one Stanley Cup in Stash's long career, but he was spared the fans' understandable jeers of frustration.

That was because they knew Mikita always went all out, from his early years as anchor for Ken Wharram, Ab McDonald, and Doug Mohns on the famous Scooter Line, or later when he showed younger Hawks how hockey should be played. He racked up 20-plus goals 14 times, en route to scoring 541 in the regular season and 59 more in the playoffs.

Mikita is the Hawks' all-time leader in games played (1,394), points (1,467), and assists (926). No wonder he got an emotional standing ovation in Chicago Stadium on October 19, 1980, when his No. 21 jersey was retired.

"I first put this Indian-head jersey on 22 years ago," Stan said, slipping it over his head and bringing down the house with a farewell line: "One more time won't hurt."

In the 1960s, on the other hand, even a superstar of Hull's magnitude didn't have to do it alone. The fact that the Hawks of Hull, Stan Mikita, Pierre Pilote, Ken Wharram, Moose Vasko, and Hall of Fame goalie Glenn Hall couldn't win another Stanley Cup is convincing proof of the league's strength, depth, and balance in those days. Losing did not diminish Hull's appeal, though, as proven by the fans' continuing adulation. He was bigger than Ernie Banks, bigger than Dick Butkus, bigger than anybody. It's impossible to calculate how much the Hawks cost themselves in particular and the NHL in general by letting Hull get away.

Shock waves traveled throughout the United States and Canada when Hull jumped to the newborn World Hockey

Association in 1972. Hull, who got $6,500 for his rookie season of 1957, wanted $250,000 a year to stay in Chicago, but Arthur and Bill Wirtz balked. Years later, Bill admitted what an expensive bit of penny-pinching that had turned out to be. Hull jumped to Winnipeg of the WHA for a $1 million signing bonus and a $250,000 paycheck. When the picture of Bobby beaming at the enlarged check for a million smackers flashed across TV screens, the salary structure of pro sports turned upside down. By driving Hull away, Arthur Wirtz unwittingly drove a stake through the heart of his prosperous franchise.

"The seven-year war with the WHA cost us $200 million," Bill Wirtz summed up for the bruised and battered NHL. "I saw NHL owners break down and cry in our meetings because they were almost busted. It cost us and the WHA so much that we had to form one league or go under."

As a pioneer in the uncharted territory of million-dollar player contracts, Hull never realized what trump cards he held with that unique blend of skating skill and fan magnetism. "If I'd known, I would have asked the WHA for $5 million," Bobby said years later. "The biggest mistake I was ever forced into making was leaving Chicago. I would have been a lot happier staying here.

"In the end, I didn't have a choice," the Golden Jet insisted. "The Blackhawks didn't offer a contract until the day I left for Winnipeg in 1972. Then it was too late. I'd given my word."

Actually, all Hull did was reach a handshake agreement with Ben Hatskin, owner of the Winnipeg Jets. Hatskin gambled that a player of Hull's stature could make the WHA an instant major league, eventually forcing a merger with the NHL. Time proved Hatskin right, but only because he picked the right man.

The Hawks got ample warning in a banner headline on the *Tribune* sports page: "Hull: If Winnipeg Pays, I'm Gone." They did, and he was, for the same five years at the same $250,000 that Arthur Wirtz had rejected as much too much.

"I told the WHA people to give me the money and I was theirs," Hull said. "If Billy Wirtz had been in charge of the Hawks then, it never would have happened."

Stan Mikita, Hull's longtime teammate, knew that the Golden Jet had made a breakthrough. "The salary structure Bobby established for us, Gordie Howe could have done 20 years before," Mikita said. "Howe was a superstar long before him, but Bobby was the man to stand up and do it. We all should bow down when he walks into the room."

Though Hull had no intention of reneging, he delayed burning his Chicago bridges until one vital detail had been settled. "Before I signed the Winnipeg contract, I made sure the million-dollar check was good," he confessed.

Was Hull worth such a staggering sum? Yes. Why? When he showed up on the ice, the crowd came to life. At his peak, he resembled a Greek god on skates; 195 pounds of sinew, a hockey machine capable of incredible strength and speed.

The Jet skated almost 30 miles per hour without the puck, faster than anyone in his day. His feared slap shot tore past cringing goalies at 118.3 MPH. When Hull set sail toward the net, blond locks flowing, fans went into ecstasy. The night Hull got the goal that put him ahead of Rocket Richard on the all-time NHL scoring list, there was so much bedlam you couldn't even hear the Stadium organ.

"If you hit the slap shot right, it could sail off the ice, through the exit ramp, break glass in the Hawks' office, and end up on Madison street," Hull grinned. "It kind of created mayhem."

But what really set Hull apart from other superstars was the way he responded to being public property. Swallowed up by hordes of fans whenever he left the Stadium, Hull would patiently work his way through the mob, signing autographs and smiling.

Bobby also subscribed to hockey's macho code, playing in pain with a dislocated shoulder, a broken nose (so grotesquely swollen that breathing was difficult), and countless other injuries.

"The kids today are stronger and faster than we were, but I don't think the heart and will to go out there and entertain is the way it was for us," Hull said. "I used to sling my stick and skates over my shoulder and walk to the pond in bitter cold. Then, before we could play hockey, we had to shovel the snow off the ice."

With all that going for him, it's easy to understand why the Golden Jet of the Blackhawks was—and to some hockey

Stan 'Snipes' at Magnuson

Keith Magnuson, a combative redhead, was a symbol of Blackhawk spirit throughout the 1970s. Maggie's willingness to take on NHL bullies in his Chicago policeman role endeared him to male fans, and his boyish grin captivated women.

Magnuson succeeded Eddie Johnston as the Hawks' coach in 1980, the year Stan Mikita retired. Like many young players, Maggie learned a lot from the smooth veteran, both on and off the ice.

"I have to admit Stan put one over on me," Magnuson confessed. "He said we were going snipe hunting and took me way out in the woods. Then he hung a snipe whistle around my neck and said, 'If the snipe don't come when you blow the whistle, just keep calling them.' I finally figured out he was ribbing me."

fans still is— the most popular athlete in Chicago history.

"He was revered," Mikita said.

Mr. Cub and Mr. Williams:
A Powerful Lot of Class

On the morning of May 12, 1970, it was raining.

But that afternoon, the sun shone on the North Side. The Cubs were playing the Atlanta Braves in Wrigley Field, and Ernie's Army of faithful fans was preparing to celebrate home run No. 500 on every continent.

Banks stepped up to the plate. Ball one. Strike one. The next pitch was a letter-high, inside fastball from Braves' right-hander Pat Jarvis and—boom!

Instead of the typical, towering fly ball off Banks's bat, this was a line drive to left-center, but it was high enough to clear the 11-foot barrier, topped by the newly installed wire basket.

For once, nice guys finished first. Only 5,264 spectators were in Wrigley Field to see Ernie's historic 500th home run, but the news was greeted by coast-to-coast cheers. Jack

Brickhouse hadn't even finished bellowing "Hey! Hey! Atta-boy, Ernie!" before glasses were being raised in salute in every Chicago saloon from Ray's Bleachers, just across the street, to Schaller's Pump, deep in the heart of White Sox territory.

You didn't have to be a Cub fan or a baseball fan or a sports fan to feel good about 39-year-old Ernie Banks reaching a milestone. Chicago was then, and still is, a racially divided city, but Banks and Billy Williams bridged that gap. Those Cub teammates had class that stood out in the clubhouse as much as their talent did on the field.

Fittingly enough, Williams hit a homer in the ninth to tie it, making Banks's big day a total triumph when the Cubs won in the 11th.

"I sat there on the bench and thought about it," Williams said. "That's a lot of home runs, and you have to remember that Ernie got most of them when the Cubs didn't have any other hitters in the lineup. In those days he only got one pitch to hit."

Despite their combined 904 home runs in Chicago uniforms (Banks 512, Williams 392), the two Hall of Famers never played on a Cub pennant winner. "My disappointment at not getting into a World Series was more for Cub fans," Banks said in 1985. "They deserved it. But we all had so much fun for so many years in Wrigley Field that I have enough happy memories to last a lifetime. We came close in 1969, but the Mets won that pennant. We didn't lose it. The respect and affection Cub fans showed me made me feel like a winner every day."

The failure to win a pennant couldn't change the way Ernie Banks looked at life. Neither could the extremes of reaction directed at him in a long, brilliant baseball career. First he had to dodge the racial slurs that greeted his first tour around the majors in 1953, the same kind of garbage directed at all black rookies by bigots who were still sore because Jackie Robinson had made it big despite their rancor. Then, after Banks became a superstar in his own right, he had to dodge occasional bullets from black militants, angered by Ernie's refusal to bad-mouth "Whitey"—or anybody else, for that matter.

A proud moment for Cub fans and all of Chicago. Billy Williams enters the Hall of Fame in Cooperstown, N.Y.

Banks just went his own way, leaving behind a legacy of smiles; home runs by the bushel basket; a pair of National league MVP trophies (1958, '59); some phrases for Cub fans to live by—"Let's play two today!" "The Friendly Confines," "The Cubs will shine in '69"; and above all, permanent recognition as Mr. Cub. That title still belongs to him, at least until his No. 14 is lowered from the left-field flagpole, and Williams's No. 26 from the pole in right, just before Wrigley Field is demolished.

Leo Durocher used to sneer when he said "Mr. Cub." Durocher's enormous ego couldn't handle the affection showered on Banks, so he cut him down at every turn. "Rally-killer" Durocher rasped whenever Ernie's battered knees couldn't beat a double-play relay to first. But the fans weren't fooled. They had been banking on Banks to start rallies, not kill them, long before Leo the Lion's stormy seven-year run as the Cubs' Captain Bligh

Another win-or-else type, Dallas Green, also tried to sweep Banks into the discard pile when he imported the "New Tradition" from Philadelphia in 1982. It took a while for Green to learn that some parts of the Cubs past were worth remembering, especially Ernie's mystique. When he did, the Cubs boss began to understand why Banks's personal flag deserved to be hoisted and why his 14 should be the first number to be retired.

Banks still signs autographs with the same old touch, but he's not living in the past. A moving-company executive on the West Coast, he finds time for golf, tennis, racquetball, and yoga. Yoga? Don't worry, Cub fans, Ernie has not gone Hollywood on you. He still greets Chicagoans with "The Cubs will be great in '88."

That kind of nonstop cheerfulness was not Billy Williams's bag. Hitting a baseball was, and still is. The Cubs' former batting instructor is the same soft-spoken guy he was, with the same No. 26 he wore for 16 years in Chicago. Always approachable and frank in the clubhouse, Williams often was taken for granted because his bat talked louder than he did.

On a team with such gifted conversationalists as Banks, Durocher, Ron Santo, Randy Hundley, Fergie Jenkins, and Joe Pepitone, Williams got little attention and less ink. He was not the type to point out to the writers that his day-in, day-out consistency at bat and in the field was often overlooked. When he went to the American League in 1974, Williams saw that Harold Baines was falling into the same pattern for the White Sox—hot bat, cold copy.

"I used to tell Harold that he had to speak up a little more, let the reporters and radio and TV guys know what's on his mind instead of holding it all in," Williams said. "I know how tough it was for me to answer questions when I was a young player. Maybe that's why the recognition was so late in coming for me."

It finally came, when Williams, his wife Shirley, and their

four daughters went to Cooperstown to watch the Sweet Swinger inaugurated into the Hall of Fame on July 26, 1987. Cub fans detected a grin on Williams's usually impassive face in the first-base coaching box as the big day drew near. Billy couldn't hide his delight, admitting that the overdue recognition erased a lot of frustration. "I knew it had to happen," he said, pointing to his career bag of 426 homers, 2,711 hits, .290 lifetime average, and streak of 1,117 consecutive games. "Those numbers speak for themselves."

So did that swing, but on the day of his inauguration, Billy Williams was the Quiet Man no longer.

"It's time for the doors of the front offices to open," Williams said when he accepted the plaque that made him a member of baseball's Hall of Fame in Cooperstown, N.Y. "Owners can make the difference by not looking at the color of a man's skin, but by examining his talent, knowledge and leadership." His strong stand added to the evidence that ex-Dodger vice president Al Campanis was wrong when he said "blacks don't have the necessities" to be managers or club executives.

The Cubs responded, sort of, by switching Williams from hitting instructor to part-time special consultant at a bargain basement $40,000 salary. Williams took it, hoping he'd get a chance to work his way up the Cub front office ladder. It was time for the Sweet Swinger to speak with more than his bat.

Bears' No. 50 One Up on 51?

The media milling around Halas Hall for the 1981 NFL draft didn't pay much attention to the Bears' second-round pick. Somebody named Singletary, a linebacker from Baylor. Good stats in the Southwest Conference, but he looks blubbery at 240 pounds and about an inch or so under his listed six feet. The scouts figure he's too short to make it in the NFL. That was the consensus.

It took a while to discover that Mike Singletary was a Samurai warrior reincarnate.

Three years later, he had nailed down the starting middle linebacker job by nailing ballcarriers to the ground with thunderous tackles. "The first time I heard the sound of Mike hitting somebody, I thought Dick Butkus had come out of retirement," said Jim Osborne, whose rookie season, 1972, was the next-to-last one for the great Butkus.

Singletary lacked the raw ability and mean temperament

Butkus Snacks on Refburgers

Dick Butkus's denial that he ever bit an NFL referee in the heat of combat was rebutted by Larry Csonka, premier running back of the Dolphin dynasty.

"I saw him do it," Zonk chuckled. "The referee came to the sidelines and there were tooth marks on his finger."

"How could that be?" snorted Butkus, the Bears' one-man Seven Blocks of Granite linebacker from 1965 to 1973. "I was wearing a white jersey and there was no blood on it."

---

of a Butkus, but that was all he lacked. He erased the talent gap between himself and bigger, faster linebackers with desire, dedication, and effort. The only Chicago player I've ever seen work harder than Singletary was Jerry Sloan of the Bulls. And not even Sloan, reknowned for his defensive ferocity, demolished opponents the way Singletary does. Until you've seen Singletary barrel in head first, separating blockers from runners and runners from footballs, you don't know what a great linebacker is.

Is Singletary better than Butkus? I think so. He has a lot more effect on the rest of the Bear defense. When Butkus ruled the middle with a glower from 1965 through 1973, opponents simply avoided him as much as possible to shred the easy pickings elsewhere. During the Butkus era, the Bears had a 48–70–4 record, never making the playoffs.

The first thing Butkus supporters will point to is the array of talent Singletary is surrounded with. Singletary, Otis Wilson, and Wilber Marshall could have replaced Bill George, Larry Morris, and Joe Fortunato as the best-ever set of Bear

No, that's not Red Grange, the Galloping Ghost of Illini and Bear fame. It's Dick Butkus, that galloping icewagon, returning an interception against the Green Bay Packers.

linebackers, but the Terrible Trio got blitzed by Marshall's 1988 raid on the Redskins' wampum—a $6 million hit. It's true that Samurai Mike had more to work with than Butkus did, but now his leadership will be tested again, as he calls the shots better than all except a handful of players in the regimented, coach-dominated game of pro football.

Off the field, as the team's player representative, Singletary held the team together during the emotional, futile players' strike of 1987. On the field, Singletary sparks the defense the same way quarterback Jim McMahon ignites the offense, though his methods are totally different. He inspires by example, willingness to work, and the force of his remarkable personality. McMahon specializes in pulling off big-play miracles, while Singletary has a knack for turning ordinary situations into big plays.

"I can't let up for a minute," Singletary summed up during the 1984 training camp. "Other guys have more ability than me, but nobody will try harder than me to do it right all the time. My ambition someday is to play the perfect defensive game." Singletary had a stack of videotapes on the table as he spoke. The rest of the Bears were heading out to sample what passes for nightlife in Platteville, Wisconsin, but he was going back to his room to pore over game film. No wonder defensive coach Buddy Ryan came to regard Singletary almost as a son. Before Ryan took his Super Bowl XX ring, thumbed his nose at Ditka, and left to coach the Philadelphia Eagles, Samurai had become an extension of Ryan's will on the field.

Unlike many pro athletes, Singletary does not require massive amounts of cajolery, back-patting, or ego reinforcement. He has some kind of inner strength that keeps him going straight ahead toward his goal. If the goal happens to be an enemy ballcarrier, the All-Pro linebacker gives him a ferocious jolt. Ever since Singletary knocked Kansas City running back Joe Delaney out of action with two stunning hits on November 8, 1981, no one has had any doubts about his ability.

The mental part of the game—translating Ryan's "46" defense from a complex set of symbols and notions other coaches dismissed as half-baked, into an understandable system that was practically impossible to score against—became part of Singletary as a rookie. Once the mental and physical parts came together, only a bitter contract hassle with Bears' owner Mike McCaskey stood between Singletary and destiny. It came dangerously close to a permanent walkout before Singletary negotiated his own deal with McCaskey. His 1988 salary of $900,000 puts him in the ballpark of Giants' linebacker Lawrence Taylor.

The Bears won their first Super Bowl with defensive stalwarts Todd Bell and Al Harris holding out, but they wouldn't have been there without Singletary. One player seldom makes the difference between winning or losing a championship in any sport, but Mike was the exception. Singletary was indispensable because his determination to be the best rubbed off on every Bear.

"I want perfection because I'm playing for the glory of God," he says.

Some athletes use religion as a ploy to cover up their real selves. Not Singletary. He puts his body on the line every play. That's the real man—and what a man.

Denis is No Menace;
He's the Happy Hawk

Center Denis Savard scored all four Blackhawk goals in a 1986 Chicago Stadium playoff game against the Toronto Maple Leafs. He's the only Hawk ever to do that in the NHL playoffs.

So what happened? The Hawks lost 5–4 and the Leafs raked them out of the first round with a humiliating 3–0 sweep. That's the way things have gone throughout Savard's career in Chicago. But instead of sulking about it, he's turned into a goodwill ambassador for hockey.

"Not gettng a chance to play for the Stanley Cup is tough, but I'm not the type to complain," Savard said. "A lot of people went out of their way to help me in 1980, when I was a scared rookie from Montreal, getting my first look at Chicago. Guys like Keith Brown, my first roommate on the Hawks, and Paul Ruck (veteran Hawks scorekeeper), my golf and race track buddy, made it easy to fit in here.

"Being friendly to the fans is just a way of paying back the good things that have happened to me."

Savard has given Hawk fans something to smile about while the team spun its skates in futile pursuit of Chicago's first Stanley Cup since 1961. His 300th career goal, on March 23, 1988, was accompanied by a pair of assists. That gave Dandy Denis 122 points, breaking his own Hawks' single-season record, set in 1981–82.

That's nice, but Savard's unique brand of stardom is better, stemming more from his attitude than his ability. He lets his zest for life show while zipping around NHL rinks, somehow making the game more enjoyable for the fans. It's a gift that Savvy dispenses freely, just like his pleasant smile. Only special athletes like Michael Jordan or Rick Sutcliffe—or Denis Savard—can do that. He's real people, and a real superstar.

Price Is Right on Andre Awesome

Andre Dawson is worth millions to the Cubs in morale alone. The slugger's 49 homers and 137 RBIs in his 1987 Wrigley Field debut enabled a last-place team to finish first in the entertainment league. So Cub brass deservedly took a lot of heat for dragging the superstar through arbitration to shave chump change of $115,000 from the $2 million contract he sought.

They finally saw the light—even before Wrigley Field got lights—and unlocked the safe to shell out a guaranteed $5.285 million to Dawson, plus bonus incentives. He'll get at least that much if the Cubs pick up his option in 1990. The way Ande feels about Chicago, and vice versa, his baseball life began at 32. The 1984 bleacher brigade of Gary "Sarge" Matthews deserted to join Andre's Army, and they were ready to invade San Diego in the summer of '87, when Padre pitcher Eric Show beaned their leader in Wrigley Field.

"You'd have thought I shot the President," Show marveled at the wrath of Cub fans. Dawson and Show buried the hatchet later, but the quiet outfielder couldn't conceal his emotion over the outpouring of affection for him. Suddenly, he was up there with Walter Payton and Michael Jordan as the third leg of Chicago's superstar triangle.

Andre Dawson kept quiet when Montreal fans booed him for failing to carry the Expos to a World Series on his broad back. He held his tongue even after getting French-fried in two languages after the rock-hard Olympic Stadium rug eroded his blazing speed.

Despite two knee operations in less than a year, Dawson had been tabbed in 1983 as the best all-around player in the majors by the toughest jury of them all—his peers. That meant he was supposed to produce miracles in Montreal, even though he couldn't pitch, hit, or field for the rest of the

Andre Dawson bites the dust after being beaned by Padre pitcher Eric Show. The Cub slugger got up, spit out the blood and chased Show out of Wrigley Field.

lineup. Frustrated by the Expos' string of late-season fades, *les Canadiens* made the taciturn 6'3", 195-pounder their scapegoat.

So Dawson was happy to get away from Montreal even at the cost of a half-million-dollar pay cut. He wanted Chicago because Wrigley Field's natural grass would soothe his aching knees. Andre quickly discovered that the enthusiasm of Cubs fans provided even more soothing balm for his psyche. "I get a standing ovation from the bleacher fans just for going out there to play right field," Dawson marveled. "In Montreal I had to hit a grand slam to get the crowd on its feet."

Dawson was concerned about having to prove himself all over again at the age of 32. As soon as his hot bat responded to Wrigley's sunshine and a steady diet of day games, that problem was solved. Performing like a superstar was nothing new to the veteran, but the reaction to his feats this time was a revelation.

He delivered a steady stream of clutch hits, homers, and RBIs, while performing flawlessly on defense. That enabled the Cubs to survive some early struggles at home by winning a few on the road, something even Cub contenders of the past had been unable to do. Suddenly, the memory of 1984 was back, and Chicago began to develop the first flush of that often fatal malady, pennant fever. Naturally, it couldn't last.

Through it all, Dawson kept his emotions on an even keel. If he was aware that his imposing presence deserved credit for turning the gloomy Cubs outlook around, he gave no hint. Everybody except opposing pitchers got the same courteous treatment. Dawson didn't issue daily bulletins on his feats, but he was always willing to discuss what makes him tick.

"Discipline," Andre said. "I know who I am, what I can do, and I try to play within my limits all the time. If you start to press in a clutch situation and get something extra into the swing, it cuts down the chances for success. When a single will help us just as much as a homer, I don't try to overpower the ball."

Dawson learned discipline from his grandmother and how to overcome adversity after a football injury in high school. He suffered cartilage and ligament damage to his left knee, the kind of thing that ended careers before new surgical techniques like arthroscopy were developed. Dawson learned to play and run in pain at Florida A&M after scouts waving big-time college scholarships stopped coming to his house in Miami.

Instead of becoming a megabucks choice in the first round, Dawson went in the 11th round of the 1975 amateur draft, signing for a $1,500 bonus. Two years later he was up with the Expos, drawing a bead on the contract that was to pay him $1 million for each season from 1981 through 1986. Dawson never figured that turning down Montreal's offer of

$2 million more for another two years would force him to play out 1987 in Chicago for a measly $500,000.

Many players, caught up in the ego-stroking money game, would have sulked and loafed their way through the humiliation of a 50 percent pay cut. Dawson doesn't think like that.

"I'm concentrating on doing what I can to help the Cubs every day," he said. "If you hit the ball solidly in Wrigley Field it will carry, whether the wind is blowing in or out."

Sting Superstars: Lee, Karl-Heinz, and Arno

Soccer fans in Chicago have no reason to kick. Two-thirds of the way through the 1980s, their team had booted home two championships, one more than the rest of the Windy City franchises combined. Of course, there were divisional titles, for the White Sox in 1983 and the Cubs in 1984, but after each team's playoff foldup, those trophies weren't worth much.

Maybe the real superstar of the Sting saga was owner Lee Stern. He took the same kind of punishment fate has been dealing out to all Chicago fans for too long, but instead of forking over a few bucks for the privilege, Stern got kicked hard in the wallet. The Sting played outdoors, indoors, in every soccer circuit except the Three-I League for 13 years. Except for a big gate here and there, the cash customers simply wouldn't buy the product despite the presence of two genuine superstars, Karl-Heinz Granitza and Arno Steffenhagen. The Sting's plight was summed up in the 1986–87 season, when they moved their peripatetic show from the Stadium to the Rosemont Horizon and still couldn't put enough fannies in the seats. First Sting coach Willy Roy and then all-time Sting scoring leader Granitza got the ax. At least Granitza went out in style, toasting Stern at a farewell champagne party for the veteran from West Germany.

Karl-Heinz deserved a taste of the bubbly. He played in both Sting Soccer Bowl triumphs, '81 and '84, led the team in goal-scoring for a decade with a booming, left-footed shot, and added a touch of class to the operation. Granitza could get testy, and new Sting coach Erich Geyer cited a tendency Karl-Heinz had for imitating Field Marshal Rom-

Karl-Heinz Granitza gets a kick out of booming this shot at Seattle goalie Jack Brand. Sting fans always got a boot from Karl-Heinz.

mel as an excuse to cut him loose. Others suspected a ploy to save a few deutche marks on Granitza's $60,000 salary.

Whatever the reason, Granitza refused to react with bitterness. "I'll never forget Chicago," he vowed. "This has been a marvelous experience, with a lot more ups than downs."

Granitza came to the Sting in 1978 and stuck around. Later in the same season, coach Malcolm Musgrove was fired with the Sting at 2–14 and the few remaining fans

Sting star Arno Steffenhagen (6) gets mugged by Tulsa's Chris McGrath.

tossing around a barbed question and answer. Q: "How good is your soccer team?" A: "It Stings."

So Roy took over for the second time as coach and promptly brought in Arno Steffenhagen, a member of the same Hertha Berlin Club that Granitza once played for. It was the right move. Steffenhagen's talent helped the Sting get off the deck and into the playoffs, while his flowing locks and mustache captivated the fans.

Arno may have resembled an extra from "Hall of the Mountain King," but his talent was undeniable. If only a few more fans had paid to see it.

TWO

CLOUT IS WHAT IT'S ALL ABOUT

Chicago's Heavy Hitters

O n or off the field, there are always a chosen few in the middle of the action. They are the movers and shakers, the ones who make things happen. In Chicago we say, "Dey got clout."

"Holy Cow!" Harry Can Caray A Tune (or a Team!)

Maybe we thought Harry Caray was immortal. That could be why the news of his stroke shocked Chicago. Here's a guy, past 70, putting out more energy in the broadcast booth than some players do on the field. And, then, after the game, Nightlife Harry would spring into action, playing just as hard as he worked. Younger sportswriters dropped out of his Rush Street tours, but Caray's entourage moved on to greet an endless swarm of well-wishers in a new bar, order another round for everybody in his booming, rasping voice, and pick up another tab.

I never saw Harry Caray let anybody else grab a tab, on Rush Street or off. No, he's not trying to buy goodwill. It's true that Caray is more sensitive to criticism than most people think, but he genuinely likes people. If some of them don't like him, he has no trouble finding another crowd, a new night spot, and renewed *joie de vivre*. That's the way Harry's been from the moment he came to Chicago as the new Sox broadcaster in 1971.

The adulation that greeted Harry's return to the Wrigley Field broadcast booth on May 19, 1987, after he recovered from his stroke, was proof of what had happened to his image during these eventful years in Chicago. Harry C. Carabina, 71 years old (give or take a year), has become Windy City celebrity No. 1. Along the way, Harry outshone such Windy City biggies as Leo Durocher, Mayor Richard J. Daley, Richie Allen, Dave Kingman, Jane Byrne, and the Fridge. The only Chicago media figure in Harry's league these days is the equally ebullient Oprah Winfrey.

The point is that Harry is big, as in gigantic. From a controversial White Sox baseball broadcaster, teaming with equally provocative Jimmy Piersall, he has become a sort of national spokesman for the common man and woman, especially the downtrodden baseball fan. Harry strikes some kind of chord in the vast majority of his audience, the ones he calls "my people." When Harry leans from his booth during the seventh-inning stretch in Chicago, he leads a nationwide singalong. His audience on superstation WGN-TV consists of more than Cubs fans. In 50 states, Canada, and the Caribbean, Caray has thousands of shut-ins, firefighters, teen-agers, groupies, and even punk rockers swaying to his gravelly voice.

Caray's act consists of one tune: "Take Me Out to the Ball Game." Harry bellows, "All right! Lemme hear ya!" and for the next few minutes, it's pure, unadulterated American corn. There may still be some skeptics who refuse to believe this is anything except a vaudeville act, but time has proved them wrong. There is no question that this man is a genuine American phenomenon. The fads and the overnight sensations have long since gone the way of the Hula Hoop and Doug Flutie T-shirts, but Harry keeps rolling along.

When Caray toppled over from a stroke at a Palm Springs poker table on February 17, 1987, the news struck Chicago like a thunderclap. The Cubs had suffered through two mediocre seasons since they won the National League East, so

Two of Chicago's all-time charisma kings, Harry Caray (left) and Bill Veeck talk it over in Comiskey Park before Harry took his golden tonsils to the North Side.

Harry once again was the main attraction, just as he had been with the White Sox. He was the glue that bonded a huge WGN audience to TV sets for a daily dose of daytime horsehide opera, and kept sponsors clamoring to spend megabucks for commercials.

But the fans didn't relate to the possible economic calamity. They worried about Harry and the bleak prospect of Cub telecasts without him. In a few days, Caray's hospital room was swamped with flowers, cards, telegrams, and every form of communication except smoke signals. The public's reaction was so overpowering that Harry's media rivals had to mask their feelings and go with the flow. When *Sun-Times* gossip columnist Michael Sneed tried a breezy approach to the story ("Attaboy, Harry"), she was hit with a broadside of angry calls and letters.

"Those boxes of mail pulled me through," Caray said. He had a lot to go through. The stroke had partially paralyzed his right side, distorted his face, and affected his memory. The familiar rasping voice was stilled, but the thought of when Caray could return to work—if ever—was far down the list of immediate concerns. "We didn't know if Dad would pull through," said his son Skip, baseball broadcaster on Ted Turner's Atlanta superstation.

Against all those odds, Caray bounced back in just over three months. It was nothing less than a triumphal homecoming when the svelte broadcaster walked up the winding concrete ramps to his TV perch, high above the Cubs' third-base dugout. He weighed 229 pounds, with blood pressure to match, when a small blood vessel broke in his brain. At a welcoming media conference, Harry happily hitched up his pants to show that, sans spare tire, he was down to 188. "The first few weeks, I didn't know if I would ever be back," he confessed. "I couldn't move my right hand and right foot and I couldn't talk."

It was Caray's iron constitution and the nation's goodwill that accounted for such rapid recovery. Caray had been counted out before, but after 45 years as a radio and TV play-by-play man, he is alone at the top. He has the same credentials that set Mel Allen, Vin Scully, and Ernie Harwell apart with their baseball knowledge and experience. Harry also has Howard Cosell's flair for TV showmanship, without the hard edge of rancor that made Hah-wahd the man you loved to hate.

None of this was handed to Caray. From the time he bluffed himself into his first radio job, he knew he was better than most of the deadly dull people who broadcast baseball in those days. Caray battled his way from the sticks to KMOX in St. Louis and 25 years of broadcasting Cardinal games. He grew bigger and better while the Cardinal radio network expanded to hundreds of stations throughout the South, but one thing remained constant: Harry viewed every game, every inning, every pitch with the eyes of a fan.

When things were going well, you knew it. When Whitey Kurowski left two Cards on base in the clutch, you knew that, too ("Pahhhhhhped it up!"). Nothing stopped Harry, not even a near-fatal 1968 accident. Knocked 45 feet through the air by a car, he landed on a rainy street and almost choked to death on his own blood. Despite two broken legs, a fractured shoulder, and a broken nose, Caray was back in action on opening day in 1969.

Harry was mysteriously fired after that season amid rumors of hanky-panky with a Busch beer heiress, which only made him more determined to show Cards' owner Gus-

Harry Lights Jimmy's Fire

The White Sox broadcast team of Harry Caray and Jimmy Piersall produced more fireworks than anybody else doing sports in Chicago. Their chemistry worked because the freewheeling Piersall was one of the few on-air partners who wasn't overshadowed by Caray's powerful personality.

"You know, Jimmy, Stan Musial once hit five homers in a doubleheader," Harry would say. "Well, I had nine kids," Jimmy would retort.

And so it went, delighting the fans, infuriating the players, and embarrassing the owners. Piersall finally gave Sox owners Eddie Einhorn and Jerry Reinsdorf an excuse to break up the team by calling ballplayers' wives "horny broads" on Mike Royko's 1981 TV talk show.

"The White Sox were a freak show," Einhorn said. "The fans thought Harry and Jimmy were the stars, and Comiskey Park was an outdoor saloon."

Yes, but it sure was fun at the old ballpark.

sie Busch and the rest of his critics. Caray worked one season on Oakland A's games for Charles O. Finley, the cantankerous genius and Chicago insurance millionaire. Then he met his biggest challenge in a floundering White Sox franchise.

The Sox lost a horrendous 106 games in 1970, with attendance sinking to 495,355. They couldn't get a Chicago station to broadcast their games, and were finally picked up by an AM radio outlet in suburban LaGrange. If the wind blew right, you could hear it. It was a situation made to order for Harry and his "Holy Cow!" In 11 stormy years on the South Side, he and Piersall packed the park, revitalized the Sox fan base with young listeners who loved the broadcasters' go-for-the-jugular style, and feuded endlessly. Not with each other, but with just about everybody else—except the fans.

Sure, they played to the grandstand, and it worked. Caray and Piersall took on dozens of Sox players, managers Chuck

Tanner and Tony LaRussa, and owner Bill Veeck and his successors, Jerry Reinsdorf and Eddie Einhorn. Piersall didn't have the power base to survive all that enmity, but Caray did. When Einhorn steered the Sox toward pay TV, Harry made the decision to move his mike from the South Side to the North Side. He began in 1982, and although the legend of "Hey Harrreee" couldn't get any bigger in Chicago, it soon was just as big in most of the rest of North America.

Although Cub fans and Sox fans are not the same kind of people, Harry's bottomless pool of charisma allowed him to transfer his enormous popularity from Comiskey Park to Wrigley Field. Now he's something like everybody's favorite baseball uncle, from the Panama Canal to Hudson Bay.

Halas U.—College of Hard Knocks

On the wall in my den is a plaque proclaiming me an honorary member of "Halas University." If there was such a place, the only major it could have offered was Advanced Survival.

George S. Halas would have survived in any business. He was tougher, meaner, and more determined than most of us. Even the Bear fans who jeered at Halas on the sidelines and labeled him a tightwad had a kind of grudging admiration for this indomitable codger.

People's opinions of him never bothered Halas. As a 165-pound defensive end or the patriarch of the National Football League, he reveled in a good fight. As a player, he'd slug it out in the line, toe-to-toe with beefy opponents. Most of them far outweighed the Bohemian kid from Chicago's West Side, but nobody could make him quit. "I'll fight every time I think I'm right," Halas said of the controversy that so often swirled around him. Since the Bears' founder seldom, if ever, acknowledged that he had been wrong, there were a lot of fights with enemies or friends.

Halas encouraged the same combativeness among his employees. "George wasn't happy unless we were at each other's throats all the time," said Stan Jones, a 12-year Bear offensive tackle. "He wanted our offensive unit to be mad at our defense, so they'd both take it out on opponents."

Don't let the smile fool you. George Stanley Halas, a tough player-coach for the 1920 Decatur Staleys, later turned them into the Chicago Bears by sheer force of will.

In his playing days, Halas would do literally anything to win, from gouging to holding. That corner-cutting experience came in handy when he struggled for decades to sell the Bears and pro football to a skeptical public. Halas was the Bears' owner, coach, general manager, ticket taker, and publicity man rolled into one during the NFL's turbulent early decades. He survived dealing with sharks like George Preston Marshall of the Washington Redskins, and in the end, outlasted , outfought, and outlived most of the pioneers who had tossed in $100 each to buy NFL franchises in 1920. Halas's payoff eventually came in the millions when television discovered the NFL after World War II. But despite his reputation for stinginess, money never was the main object of Halas's lifelong battle. He fought to keep his league alive, to get the Bears to the top, and to keep them there. The clash of armor was music to the crusty old coach, though in his later years he mellowed enough to take a satisfying backward glance at his handiwork, which included a 40-year coaching career and a 326–151–30 record.

Not many people left such an impressive monument behind them. One of Halas's last and best moves was bringing Mike Ditka back to rekindle the Bear dynasty that had given the Monsters of the Midway a fierce, proud tradition. Almost as fierce and proud as George Stanley Halas himself.

Cast-Iron Coach, Steel-Trap Mind

Mike Ditka didn't gum up the works for the Bears. Well, maybe he did in San Francisco, giving a female 49er fan an earful of green gum in the midst of a painful 41–0 Bear-bashing. Watching the erstwhile invincible Bears turn vincible with the whole nation tuned in is enough to make their fans throw up, so merely throwing gum could be considered admirable restraint by Iron Mike.

Of course, we didn't have to listen to the verbal brickbats Ditka lobbed at the Funsters of the Midway while they tumbled from Super Bowl XX executioners in 1986 to XXX-rated raps from outraged fans after first-round playoff knockouts in '87 and '88. Ditka did his best to keep the Bears hungry, but the adulation—and the money—showered on the NFL champs, along with the annual Jim McMahon injury, foiled the coach.

Ditka benched Super Bowl starters Otis Wilson, Gary Fencik, Matt Suhey, Fridge Perry ("Who'll hit 400 first—Wade Boggs or the Fridge?" Brent Musburger mused on CBS) and others; roasted receiver Dennis McKinnon for zinging the leaky Bear pass coverage; then took on the whole state of Minnesota by slapping his famous "Rollerdome" label on the Vikings' Homerdome Home, but just couldn't beat the NFL Players Association all by himself.

"After the strike, we sometimes didn't even know where to line up on defense," Ditka admitted after the agony of 1987. "Let's face it, we just ain't good enough."

Not even Ditka's election to the pro football Hall of Fame could ease the plain completely. He finally found solace in a few laughs, and it's a good thing Mike Ditka has a sense of humor. He needs it to walk the emotional tightrope that stretches out ahead of him every season. Being a coach in the NFL is tough enough. When you're the coach of the Chicago Bears, it's tougher. All those ghosts from the past are there every time the Bears huddle: Grange, Nagurski, Feathers, McAfee, Stydahar, Turner, Luckman, Osmanski, Atkins, Sprinkle, Butkus, Sayers. Now there's Mike Ditka, spiritual heir of the Founding Father, George Halas.

Ditka has a tough act to follow. Even more than equaling the records hung up by Halas, Ditka's challenge is finding a

The reincarnation of George Halas, Coach Mike Ditka reasons with an errant Tom Thayer in practice.

way to make today's Bears play the way Ditka did. From a talent standpoint alone, that's difficult, because Ditka was a superb tight end. If the Pitt All-American had known how to pace himself, he would have lasted longer and not left the active ranks with so many scars on his knees, hips, feet, shoulders, and assorted other body parts.

That was something Ditka the player never could do. Maybe the hardest adjustment he had to make in coaching was learning that raging intensity with no letup will burn out a team before it can burn up the gridiron. The Bears will be the first to admit that Ditka expects more than they have to give, at least in the effort department. To their surprise, the ones who buy Ditka's theory of football as a crusade often find that both their talent level and their enthusiasm hits new heights.

"Guys who don't want to work or sacrifice won't be here," Ditka told them the first time a Bear squad assembled around the new coach in 1982. Most had heard the same song, with slightly different lyrics, from other coaches, so they didn't pay much attention until Ditka began to ship players out. But nothing much seemed to work in Iron Mike's Chicago debut, a disappointing 3–6 record for the strike-shortened 1982 campaign.

The fans' unhappiness paled alongside Ditka's fury. Things got even worse in 1983, when a 2–5 start put the new coach's regime in peril and his head on the chopping block. The fans were beginning to think that Ditka's intensity, the same quality that made him a brilliant player, was too far out of control to let him function as a head coach. When he TKO'd a metal locker after a bitter overtime loss in Baltimore, many wrote him off as a nut.

That's when Ditka saved himself, and most likely the whole Bear franchise, by falling back on his sense of humor. The players expected the worst when the firebrand coach opened his pregame meeting in the Soldier Field locker room the following week, October 2, 1983. They figured going out to face the Denver Broncos would be less of an ordeal than another Ditka harangue, but he had a surprise in store for them.

Brandishing the elbow-length cast on his right hand, Ditka said only, "Fellas, let's win this one for Lefty." The laugh produced a badly needed lift: storming to a 24–0 halftime edge, the Bears won handily, and Ditka's coaching career turned a critical corner. He was no match yet for his Dallas mentor, Tom Landry, or for Halas, but Ditka was rapidly discovering there was more than one way to survive in the NFL crocodile pit.

"I've got to relax, and I will," Ditka vowed, contradicting himself one sentence later. "My intensity level has to do with what I feel inside."

When those feelings boil over, nobody, not even Ditka himself, can keep this complex character in check. The suave, sophisticated, post–Super Bowl version of Ditka still bears a strong resemblance to the tiger who stalks the sideline on game days. Now when the safety valve blows, Ditka grabs players by the jersey to bark orders or hurls clipboards and headsets, riveting every eye in the stadium on him, especially the unblinking one on the zoom lens of a TV camera.

"It's silly to keep a camera on a coach, especially this coach," Ditka said after the whole country got a close-up of his sideline tantrum in a 1986 Monday night game against the Detroit Lions. "Lots of coaches put people to sleep. Put the camera on me and the fans want to go out and buy guns."

Theatrics? Maybe. Uncontrollable temper? Perhaps. But from the instant Ditka grabbed tight end Emery Moorehead in a semi-stranglehold, the sluggish Bears came to life that night, roaring from behind to overtake the Lions 16–13. At that moment, Ditka completed the transition from a frustrated losing coach to the front rank of NFL coaches. He had learned how to use his emotions to make the Bears play harder in a situation where they needed an emotional kick in the pants.

Of course, Ditka's favorite sparring partner, quarterback Jim McMahon, was out of action by then, so the Bears had no chance to repeat as Super Bowl kingpins. Ditka went with miracle worker Doug Flutie instead of experienced Steve Fuller in their first playoff game, and came up empty. The Redskins' defense did a war dance on Flutie in a 27–13 upset that shocked confident Bear fans.

But the drafting of Michigan quarterback Jim Harbaugh and the firing of Ditka ally Jerry Vainisi proved that owner Mike McCaskey had the final say. The Bears were in a volatile, explosive situation on and off the field, Mike Ditka's kind of situation. No wonder he signed for three more years, through 1990. The $2 million salary is less than Mike will make from his restaurants, commercials, videos, and other outside perks. It's the challenge that turns him on.

"Nobody else could coach the Bears the way I do," he maintains.

True.

McCaskey, A Chip Off Halas Block

Don't underestimate Michael B. McCaskey. Ignore the button-down collar, the tasteful tie, and the well-tailored suit. Take a look at the piercing blue eyes. George Halas used to fix opponents with the same steely gaze before pouncing on them. Until the day he died at 88, Halas was one of the toughest old birds ever to inhabit this planet.

His grandson, Mike McCaskey, has inherited a lot of that flint and steel. "When it comes to money, I'm my grandfather's grandson," McCaskey said after succeeding Halas as the Bears' president and chief executive officer on November 11, 1983. McCaskey soon demonstrated that he was part Halas

Bear boss Mike McCaskey welcomes Michigan quarterback Jim Harbaugh into the den. McCaskey ended the Doug Flutie fiasco by insisting on Harbaugh in the 1987 NFL draft.

in many other ways. The name Iron Mike had already been awarded by the media to coach Mike Ditka, but McCaskey staked a claim on his own handle: Iron-Willed Mike.

McCaskey showed there was steel, not spaghetti, in his backbone in 1984 at the Bears' Platteville training camp, deflecting questions about Ditka's job security—or the lack of it—by insisting that he knew the timetable, so nobody else had to know, at least for the moment. "Wait and let things work out," McCaskey said. "I expect Mike to be coach of the Bears for a long time to come."

McCaskey chose to wait until just before the 1984 NFC Championship game in San Francisco to offer the head coach a new pact. And in case anybody was unaware that the new Bear boss would do things his way, he delivered the message before leaving camp.

McCaskey and his staff were staying in a small hotel on the outskirts of Platteville. He asked the room clerk to send all bills to the Bears' office, standard procedure for VIP travelers. When McCaskey was told to flash some cash or credit cards, he responded with a tantrum worthy of a Halas halftime speech. After the walls stopped virbrating, every-body in earshot knew this was a man not to be trifled with. A little over two years later, just after the Bears had been knocked out of the NFL playoffs by Washington, General Manager Jerry Vainisi discovered the same thing.

Those who felt the biggest jolt when McCaskey dropped Vainisi overboard early in 1987 were Bears fans. Still reeling from the 27–13 first-round playoff scalping by the Redskins on January 3, Chicago was rocked again by the news of Vainisi's firing. Many fans had accepted at face value the McCaskey-as-superwimp-straw-man portrayal in Jim Mc-Mahon's best-selling book. It was far too easy for the rebel-lious quarterback, who loves to needle any symbol of au-thority, to whale the stuffing out of McCaskey in print. It was also inaccurate.

Truth to tell, McCaskey is nobody to mess with. Even with-out Halas's millions, his grandson has Halas's genes, espe-cially the combative ones. Papa Bear never bothered to hide the street fighter that lurked just under his tough old hide. Even near the end, between pauses to do sugar-coated vi-deotapes of the way it wasn't, for posterity's sake, Halas could still unleash his notorious temper. He made sure his legacy would continue to mold the Bears by hiring Mike Ditka, a Halas-style battler.

The supreme irony of all this is that McCaskey, the heir apparent to the Halas empire, is swinging the ax to rid the Bear organization of any lingering traces of the Halas re-gime. It will be done McCaskey's way from now on. If his tactics, methods, and aims bear an eerie resemblance to Papa Bear's, don't say you weren't warned. Everybody thought the new boss was kidding when he laughingly called himself the "Jim McMahon of the boardroom" while the rest of the Bears were still reveling in their Super Bowl XX triumph. "In the next few years we are going to have to be prepared to lose some people from our organization," McCaskey warned. The suave 44-year-old Yalie had decided already that one man would have the last word on the Bears' future: Mike McCaskey. Those with more allegiance to someone else—like Vainisi to Ditka—would have to go.

Again, the media dismissed McCaskey's running feud

with the Chicago Park District over custody of Soldier Field skyboxes as a childish spat. It was no laughing matter to McCaskey, who used that incident as a springboard for his campaign to get a new stadium built for the Bears. Ever since then he has been playing hardball with the city to make it happen.

The final piece of evidence that McCaskey is determined to be completely in charge was his 1987 draft prediction, dismissed by many, as a throwaway line. "We already got McMahon, Flutie, Tomczak, and Fuller," Bear fans kept telling each other between gulps of beer. "The last thing we need is another quarterback, right?" Wrong. Too late, they recalled McCaskey's words: " I guarantee you we'll draft a quarterback." Welcome aboard, Jim Harbaugh. And if anyone still doesn't know who's in charge here, he's too dumb to add up the facts, subtract the non-McCaskey people from the Bears, and multiply the effect of McCaskey's power. When the dust settles around those new-math realities, Bear fans may still be divided, but the front office won't be. His employees will support Mike or take a hike.

The Jim and Zim Show: Will the New Cub Duo Do?

Ex-Cub manager WGN spieler Jim Frey and ex-almost-everybody's manager Don Zimmer know their new roles have to provide new results for Cub fans. If general manager Frey and manager Zimmer try dishing out the same old baloney, the victory-starved faithful will make a salami sandwich out of them.

Frey was plucked from WGN airwaves to pick up the pieces of the shattered Dallas Green regime. Just like life, baseball is a funny game. Green canned manager Frey and third base coach Zimmer as a team on June 12, 1986. Now they're teaming up again to double-team the Cubs. Zimmer was Frey's first choice and Tribune Company brass went along, despite protests that qualified black candidates like Billy Williams, Frank Robinson, and Bill Robinson weren't considered.

"You have to consult the people who pay the bills, but it's my job to put a winner on the field," said Frey, who managed the Cubs to their only NL East title, in 1984. "I hired Zim because he's the best man, not because we're friends."

Still, their friendship should help Jim and Zim weather the second-guessing storm if some of their brainstorms backfire. Unloading relief ace Lee Smith was a gamble; so was bringing in aging Goose Gossage to replace him in the bullpen. At least Frey isn't afraid to make a move. If he discovers that the Cubs can't wait until all that promising young talent down on the farm grows up, Frey will trade some over-the-hill Cub starters for pitchers.

Zimmer, indelibly labeled "a gerbil" by Spaceman Bill Lee, wants to manage the Cubs, not dwell on the past. "When the umpire hollers 'Play ball,' I'm the man in charge," he said. So go charge, Zim.

The new Cub brain trust, Don Zimmer (left) and Jim Frey, tries to figure what's cookin' with the Cubs.

Chicago Gives Dallas Back to Philly

If the Cubs had not choked up in San Diego during that lost weekend in 1984, the Chicago reign of Emperor Dallas could have lasted longer than that wholly Roman umpire, Ron Luciano.

Neither Dallas Green nor the Cubs recovered from the 0–3 playoff fiasco, snatching a World Series banquet away from starving Cubs fans, who had been subsisting on leftover crumbs from 1969. They had to go back on a starvation diet for the next two years while the Mets and Cards caved in Green's Cub house of cards. Green wanted to try the same radical approach that had worked for him in Philadelphia: move into the dugout as the 1988 Cub manager; kick butt and restore that 1984 pennant fever; hand-pick a successor and go back to the front office, taking bows all the way.

Instead, Green found his power base softening, so he quit in a huff. That wasn't so bad, but a silly, name-calling, finger-pointing exchange with Gene Michael, the inept Cub manager Green had seemingly hired out of the American League Red Book, wrote a dreary ending to the Dallas connection in Chicago.

When Green decided to go for it in 1984, transforming the Cubs almost overnight from NL doormats to media darlings, the rewards also were instantaneous. Cub fans discarded the despair they'd been draped in since the Great Foldup of 1969, snapping up every available seat in the cozy confines. Then came the ultimate gamble, prying Rick Sutcliffe loose from Cleveland for two potential stars, Joe Carter and Mel Hall.

"We have a chance to win this thing now," Green told a meeting of his brain trust when the Indians' offer was made just in time to beat the June trading deadline. "Who knows what will happen later with these free-agent salaries so far out of line? Let's get Sutcliffe and the other guys."

The "other guys," catcher Ron Hassey and reliever George Frazier, played bit parts in the dramatic summer of 1984. It was the wildest outdoor carnival in Chicago since the amazing April, miraculous May, joyful June and July, and astonishing August of 1969 were followed by the Cubs' September swoon. Sutcliffe was savior, superstar, and celebrity all in one, making Green look like a genius by racking up a 16–1 record after the trade, the last 14 wins in a row.

Not even the most rabid, anguished Cub supporter could find it in his heart to blame Green for the melancholy epitaph to this incredible season. With the whole country pulling for them, the Cubs charged to within one game of the World Series. Then the dream collapsed like the stock market in October 1987.

The Wall Street calamity of October 19, 1929 triggered a worldwide panic that turned into the Great Depression. But, typically, Cub fans got an early start because their depression had begun 17 days earlier, on October 12, 1929. That was the day Hack Wilson lost a fly ball in the sun, turning it into an inside-the-park homer. It was the key to a World Series record 10-run seventh inning for the Philadelphia A's, wiping out both an 8–0 Cub lead and the Cubs themselves.

Green had come to Chicago in 1981, full of fire-and-brimstone zeal to erase those painful memories by winning a World Series with the Cubs, just as he had with the Phillies in 1980. First, all that stuffy, moldy Cub tradition had to go. The slogan was "Building a New Tradition," and Green's first target was the 35 years of nostalgic, lovable losing in the shadow of Wrigley Field's ivy.

"Some of those guys on the 1969 Cubs made a living out of coming close to one pennant," he snorted in disbelief. "They were professional losers. The 1964 Phillies folded, too, but nobody wanted to admit they were on that team."

Green had a point. What he failed to realized at first was that Chicago was not Philadelphia. Wrigley Field might well have been a relic, but it had more going for it than even Green's determined bid to banish the past could overcome. In his attempt, though, Dallas made some big mistakes in the vital area of tact and diplomacy. Suburban fans didn't jump on his "Let There Be Lights" bandwagon until the 1984 resurrection made coming to Cubs games as trendy and chic as Brie and Chablis.

The fans' resistance, along with plenty of media criticism, only stiffened Green's resolve to stuff a winner down their undeserving throats. He needed a superstar to lead the charge, and courted Dodger discard Steve Garvey with $4 million of excess profits from the new owner, the Tribune Company. Unfortunately, Green ended up with another ex-Dodger, Ron Cey, at Garvey prices. It was Cey's stiff-necked aloofness almost as much as the third baseman's lack of production that poured vats of boiling second-guess oil on the expensive transaction. Aside from some sizzling bat streaks that kept his homer total respectable, Cey's four-year stay was not a smash. Regardless, the Penguin could have become Chicago's Big Bird with a clutch hit in just one situation. Cey batted with the bases loaded and the score tied in the ninth inning of Game 4 of the 1984 playoffs. Ex-Cub lefty Craig Lefferts of the Padres got him on a routine grounder, killing the rally.

Two disappointing seasons on the heels of 1984 revived some of the old heat. A flock of wounded pitchers, notably Sutcliffe, made fans eager to forget 1985, but when the healthy Cubs made their fans sick in '86, Green made another switch, turning to a youth movement. For the first time in his six years on the Chicago scene, Dallas entered 1987 with some young talent from the system. Those prospects persuaded fans that Green's patient rebuilding of the farm clubs was the way to go.

Along with shortstop Shawon Dunston, the Cubs tapped pitchers Jamie Moyer and Greg Maddux and outfielders

Veeck's Bear Plan a Wreck

One reason Bill Veeck couldn't afford to keep the White Sox was the rejection of his 1979 plan to lure the Bears from Soldier Field to Comiskey Park. Veeck proposed portable, pie-shaped temporary stands to bring Comiskey's capacity to 52,000 for football.

His architect's model had the field running from home plate to center field, unlike the Chicago Cardinals's layout, when it ran from the first-base line to left field. The Bears turned him down, even though Veeck would have bought the football stands and given them a cut of parking and concession revenues.

"The Bears are spending my tax money to compete against me at Soldier Field, and that annoys me," a disappointed Veeck said.

Doing what he did best, Bill Veeck thumped the tub for another White Sox season. His sidemen are Pat Hoy (left) and Edward Lee.

Dave Martinez for key roles. With Sutcliffe regaining some of the old magic, and veterans Ryne Sandberg and Jody Davis as stabilizers, only a spark was needed to light the pennant-fever fuse once more.

In Andre Dawson, Green found the right match. The comic-opera preceding Dawson's signing in spring training was just part of the charade acted out by baseball to deflate free-agent salaries. Players and greedy agents brought much of it on themselves with ridiculous demands, but Cub fans weren't complaining. With Dawson in the fold, hope sprung anew, along with Wrigley Field's ivy. When the Cubs flubbed again, Green was gone. Can the new boss do what Dallas didn't?

Veeck as in Heck of a Human Being

Bill Veeck was one of Chicago's best, in or out of the sports world. At times, it's still hard to accept the fact that he's gone. Between Veeck's terms as Sox owner, covering baseball in Chicago wasn't a barrel of laughs. The Cubs were still reeling from the Great Foldup of '69, with manager Leo Durocher grappling in vain to find a way to get them over the hump. The Sox were just plain staggering in 1970, on their way to an all-time low of 106 losses.

Bill Veeck was in Easton, Maryland, then, but he flew in on January 10, 1970, when Bulls' general manager Pat Williams held a Stadium promotion—"Pack 'em in Tight for Bill Veeck Night." Veeck helped restage his famous midget pinch-hitter stunt and gave Williams some free advice.

That was Veeck's specialty, helping people out. He gave baseball a lot of free advice over the years, most of it ignored by the stuffed shirts who ran the game with closed minds. Bill really enjoyed harpooning the baseball establishment, tweaking the noses and puncturing the pretensions of the baseball hierarchy. Next to putting on a promotion that lured thousands to his ballpark, or winning a pennant, that was his mission. And that's probably why his plaque still hasn't been placed in baseball's Hall of Fame, where it belongs.

Upon returning to save the White Sox for Chicago in 1975, Veeck would hold court with a phone at his elbow, beer mug in one hand and cigarette in the other, in Comiskey Park's Bards Room, where the writers ate their pregame meals.

Just being in a ballpark, especially Wrigley Field, where he grew up, was a tonic for Veeck. I never heard him complain about pain, though his leg had been amputated and he was far from healthy. He still had his zest for life and much to contribute when he died on January 2, 1986. And you're not a real Chicago fan if you don't miss him.

Clouds Crowd Sunshine Boys

Jerry Reinsdorf and Eddie Einhorn would probably do it again, even if a witch had whispered what they'd be letting themselves in for by buying the White Sox from Bill Veeck in 1981. They know now that the hoped-for riches from pay TV may be as illusory as another Sox pennant, but there are other rewards. Take away the ego factor and the roster of owners, and any big-league sport would soon be populated by accountants, corporate executives, and similar termi-

Opening a new era for the White Sox, Jerry Reinsdorf (right) accepts keys to Comiskey Park from Bill Veeck.

nally dull types. Maybe Jerry and Eddie don't live up to their former "Sunshine Boys" billing nowadays, but they're not dull.

With what has been happening on the South Side since the 1983 playoff decline and fall, rosy optimism is hard to justify. Still, Reinsdorf and Einhorn, a.k.a. Reinhorn and Einsdorf, are tough competitors, even if some of their players aren't. Combativeness is a handy trait whenever things don't go well for the Sox, because a whip and a chair is standard equipment to conduct stormy board of directors meetings.

The problem with the Sox is easy to diagnose, hard to solve. When you're in head-to-head competition with the Cubs for cash customers, newspaper space, and radio and TV time, a contending team is not a luxury, it's a matter of survival. The territory up for grabs takes in the entire Midwest, because bus-, train-, and even planeloads of fans descend on Chicago all summer for a day or a weekend. A baseball game is high on most of those crowded agendas, but it's either Cubs or Sox.

For some reason, out-of-towners assume getting to Wrigley Field is easier. Many Chicagoans have their own reasons for perpetuating this myth, especially since the Dan Ryan expressway was torn up for construction. Another headache Reinsdorf and Einhorn inherited from Bill Veeck is the fans' fear of traveling to the South Side, especially at night. Unless the Sox are contenders, those who are not hard-core baseball junkies go elsewhere on summer nights.

So the back-to-back gates of two million-plus in 1983 (2,132,821) and 1984 (2,136,988) brought only temporary prosperity to aging Comiskey Park. Even while crowds flocked to 35th and Shields before, and especially after, the Golden Anniversary All-Star gala of 1983, Reinsdorf was thinking ahead. Baseball's oldest living big-league park was dying of rusting girders and crumbling concrete. "It cost us millions just to keep this place together," the Sox chairman said. "We solved the drainage problem and put in a new $5 million scoreboard, but any structure more than 75 years old is a money trap. Maintaining Comiskey Park is too expensive. We have to have a new stadium." As if to prove his point, some hurry-up repairs had to be made before the crowd could be allowed in for the 1987 City Series clash.

But crowds of 40,000 were only a memory after the Sox failed to defend their AL West title, stumbling to an embarrassing 74–88 record in an also-ran 1984 campaign. Attendance has been plummeting since then, so the atmosphere of crisis returned. The Sunshine boys, who took the Sox close to the summit in a hurry and enjoyed the accolades while the "Winnin' Ugly" Sox roared down the stretch in the summer of '83 to win by a whopping 20 lengths, now are trying to brake the skid.

Reinsdorf and Einhorn have taken a lot of heat since their team folded in the 1983 playoffs, being accused of everything from plotting to sell out Sox fans for a Denver jackpot to watering down the Comiskey Park beer. Einhorn also left himself open to critics by predicting that his SportsVision TV setup was the wave of the sports future. Customer resistance to high monthly fees, plus the inability of Chicago politicians to agree on a plan for wiring the city, proved him wrong. With the Cubs blanketing the country on superstation WGN, the Sox had to add more free games on UHF Channel 32 just to get some exposure in Chicago.

And Reinsdorf and Einhorn were equally guilty of turning the baseball operation over to Hawk Harrelson in 1985. From the ill-conceived "The Hawk Wants You" promo campaign to the jerry-built "double coach" system Harrelson installed, his regime was a total disaster. Add to that the debacle of the Addison, Illinois, stadium that never was, along with speculation of a move to St. Petersburg, Florida, and it's a wonder both Reinsdorf and Einhorn didn't throw in the towel.

Whatever Sox fans think of chairman Jerry and president Eddie, the two deserve credit for putting up a good fight. Chicago should have a team in both leagues: the Cubs in sunshine and the Sunshine Boys after dark.

For Better or Wirtz, It's Arthur and Bill

As a tag-team wrestling duo, they would have been cast as villains. "The Wirtz Empire," wearing black hats and menacing scowls, would be a natural label for this father-and-son combination that had more to say about Chicago sports history than anyone else in their era.

The Halases, the Comiskeys, the Wrigleys were all one-sport operations. Not so with Arthur Wirtz, who gained control of Chicago Stadium during the Great Depression.

Wirtz had the vision to see what could be done with big arenas centrally located in sports-hungry cities. He took over in 1934 by trading the Olympia in Detroit to James D. Norris, another heavyweight sports promoter, for the keys to the Stadium.

Wirtz Fumbles the Hull Show

"The Bobby Hull thing was one of the worst mistakes Arthur Wirtz ever made," said Ben Hatskin, the man who gave Hull a $1 million bonus to sign with the Winnipeg Jets. "Bobby would have played for the Blackhawks a lot cheaper than he played for us."

Hatskin applied for a National Hockey League franchise in Winnipeg and was told it would cost $7.2 million. Instead, he bought a World Hockey Association franchise for $25,000 in 1972, signed Hull, and challenged the NHL to a costly war.

"Without Hull we had no chance," Hatskin noted. "Once we got him, other players jumped. It probably cost the NHL and WHA $100 million before we got together."

Jim Norris (left) and Arthur Wirtz didn't exactly make Bobby Hull jump through hoops when the highly-touted rookie joined the Blackhawks in 1957. Hull had the last laugh in 1972, touching off a hockey war by jumping to the Winnipeg Jets for $1 million.

Norris and Wirtz had a long, often stormy relationship in hockey, boxing, and other business ventures. The Chicago-based International Boxing Club, owned by Norris, challenged New York promoter Mike Jacobs for supremacy in staging big-money bouts during the 1940s and 1950s. Television added both spectators and dollars by the millions, and Wirtz didn't hesitate to cash in.

Arthur Wirtz had learned how to survive and prosper during the Depression, buying and managing properties so skillfully that he created a real estate empire. Chicago Stadium, the pride and joy of legendary hustler Paddy Harmon, became a major, profitable part of his holdings. Over the years, Wirtz's financial acumen brought him the respect—and the clout—that Chicago power brokers share with those who earn their way to the top rung.

But when Wirtz's multiple dealings involved him more and more in sports, his reception was not quite as cordial. Over the years, fans discovered that Stadium events were geared to extract whatever the traffic would bear, from parking to concessions to the ticket sellers' habit of waiting until a five-dollar bill slid through the window before "discovering" a few choice seats.

Wirtz dealt with many tenants for decades, and few of them regarded him as a benevolent landlord. His robberbaron image was made to order for Chicago newspapers in their frantic fight for survival before World War II. Sportswriters gleefully printed the quotes of promoters, team officials, and other would-be Stadium renters, painting a picture of Wirtz as a tight-fisted nickel nurser.

The NBA expansion franchise called the Chicago Bulls was one of those dissatisfied renters. After playing their initial season in the Amphitheater at 42nd and Halsted streets, the Bulls moved to the Stadium in 1967. They dangled on a shoestring for five years, well after the prime mover, Dick Klein, had been dumped by his fellow owners.

Klein had no one else to go to in 1967 except Wirtz, because a mysterious midnight blaze swept through the original McCormick Place on January 16 of that year. Loss of the gigantic lakefront exposition hall meant that trade shows had to switch bookings to the antiquated Amphitheater. Business being business, the Amphitheater bumped the Bulls for more profitable clients.

That kind of situation was made to order for Wirtz. He welcomed Klein and the Bulls aboard for a sliding-scale rental agreement that eventually cost the struggling NBA team up to $250,000 a year. Wirtz had been doing things his way for so long that nobody thought much of it. The Chicago multimillionaire wound up owning the hockey Blackhawks, as well as the Bulls, assuring a profitable bottom line for the 20,000-seat Stadium.

As an owner, Wirtz only enhanced his image as a tightwad. It was Wirtz, after all, who refused the Golden Jet, Bobby Hull, a $250,000 salary in 1972 and drove him to Winnipeg and the World Hockey Association.

Wirtz's close ties with other hockey, basketball, and arena owners across the country meant he was able to squeeze many other Stadium attractions for top dollar because the going rate for everything from a religious revival to the Roller Derby was shared by this tight network of Good Ol' Boys. The manipulations of this inner circle eventually cost the Wirtz estate a bundle after Arthur's death on July 21, 1983.

A lawsuit against Wirtz dragged on for more than a decade, and he was found guilty of antitrust violations in blocking the 1972 sale of the Bulls to Milwaukee businessman Marv Fishman. The trial record showed that Wirtz had conspired with his hockey and basketball allies to have Fishman's bid rejected by the NBA. While the case languished, Wirtz suffered a stroke and was speechless and partially paralyzed until he died.

"Very few people know the way Dad suffered in those last few months," Arthur's son and heir, Bill Wirtz, said. "I saw the way he watched everybody and listened to everything in his hospital room. Then he'd write us a note on his pad. He was so active and so in charge of things all his life, that it must have been terrible for him to endure."

So the torch passed to Bill Wirtz, a respected hockey figure who is one of the few members of both the United States and Canadian hockey Hall of Fame. He is still tagged by many fans with the Wirtz family tightwad label, but Bill bears little resemblance to his imperious father. A down-to-earth sort, he's earned the goodwill of Chicago reporters by talking frankly and on the record about many controversial issues.

What's the Motta with the Bulls?

Nothing was the Motta with the Bulls when that bantam rooster was in charge. Dick Motta's teams were among the most exciting, controversial, successful packages of dynamite ever to detonate on the Chicago sports scene.

Every time Motta's Bulls were home, it was like a heavyweight title bout in Chicago Stadium, the air charged with pregame tension. And with Norm Van Lier, the bantamweight champion of the NBA, the fans often were treated to a boxing-basketball doubleheader. Maybe there were more hockey brawls in the Stadium during the Motta era, but when the basketball boards were placed atop the ice, a ring occasionally would have come in handy.

Motta dropped out of nowhere onto the Chicago sports stage in 1968. There was little interest in the Bulls then, and even less in an obscure coach from Weber State (Where's

Coach Dick Motta (right) stopped smiling when his battling Bulls took the floor in Chicago Stadium. Left to right, Bob Weiss, Chet Walker, Norm Van Lier, Howard Porter, Jerry Sloan and Tom Boerwinkle played for one of the most entertaining teams in Chicago history.

that?) in the Big Sky (What's that?) Conference. Chicago didn't recognize Motta's influence overnight, but the 5'9" firebrand made his presence felt quickly all around the NBA. From the first time referees felt the lash of the freshman coach's tongue, Dick Motta was a marked man.

"They say we're a dirty team, so that gives everybody in the league an excuse to slap, punch, and gouge us," Motta was soon moaning. It was the central theme of his stormy eight-year tenure as head coach of the Bulls, ringmaster of their circus, and architect of their ferocious defense. Motta's main motivational technique was both simple and effective: It's us against the world. Circle the wagons. They're out to get the Bulls.

Coaches without Motta's ability to communicate would have fallen flat on their alibis while trying to sell that approach. Somehow it worked for him. In an astonishing, bumpy roller-coaster ride with the Bulls Motta lifted his players to the heights time after time, extracting the maximum physical and mental contribution.

Motta was a fascinating man to be around because he was such a paradox. An essentially private person, introverted by nature, most of the time he was completely different on the job. For players who matched his burning desire, Motta became almost a father figure. Guard Jerry Sloan was the outstanding example. His will to win drove Sloan into near frenzy on the court. Motta summed up the defensive dynamo's value succinctly: "Jerry Sloan is the Bulls' franchise." Motta thought so because Sloan was an extension of the coach's will during games.

But for those who couldn't or wouldn't show that blend of desire and commitment, Motta had little patience. The list of players he unloaded was topped by Clifford Ray, the center who could have won the NBA championship for the Bulls in 1974–75, the year it got away.

Once he had stamped his character on the team, turning them into winners with bone-jarring defense and patient, patterned offense, Motta could have been a Chicago hero. Instead of cashing in the way Mike Ditka is doing now, Motta shunned the limelight, guarding his privacy. He was too honest to deny that Chicago ranked far behind his native Utah as the place where he'd rather live and work.

Despite his almost paranoid distrust of the press, Motta was open and communicative about basketball. That cost him thousands of dollars in fines (paid for him by the Bulls), but the emotional coach simply couldn't stop saying what was on his mind. Since Motta's opinion of the referees and the NBA in general was uniformly low, he was not the most popular guy in the league. Reporters could always count on a rainy-day story by repeating one of Motta's blasts to another coach or to a player, then jotting down the angry response.

Motta finally began to mellow, or at least to control his temper, after sitting out a week-long 1974 suspension for shoving referee Ed Batagowski. "I had to let it go," he said. "They [the refs] were looking for me and waiting until I stood up from the bench. I can't let that destroy my team."

No, the Bulls during Motta's tenure were never dull.

Lee Stern: Stung by His Own Sting

Here's a guy responsible for the ultimate Chicago Sting. Lee Stern went for a $12 million bundle while trying to prove the old W. C. Fields adage about a soccer fan being born every minute.

Not in Chicago, they're not. Stern has the scars on his psyche and the deep dents in his wallet to prove it. The Sting owner, by his own admission, has dropped almost a million

Lee Stern, founder, godfather, and financial angel of the Chicago Sting, took a bath in red ink, but refused to stop pushing big-time soccer.

bucks a year trying to sell outdoor and indoor soccer in Chicago. "If I knew it would cost me $10 million just to win our first Soccer Bowl [in 1981], I'd have gone home," Stern recalled of the North American Soccer League franchise he brought to Chicago in 1975. "I got some thrills out of it, and so did my family."

It was expensive titillation. The Sting won a second Soccer Bowl in 1984, and the NASL promptly folded under the pressure of enormous financial losses. Stern refused to give up, taking the Sting back to the Major Indoor Soccer League in 1984 for a last-ditch effort to convince Chicago to get its kicks from soccer. In Europe, Asia, Africa, and South America, soccer produces frenzy and riots. Around here, it triggers yawns, except among a slim cadre of hard-core perennials.

"We all ask ourselves why," Stern shrugs. "When Madison Square Garden bought the Washington Diplomats, it was supposed to be the big breakthrough in America. Sonny Werblin said their one game a week would be a major event, with TV and promotions. It didn't happen. They lost $2 million in a year and got out." The lack of media coverage in Chicago is part of the problem, Stern insists. "When the Sting won the '81 Soccer Bowl, Channel 7 put on a 'Love Boat' rerun instead of showing the game here. We were met by thousands of people at the airport, had a parade down LaSalle Street, and got the key to the city from Mayor Byrne. Fans still didn't turn out, even when we won another championship in 1984. With eight million people playing soccer in

America, maybe we're just not marketing it right," concludes Stern, a Chicago commodity trader who also owns a piece of the White Sox. Finally, in outright frustration, Stern sarcastically offered to sell the team for a nickel in 1988, and more than a few fans tried to take him up on it. Given the lack of tickets being sold, and the tottering condition of the MISL, perhaps he should have accepted the cash.

Selling soccer as part of a glitzy entertainment package is the thrust of the full-scale effort by Stern and his new partner, Lou Weisbach. They're hoping to pack the Rosemont Horizon for concerts by show business biggies and throw in the Sting game. The theory is that some of the crowd will get hooked on the fast-paced MISL brand of soccer, sort of human pinball with crazy caroms and frantic action. If it works, Stern will sell his majority interest in the Sting to Weisbach. If not? Lots of luck, Lee.

THREE

IT'S NO SIN TO WIN

Chicago's 10 Best Teams

S ome of you downtrodden rooters might find it hard to believe Chicago had 10 teams that were best at anything except breaking their fans' hearts. Well, you're wrong, and here's the evidence to prove it.

1919 White Sox: The Great Thumpers

This was the best team in Chicago sports history.

But when eight White Sox conspired with New York gambler Arnold Rothstein to throw the 1919 World Series, they changed the direction of baseball. If the Gang of Eight hadn't gotten themselves banished from baseball, the New York Yankees might not have been the sporting colossus of the Roaring Twenties, even with the mighty Babe Ruth. These Sox, not the Yankees, could have dominated the American League.

Instead of the legacy of losing that the 1919 South Siders left behind, they should have been folk heroes. After all these years, it's hard to imagine how many pennants such a collection of awesome hitters and overpowering pitchers was capable of stringing together. From the standpoint of

He's wearing shoes, but it's the immortal Shoeless Joe Jackson, bantering with White Sox fans in 1919. Even after they knew he'd sold them out in the World Series, Sox fans couldn't stop longing for his awesome talent.

raw talent, what a team those 1919 Sox were. Two Hall of Famers, catcher Ray Schalk and second baseman Eddie Collins, were in the starting lineup. Pitchers Eddie Cicotte (29–7) and Claud (Lefty) Williams (23–11) were the twin aces of the 1919 Sox staff. Both would have made the Hall of Fame, barring career-ending injuries, if they had not chosen to wear Black Sox by taking part in the Series-fixing scheme. Urban (Red) Faber and Dickie Kerr were the other mound mainstays. Faber's 254 big-league victories got overdue recognition when the old-timers committee awarded him a Cooperstown plaque in 1964.

With or without shoes, left fielder Joe Jackson was a magnificent hitter, the cornerstone of a team that won AL pennants in 1917 and 1919 and was capable of winning three or four more. Those who saw Jackson play knew they were watching someone special, a baseball artist who could not read or write. What he could do was tattoo a pitch with that picture swing. Shoeless Joe hit a mere .351 in 1919, a full five points under his lifetime average. The left-handed batter (who threw right) hit .408 and .395 for Cleveland in 1911 and 1912, his first two full seasons in the majors. Even with the shadow of the scandal hanging over him, Jackson batted .382 in 1920, with 42 doubles, 20 triples, and 12 homers.

The slugging leftfielder was the superstar, though the 1919 Sox, White and Black, were loaded with other people who could play. Even the straightest arrow of them all, gentlemanly Eddie Collins, had a touch of larceny in his heart, swiping 33 bases in 1919. Collins batted .319, played a dandy second base, and, along with Schalk, helped keep morale up amid a storm of fix rumors that tarred the whole team with the same brush.

The most remarkable thing about this bizarre season is how well the Sox functioned as a unit. They were torn by dissension and split into two factions—the Good Guys and the Bad Guys. Despite that, they won 88, lost 52, took the AL pennant by 3½ games over Cleveland, and doubtless could have knocked off Cincinnati if everybody had been trying in the World Series.

The Sox hung up some remarkable numbers that season. They paced both major leagues in hitting with a hefty .287 team average. The pitching staff also topped the AL with 87 complete games, 14 of them shutouts. Sadly, too many members of that memorable team were unfairly branded. Pitcher Dickie Kerr's story was the saddest of the bunch. The spunky little left-hander won two games in that dumped Series of 1919, even with monkey business going on behind his back. Then Kerr (21–9) rebounded in 1920 by joining Faber (23–12), Williams (22–14), and Cicotte (21–10) as the first quartet of 20-game winners on the same team in the same season.

Instead of showing his gratitude for Kerr's grit, Sox owner Charles A. Comiskey kicked his pitcher in the teeth. The lefty "slipped" to 19–17 in 1921, but still had won 53 games in a three-year stretch. Comiskey paid Kerr $6,500 in 1920 and refused to give him a raise in 1921.

Understandably, Dickie figured his brand of winning work was worth a little more, so he requested a two-year contract at a modest $8,500 a season. The response? A resounding no from big-hearted Comiskey. When Kerr refused to sign, he had nowhere else to go, so he was out. The White Sox owned him, body and soul.

Commissioner Kenesaw Mountain Landis, the czar hired by frightened baseball moguls from the federal bench to clean up their tarnished game, then got into the act. Judge Landis, believe it or not, suspended Kerr merely for playing a semipro game against the banished Black Sox. Comiskey let Kerr return in 1925, but the little southpaw's skills had eroded at age 32. He went 0–1 in only 36⅔ innings, and his career was over.

This sad story has a happier ending. Instead of turning into a bitter old man after such treatment, Kerr became the kind of minor-league manager who took young players under his wing. In 1940, at Daytona Beach, in the Class D

Florida State League, Kerr did more for baseball than the game ever had done for him. The classy manager refused to let a left-handed rookie pitcher quit in disgust after a shoulder injury. He told the kid he could hit, put him in the outfield, and kept his spirits up. Less than two years later, the ex-pitcher was terrorizing National League pitchers on his way to the Hall of Fame. His name was Stan Musial.

So Kerr got a piece of the Hall, at least, when Musial insisted he be there to watch Stan the Man enter in 1969. That's more than the eight Black Sox fixers could say. Dickie Kerr was a better man than any of them.

Some purists still argue for the 1917 White Sox as the best ever. It's true that this group won 100 games and the World Series, knocking off John McGraw's stuck-up New York Giants 4–2. The starting lineup and much of the mound corps was the same as in 1919. But calling this bunch the best just because they were the only White Sox squad to reach the century mark in victories is a mistake in my book. Since that's what you're reading, the nod goes to the 1919 Pale Hose.

The 1985 Bears: A Halas of a Team

Bear fans had questioned the judgment of George Halas for a long time before Papa Bear died in 1983. They had a lot to grumble about during Halas's declining years as head coach. After winning the last Halas-coached National Football League title in 1963, the Bears went downhill much faster than their venerable owner.

Despite adding a pair of superstar rookies, Gale Sayers and Dick Butkus, in 1965, the Bears kept floundering. Halas retired after posting a 7–6–1 log in 1967, closing the book on 40 years as head coach with 326 wins, 151 losses, and 31 ties.

Halas struck out on three straight successors: Jim Dooley, Abe Gibron, and Jack Pardee. Jim Finks's hand-picked choice, Neill Armstrong, couldn't do it, either, so the Bears were in even worse shape when Halas opened a letter from Mike Ditka, applying for the head-coaching job. Halas hired Ditka away from an assistant post with the Dallas Cowboys

Yes, a Chicago team really did go all the way. It was the Bears, who lost only once in the 1985 NFL season, then crushed the New England Patsies 46-10 in Super Bowl XX.

on January 20, 1982. When Ditka returned to Chicago, the old-time Bear tradition came back with him. Too bad Halas couldn't have lived a few more years to see the Bears become the Bears again.

In a sense, Halas made sure that his ferocious will to win would come back from the grave when he hired Ditka. Papa Bear knew he was on the way out, and cancer finally ended the 88-year-old NFL pioneer's remarkable career on October 31, 1983. Ditka had some rough times in the early going, letting his volatile temper get the best of him after tough losses. Bear fans, some players, and even Ditka himself began to waiver in the belief that Iron Mike could be the second coming of Halas.

But the Bear owner supported his hand-picked coach with every ounce of waning strength. By the time Halas died, Ditka was turning the corner. He survived his critics and his worst enemy—himself—by boring straight ahead, the way he had as a player, getting rid of the whiners, pretty boys, washed-up hangers-on, and those with not enough talent to match their desire.

Still, it was a narrow escape. Ditka admitted he probably couldn't have survived a loss to Philadelphia on October 23, 1983, after a tension-packed 2–5 start to the season. The

Bears squeaked past the Eagles 7–6, Jim McMahon soon wrested the starting quarterback job from Vince Evans, and things began to happen. The Bears were almost ready in 1984: even with McMahon TKO'd by a kidney injury, they reached the NFC Championship Game.

New Bear boss Mike McCaskey had been pussyfooting around the question of another contract for Ditka all season. After the Bears whipped Washington 23–19 in the 1984 playoff opener, McCaskey rode the emotion sweeping through Chicago by signing the coach for three more years. That and the revenge factor supplied by a 23–0 loss to the 49ers in the NFC Championship game was all the ammunition Ditka needed to be ready for 1985.

The Bears didn't look too ready in the first half of their Soldier Field opener against Tampa Bay. The Bucs sprinted to a 28–14 halftime lead, and it took a big play to turn things around. Naturally, the defense provided it when Richard Dent deflected a swing pass to Leslie Frazier, who hotfooted 29 yards for the fuse-lighting TD. McMahon took the Bears the rest of the way to a 38–28 comeback win, hitting 23 of 34 passes for 274 yards.

The combination of McMahon's offense and the "Junk-yard Dogs" brand of demolition defense swept the Bears to five straight victories. Not since 1963—the year they won the NFL championship—had the team gotten off to a 5–0 start. Ditka the tight end had been a force on that team, and Ditka the coach proved even more important to this team.

Chicago began to believe when the Bears scalped the Red-skins 45–10 in Soldier Field on September 29, but the real test came two weeks later. It was in San Francisco, on the same Candlestick Park turf where the Bears had been counted out nine months earlier. This time Buddy Ryan's vengeful defense sacked 49er quarterback Joe Montana seven times, beat up the Super Bowl champs 26–10, and flew home with a planeload of confidence.

The whole country caught Fridge Fever on the unforgetta-ble October 21 version of Monday night football. Rookie Wil-liam Perry's 325-pound bulk in the backfield delighted the fans and flattened the Green Bay Packers, 23–7. Perry twice wiped out Packer linebacker George Cumby on Walter Pay-ton touchdown plunges, but that was only the appetizer.

Perry provided the meat on the scoring sandwich by barreling over from one yard out himself for another TD. While it lasted, the Perry phenomenon was a marketing miracle. The personable Fridge peddled everything from refrigerators to whatever would fit inside them. The Bears kept rolling despite jealous taunting of the wealthy rookie by Dan Hampton and other veterans. That dissension took its toll a year later, but nothing could stop the 1985 Bears. Well, almost nothing.

The Miami Dolphins gave them a humiliating 38–24 punch in the ego before another Monday night audience on December 2. Coming off back-to-back shutouts of Dallas (44–0) and Atlanta (36–0), the Junkyard Dogs were a mite too cocky. Quarterback Dan Marino taught them a much-needed lesson, riddling the secondary for 31 first-half points. That was more than the Bears had yielded in the previous six games, ending their string of 13 quarters without permitting a TD.

Not surprisingly, Ditka and Ryan almost brawled at halftime while the players watched open-mouthed. It took time to heal the wounds, but three games were left and the Bears rebounded to win them, heading into the playoffs with renewed confidence. Three playoff games later, via a combined 91–10 slaughter of the New York Giants, Los Angeles Rams, and New England Patriots, the Bears got their claws on the Vince Lombardi Trophy. What the 18–1 world champs did in blanking the Giants 21–0 and then the Rams 24–0 was even more remarkable than their 46–10 pummeling of the Patsies in Super Bowl XX.

The 1984 Cubs: A Lost Weekend

Let's not dwell on the end of 1984, Cub fans. You've suffered enough. Remember instead what it was like in the summer, when the Cubbies were flattening everybody in sight, Harry Caray's beer-bellow-polka was No. 1 on the hit parade from Key West to Point Barrow, and Chicago rocked to the exploits of Ryno and the Red Baron, Rainbow and the Sarge, Deer and Bull and Penguin, Big Bad Lee and Jo-dee! Jo-dee! Jo-dee!

How sweet it almost was. Already a golden haze of nostalgia is settling over the ghost of the 1984 Cubs, even though many of the same guys came back to make another futile charge. Still, there is a fundamental difference in the makeup of today's Cubs and the hardy '84 band that got to within one step of the summit, then pitched (not to mention batted and fielded) their fans off the cliff in San Diego.

That weekend (and just two paragraphs ago, I vowed not to mention it) assured the '84 Cubs a place in their fans' hearts right next to the niche where the 1969 Cubbies rest in peace. Although Dallas Green gritted his teeth at the thought, the Cubs turned back into lovable losers almost overnight.

Such a foldup wasn't supposed to happen, because manager Jim Frey had a veteran starting lineup, with aging Larry Bowa, Ron Cey, and Gary Matthews; seasoned Jody Davis, Leon Durham, Keith Moreland, and Bob Dernier, and young Ryne Sandberg. None of the pitchers were fuzzy-cheeked kids, either.

It's a shame all the upbeat stuff came first in 1984, only to be buried under the postseason avalanche of gloom that shrouded Chicago. The Cubs already had put their ecstatic worshipers into the '84 World Series—psychologically, at least—by stomping the Padres twice in the Wrigley Field playoff games. That made the trip to San Diego a formality. The only question was whether the hot Cubs would sweep these creeps or grant them the face-saving solace of winning once before wrapping up the National League pennant and storming out to twist the Tigers' tail in the World Series. After all, the Cubs had been playing .333 ball on the road for years. That's all they needed to wrap up their first NL flag since 1945. So it was a cinch, wasn't it?

The letdown felt like tumbling into a bottomless pit. In just three games, the Cubs somehow lost six times, getting whipped by the Padres three straight and beating themselves three times. By comparison, the Cubs' gradual fade under the relentless pressure of the 1969 Mets' stretch charge was almost easy to take.

This was total disaster, an H-bomb landing right on Ground Zero in Wrigley Field, where Cub fans had confidently expected to stage a rematch of their 1945 World Series against Detroit.

Champagne and tears of joy mingled in Chicago when Jody Davis (left) caught Rick Sutcliffe's strikeout pitch to wrap up a 1984 division-clinching triumph over the Pirates. That's Jack Brickhouse in the background, wondering why it hadn't happened years ago.

That was partly a reflection of what a sensational season the Cubs had enjoyed until their last, lost weekend. By acquiring pitchers Steve Trout, Scott Sanderson, and Dennis Eckersley one by one, resident genius Dallas Green had taken a giant step toward solving the Cubs' longest-running headache—the lack of reliable starting pitchers. His best— or maybe worst—move came just before the June 15 trading deadline, although Green almost torpedoed it with a rookie blunder. He forgot that outfielders Joe Carter and Mel Hall hadn't cleared waivers before he sent them to Cleveland for pitchers Rick Sutcliffe and George Frazier and catcher Ron Hassey. The Cubs also tossed minor-league pitchers Don Schulze and Darryl Banks into the pot.

"I really butchered that one," Green conceded, aware he would have been laughed out of town if the blockbuster deal had collapsed because of his failure to shuffle the right papers. Fortunately for Green and the Cubs, Indian chief Phil Seghi stuck to the bargain. "A deal is a deal," Seghi said.

Such a deal. Sutcliffe's mound mastery made him the king of the Wrigley Field hill almost overnight. The strapping right-hander has a big heart, an easy smile, and sense of obligation to the fans that's missing in all except a handful of today's baseball-playing capitalists.

"Rick Sutcliffe is a class guy," noted Ben Bentley, the Chicago sports philosopher and referee of "The Sportswriters." "Why did people love the [1984] Cubs so much? Winning was important, but their fans even love losing Cub teams. This team was different because it was a bunch of handsome, nice guys. They looked good in pictures and they looked good on the field. The whole country went nuts for them."

True enough. By July, the bandwagon was full of newborn and recycled Cub fans, crowding out the long-suffering regulars in the bleachers, in the grandstand, and especially in Chicago saloons, where they trumpeted their undying fervor and baseball expertise. Most of them had been true-blue fans for about 10 minutes and what they knew about baseball had been gleaned from Harry Caray in that afternoon's telecast, but what the heck. The Bleacher Bums grumbled about the invasion of their Wrigley Field refuge, although they soon were caught up in the frenzy swirling around a team that suddenly had become a total winner.

"The fans have turned Wrigley Field into a circus," Sutcliffe marveled. "It's fun just being here. When we're trailing and get a man on base, the whole park is up, trying to help us get a rally going. These people in Chicago are amazing."

It wasn't exactly a replay of 1969, when the Cubs jumped in front of the NL East on Opening Day. In 1984 the fans weren't expecting too much, indicating that experience is not always the best teacher. Everything changed when Ryne Sandberg brought the Cubs back from the dead on June 23 with consecutive homers off Card relief ace Bruce Sutter.

From then on it was an emotional skyrocket to the top. The Cubs brushed aside the Mets and everybody else on the way to the September 24 clincher in Pittsburgh. Naturally, Sutcliffe wrapped it up when the Cubs won their first-ever division crown. Long before then, Chicago had gone completely bananas in a jubilant spree that peaked after the last home game of the season. The fans simply refused to go home, so manager Jim Frey led the Cubs from their clubhouse for a victory lap around the field. Towel-clad players jumped out of showers, scrambled into uniform and joined Pied Piper Frey.

It was a love feast, pure and simple. Exactly two weeks later, when the Cubs had finished blowing the pennant in San Diego, the front-runners jumped off the bandwagon, snarled, "I told you so!" and disappeared. The real fans licked their wounds, raised a toast to the exciting season that 1984 had been, and prepared to do what Cub fans do best: wait till next year.

Hot Stuff on Ice:
Hawks Jet to 1961 Stanley Cup

The year 1961 almost seems like ancient history. It was only 16 years after the Cubs had captured their last National League pennant: now it's going on a half-century since the Cubbies did it. For Blackhawks fans, the mathematics are just as depressing. The 1960–61 Blackhawks were the last to win the Stanley Cup. Bob Murdoch, who took over as coach 27 years later, for the 1987-88 season, was the eighth man to stand behind the Hawks' bench since Rudy Pilous took them to that long-ago National Hockey League playoff triumph. That includes the durable, if not too popular, Bob Pulford, who has had three separate tours at the helm.

Most Hawks' fans with long memories insist there were better Chicago teams on Stadium ice all through the '60s. An entire new generation of fans has grown up since then, suffering with their ice-cold hockey team the same way other Chicagoans have been moaning about the baseball, football, and basketball squads. The Blackhawks have had many more valleys than peaks since the Stanley Cup last showed up on home ice.

But it was "Here Comes the Hawks, the Mighty Black Hawks," during the 1961 playoffs. While fans sat transfixed by the exploits of a new superstar, Bobby Hull, they couldn't help dreaming of the Chicago hockey dynasty that surely would take shape. In the noisy beat of that stampede to the Stanley Cup, discordant notes were few. Nobody knew it wouldn't happen again.

The 1960–61 regular season wasn't that much of a tipoff

to the Hawks' playoff success, though. Even this team couldn't lay to rest the fabled Curse of Muldoon before coming to life in the playoffs. The curse was slapped on the Hawks by their first coach, Pete Muldoon. Fired after his 1926–27 debut, Muldoon stormed off with a vow that the Blackhawks would never win the regular-season NHL championship. His spell lingered for 40 years, until the Hawks finally exorcised it in 1967 with a sparkling 47–17–12 record, 17 points better than the second-place Montreal Canadians, before they took a knockout punch from Toronto in the first round of the playoffs. In 1960–61 the Hawks rang up a modest 29–24–17 record under Pilous, finishing third behind Montreal and the Maple Leafs. In those days, believe it or not, only four teams made the NHL playoffs. The Hawks stunned Montreal, shooting for its sixth straight Stanley Cup, in the first round. The Detroit Red Wings knocked off Toronto in the other semifinal, setting up the first all-American Stanley Cup showdown since the Wings and New York Rangers had tangled in 1950.

This one was tough, but the Hawks won the pivotal fifth game 6–3 in the Stadium on April 14, 1961. Two nights later they folded the Wings 5–1 in Detroit to break a 23-year drought by sipping champagne from the Stanley Cup for the third time in NHL history.

It was the storybook ending for a season that his teammates had dedicated to Hawk defenseman Ed Litzenberger. Litzenberger had been badly hurt in a car crash that killed his wife. When he returned for the 1960–61 season, the Hawks elected him captain. That emotional lift, plus the scoring punch of three high-powered lines and Glenn Hall in goal, turned the Hawks' promise into reality. The Million-Dollar Line featured Hull along with Red Hay and Murray Balfour. Ken Wharram, Stan Mikita, and Ab McDonald made up the Scooter Line, and the other unit employed Litzenberger, Eric Nesterenko, and Tod Sloan.

Hull, in his fourth NHL season, led the way with 31 goals, but relentless shadowing limited the Golden Jet to just four more in 12 playoff games. Oddly enough, defensive stalwart Pierre Pilote was the Hawks' top playoff pointmaker, contributing three goals and a dozen assists.

But the outstanding performer for these Stanley Cup

champions had to be goalie Hall. The hot netminder stunned the haughty Canadians with back-to-back semifinal shut-outs, sending the Hawks into the showdown round at peak confidence. Coach Pilous moved Nesterenko up to the Hay-Hull line and all three scored a goal in the Stadium to oust Montreal 3–0. The defensive work of Pilote, Moose Vasko, and Reggie Fleming, among others, was outstanding. Still, much of the credit must go to the Hawks' fidgety goal-keeper. It all added up to Chicago's third—and last—Stanley Cup coup.

The 1974-75 Bulls: Monsters of Madison Street

The trade for Nate Thurmond was supposed to be the final stone in the monument grateful Chicago fans would build to hail the 1975 National Basketball Association title, which should have been the first one for the Bulls. Instead, it turned out to be the final nail in the coffin of coach Dick Motta's dynasty.

Instead of becoming a milestone in Bulls history, Thur-mond became a millstone around their necks. He was Nate the Great in San Francisco, where the 6'11" center shared billing with the Golden Gate Bridge as the Bay Area's favor-ite towering edifices. In Chicago, Thurmond turned out to be the chief suspect in the most disappointing finish since the 1969 Cubs.

Nobody figured on that when the Bulls landed Thurmond from the Golden State Warriors on September 3, 1974, for center Clifford Ray, a cool half-million dollars, and a num-ber one draft pick. Motta had been saying while the Bulls were winning 51, 57, 51, and 54 games in the previous four seasons that a dominant center was the only thing he needed to take his team all the way. That they didn't go all the way wasn't Nate the Great's fault. The same strengths that Motta used to keep the franchise in Chicago led to the undoing of the feisty coach.

Chicago had been ready to bail out on pro basketball for good before Motta galloped out of the West and into the spotlight in 1968. Unfortunately, coaching success convinced Motta he could function as a general manager, contract negotiator, and judge of talent. The record shows he couldn't, with the disastrous Thurmond trade serving as exhibit A. Even so, when the 1974–75 championship dream turned into a nightmare, nobody tried to pin the scapegoat rap on Nate, not even Motta.

The sad truth was plain to see. Thurmond was a mobile center, a free-wheeling shooter, and a scorer who also played tough, physical defense. He had the credentials to put a powerful Bull team over the top. Or so it seemed when a Rolls-Royce delivered the veteran pivotman to Arthur Wirtz's Lake Shore Drive digs for his introductory press conference. Motta predicted the Bulls wouldn't have to change their style for Thurmond because "the ball always goes into the center."

But Thurmond's 11-year NBA scoring average of 17.4 points a game dwindled to 7.9 with the Bulls, knocking the Motta theory into a cocked hat. Motta's system needed a high-post passer in the pivot. Before the playoffs began, center Tom Boerwinkle was back in the starting lineup, with Thurmond a baffled benchwarmer. Instead of becoming the Bulls' big bully, Nate stopped moving inside and started missing from outside.

"I had no idea this offense was so delicate," he confessed.

A competitor, Thurmond blamed himself for the adjustment problem, but the seeds of Bull disaster had been sown by Motta in 1973. The coach told the owners that either General Manager Pat Williams had to go or Motta would go. Not surprisingly, they dropped Williams overboard, partly because of his habit of redistributing their wealth by renegotiating contracts. Now firmly in charge, Motta reneged on Williams's spoken promises to forwards Chet Walker and Bob Love, and guard Norm Van Lier.

Walker finally got a $200,000 deal, but Love and Van Lier were holdouts when the Bulls opened 1974–75 training on September 16 at Wheaton College. Van Lier didn't return until November 9, and Love stayed away until December 1. Their absence, along with the Motta's decision to sign no-talent rookie Cliff Pondexter instead of intimidator Maurice Lucas, eventually cost the Bulls the NBA championship.

The warning siren wailed early in Boston Garden, where

the Bulls built up a 26-point lead, then barely escaped with a 105–104 decision. They were only 19–17 when 1975 opened, and even a strong 28–18 finish left them one game short of locking up the home-court playoff edge.

From January 21 through February 28, though, the Bulls were almost unbeatable. An 18–2 rampage cemented their first Midwest Division title, but they ended the season by limping to 13 losses in 21 games.

That slump proved fatal in the playoffs, enabling the 48–34 Warriors to earn the odd game of any Western Conference series at home. In the seven-game Bulls-Warriors war waged in the Western Conference finals, that was a decisive advantage for Golden State. The exhausted Bulls didn't have the reserve strength to cope with coach Al Attles's mass-substitution tactics. Future Hall of Famer Rick Barry led by word and deed while the Warriors slugged the Bulls with their bench, leaving them exhausted, beaten, and embittered.

All of Motta's chickens came home to roost at the end. Dissension tore the Bulls apart, ending the Motta era with a whimper instead of the farewell bang it deserved. The frustrated Chicago coach couldn't resist lobbing a verbal hand grenade of his own after the 83–79 seventh-game loss in Oakland that froze the Bulls one step short of the 1975 championship series.

"When you vote on playoff shares, remember who was here at training camp and who wasn't," Motta snarled at his dejected team. Naturally, they ignored his fatherly advice, firing back with verbal broadsides of their own. Walker's whimsical description of the Bulls as the "Oakland A's of basketball" was on the mark, with one major difference—Motta's team won no titles.

Until that apocalyptic finish, the Bulls had at least turned on Chicago fans, making pro basketball the hottest ticket in town. Not until heaven-sent Michael Jordan arrived a decade later could the franchise begin full recovery from that devastating playoff defeat. After Motta's departure in 1976 the Bulls went through nine coaches in 10 years, a dreary parade of futility. Not even Jerry Sloan, the hardnosed guard who was to the Bulls what Mike Ditka was to the Bears, could turn it around in his three seasons as head coach.

The 1983 White Sox: Ugly or Not, They Won

Then–Texas Ranger manager Doug Rader will go down in history as the man who called it "Winnin' Ugly" when the White Sox ran away from his Rangers and the rest of the American League West in 1983. On the South Side of Chicago, nobody cared how they did it. It had been so long since the Sox had won anything that the fans adopted Rader's remark as their battle cry. That's how baseball nicknames are born. The Brooklyn Dodgers got theirs when a writer noted that fans "had to be real trolley dodgers" to elude heavy streetcar traffic on Flatbush Avenue.

Sadly—and almost traditionally for Chicago teams—the Sox ended this entertaining season by losin' ugly in the playoffs. But before they turned into birdseed for the Baltimore Orioles, the White Sox played some of the best baseball seen in Comiskey Park since the 1919 Pale Hose had stopped trying.

For the first time since the reign of Richie Allen and Bill Melton in the early '70s, followed by the Richie Zisk–Oscar Gamble one-two punch in 1977, the Sox had sock. Their 1983 team total of 157 home runs fell short of the club-record 192 clubbed by those 1977 South Side Hit Men, but it was an impressive power show. By way of contrast, during the 1910 Comiskey Park debut for the White Sox, they celebrated with seven—count 'em, seven—homers all season.

But in 1983, Big Boppers studded the lineup, notably Greg (Bull) Luzinski and rookie sensation Ron Kittle. Those guys really played longball. The Bull joined Jimmie Foxx and Ted Williams as the only sluggers to loft more than one homer atop the Comiskey Park roof. Luzinski bombed three of those moon shots into orbit in 1983, adding another the following year. Kittle slammed two roofers in 1983, then three more in '84 to take the all-time lead in that category. Engineers calculate that to clear the Comiskey Park grandstand roof, which towers 70 feet above the ground, a batted ball must travel a minimum of 474 feet from impact to the landing point outside the park. It's such an awesome feat that ex-Sox general manager Roland Hemond, an undemonstrative sort, confessed to an attack of goose bumps when Kittle connected. "We'll have to tell our maintenance crew

Floyd Bannister, lefty mound mainstay in the White Sox drive to a 1983 AL Western Division crown, congratulates stylish southpaw Billy Pierce by giving him the shirt off his back. Pierce's No. 19 was retired by the Sox, so Banny switched to No. 24.

not to walk on the roof during a game," Hemond dead-panned. "It's not safe."

No casualty reports were issued from the roof in 1983, but the rest of Comiskey Park was a danger zone for opposing pitchers. Five Sox homered in double figures, with Kittle (35), Luzinski (32), and Carlton Fisk (26) leading the way.

Still, it took more than brute strength to win 99 games, the second-highest total in Sox history. Only the 1917 world champs did better, chalking up a 100–54 record under manager Pants Rowland.

The Sox were a well-balanced team, but they sagged in May, hanging manager Tony LaRussa's job on tenterhooks. LaRussa's fate rested in the hands of Bobby Winkles, Sox director of player development, who was called on early in the 1983 season by owners Eddie Einhorn and Jerry Reinsdorf to evaluate the club. Fortunately, Winkles had enough savvy to sense some potential, despite a stumbling 16–24 start, the disruptive feud between LaRussa and veteran catcher Fisk and the wolfpack that howled nightly for the manager's hide from the Comiskey Park stands.

It's no mystery how LaRussa and his players overcame those problems. They started with solid, if not sensational, defense, backing up a formidable trio of starting pitchers that combined for a 62–27 log. LaMarr Hoyt (24–10), Richard Dotson (22–7), and Floyd Bannister (16–10) were so steady down the stretch that the lack of a short relief ace was no problem. There was good speed on the bases, as well, with Rudy Law pilfering 77 hassocks and Julio Cruz swiping 57.

Add the booming bats of Kittle, Luzinski, Fisk, Harold Baines, and Greg Walker and you have a team good enough to steamroll its division by an AL record margin of 20 games over second-place Kansas City. Once they hurdled the division barrier by sweeping a June 12 doubleheader in Oakland, the Sox were the best team in baseball. They were 25–31 before that decisive double dip, 74–32 after it.

By the time Rader unleashed his "winnin ugly" bleat in mid-August, the AL West race was already over. All his remark did was make winning three of four in a supposedly crucial series at Texas a little sweeter. The Sox left town with an eight-game bulge over Rader's faders.

That surge of superconfidence made the Sox and their fans feel good about the upcoming AL playoff against Baltimore. Nancy Faust wore out her fingers playing the "Na-Na-Hey-Hey-Good-bye" victory salute on the Comiskey Park organ while the Sox frolicked to a 22–9 August and a 24–6 September-October.

Chicago was late jumping on the Sox bandwagon, but Sox fans made the joint jump when the runaway hit full stride. Most of them even stopped booing LaRussa, while Sox players cashed in on commercials and promotions, such as the poster celebrating Luzinski's three roof jobs.

The Bull rashly predicted a playoff sweep of the Orioles during a Daley Plaza pep rally, but the Birds, who had been there before, knew better. They turned Luzinski's boast into bullfeathers by taking the best-of-five playoff set in three straight after Hoyt won the October 5 opener in Baltimore. It was the 100th Sox victory of the season—and their last. After that, Sox fans had to concede the playoffs were for the birds. Another familiar ending to a very different season.

The 1940 Bears:
Midway Monsters Go All the Way

The 1930s was the decade of the Bears. Even if they go back to the Super Bowl from now to 1990, the Bears of the 1980s will only approach the sustained excellence Coach George

Here's the real stuff, the 1940 Bears. No holdouts among these Monsters of the Midway, who flattened the Washington Redskins 73–0 to provide Chicago's all-time sports thrill.

Halas put on the field in that golden era of Chicago pro football.

Just consider the Hall of Fame array who wore the Blue and Orange colors Halas had brought along from the University of Illinois. Red Grange, Bronko Nagurski, Sid Luckman, George McAfee, Paddy Driscoll, Bill Hewitt, Joe Stydahar, Danny Fortmann, George Musso, Link Lyman, George Trafton, and Beattie Feathers played all or part of their careers with the Bears in the 1930s.

Neither the 1985 Bears nor any other single-season lineup in NFL history can match those greats for sheer ability. As for toughness, the Bears of the 1930s could pit that intangible against any wild bunch from any planet in the universe and hold their own. Not for nothing were they known as the Monsters of the Midway.

In large measure, Bear toughness was a reflection of their owner. Life was a brawl and football was life to the combative Halas. Rookies who couldn't meet Boss Bear's standards in the famous "nutcracker" drills under a broiling sun at the Rensselaer, Indiana, training camp sometimes staggered to the sidelines and went home without waiting to be cut. You had to want to play for Halas, because he wanted to win.

And win the Bears did, going to the NFL Championship game four times in the 1930s. They wore the crown in 1932—the first indoor title clash, a 9–0 Bear triumph over the Portsmouth Spartans in Chicago Stadium—and in 1933. That one was almost carbon copy of the 1963 classic, when the Bears beat the New York Giants 14–10. On the same Wrigley Field turf, the Bears came from behind to whip the Giants 23–21 in the brutal 1933 battle. The Bears of the late

'30s were better than their 1963 successors.

They were so good, in fact, that the 1940 Bears might have been the best football team ever to take the field anywhere, college or pro. In those days of limited newspaper and radio coverage, brilliant players often went unnoticed. Those who rose to stardom in an era of two-way football had to play 60 minutes of bruising contact on offense and defense. Only the best of the best came back for more.

Sid Luckman, spotted by Halas as a slick halfback at Columbia, needed part of his 1939 rookie season to learn how to become a sensational NFL quarterback. Columbia Sid watched Carl Brumbaugh operate under center for four games in the Bears' newfangled T formation, then stepped in to lead them to four straight title games and four NFL championships in the next seven years.

In that legendary era, 1940 had to be The Year. Luckman was in command of a veteran lineup, and Halas bolstered it with an incredible crop of rookies: Bulldog Turner, George McAfee, Ken Kavanaugh, Scooter McLean, Hampton Pool, Lee Artoe. Sophomores Luckman and Bill Osmanski melded with these newcomers plus proven performers such as Ray Nolting, Joe Maniaci, Joe Stydahar, Gary Famiglietti, and Automatic Jack Manders.

Looking up and down that roster makes the Bears' 73–0 demolition of the Washington Redskins in the 1940 NFL final seem less like a miracle. More than anything, it was the coming together of magnificent athletes at the precise moment to produce the perfect game. Nothing like it has been seen before or since in pro football or perhaps in any other sport. The test of time could well determine it to be the greatest performance of them all.

The most baffling aspect of that 1940 season is how the Bears managed to lose three times. They were beaten 21–7 by the crosstown rival Chicago Cardinals in Comiskey Park on September 25, then dropped two road tests in November—17–14 at Detroit and 7–3 at Washington. Yes, they lost 7–3 to the same team on the same Griffith Stadium turf under which they would bury the Redskins 73–0 just three weeks later.

If you figure that the close defeat in Washington had a lot to do with the Bear barrage that scalped the 'Skins in the rematch, you're right. Papa Bear Halas, a crafty devil, made sure of that.

Cubs Win! (Ten NL Pennants); Cubs Lose! (Eight World Series)

Believe it or not, the Cubs have had dynasties in their storied National League history. They won the first NL pennant in 1876. Under Adrian (Cap) Anson, the Cubs—then known as the White Stockings—took five NL flags, three straight from 1880 to '82. Frank Chance, "The Peerless Leader," managed four Cub pennant winners in five years, from 1906 through 1910. The Cubs managed to put together one more dynasty of sorts, winning the NL pennant every three years, regularly as clockwork from 1929 to 1938.

Sadly, the only time the Cubs—by then known as the Cubs—had a chance in the World Series was with Chance. He led Three-Finger Brown, Joe Tinker, Johnny Evers, and all that gang to back-to-back Series triumphs over Ty Cobb and the Detroit Tigers in 1907 and 1908. The best team in Cub history has to be the 1929 bunch. In 1929, manager Joe McCarthy had the horses to work with in Wrigley Field, and he put them through their paces. He shipped fading Grover Cleveland Alexander back to battle the bottle in St. Louis, handled Hack Wilson's binges tactfully (he kept the 5'6" slugger in line by telling him, "Hack, as long as you hit, I

Piercing Question

Who was the only player to be in uniform for the last Cub World Series in 1945 and the last White Sox World Series in 1959? It was stylish southpaw Billy Pierce, an 18-year-old Tiger rookie when they outlasted the Cubs in '45. Pierce saw no action in that one, and Sox fans still second-guess Manager Al Lopez for not using him against the Dodgers in '59. Pierce had to wait until 1962 to win his second World Series start for San Francisco, beating Whitey Ford and the Yankees 5-2 in the sixth game.

Whooping it up in clubhouse celebration after the Cubs clinched the 1945 NL pennant are Manager Charlie Grimm (top) and trainer Andy Lotshaw (bottom). Grimm and Lotshaw, two of Chicago's legendary characters, saw it all, both top and bottom.

don't care what you drink"), and won the pennant by a whopping 10½ games over Pittsburgh. With hitters like Wilson, Rogers Hornsby, Jolly Cholly Grimm, Riggs Stephenson, and Kiki Cuyler and pitchers such as Charlie Root, Pat Malone, Guy Bush, and John (Sheriff) Blake, it was easy. Even an arm injury that limited Gabby Hartnett to 22 at-bats all season didn't slow the pennant express.

The four Cub pennant winners in 1929, 1932, 1935, and 1938 were all strong teams with veteran casts of outstanding players, some in the Hall of Fame class. But in the end, it was the same old thing that prevented this collection of winners from dominating the NL in the '30s in the same way the Yankees were trampling American League opposition: muddle-headed ownership.

When mild-mannered Philip K. Wrigley took the reins after his father, William, died in 1932, the Cubs were the NL's dominant organization. They had talent on the field and the Wrigley Gum millions to buy more. A comparatively small investment in the farm system would have kept the Cubs on top for years to come.

Their mistake was in sticking with Wrigley family retainers such as Grimm and Hartnett instead of hiring a strong general manager in the Branch Rickey mold to blueprint the future. That compounded the costly mistake of letting manager Joe McCarthy get away after he took the Cubs to the 1929 pennant.

Cub fans blamed McCarthy for refusing to make Hack Wilson the goat of the A's devastating 10-run rally in the fourth game of the '29 Series that wiped out an 8–0 deficit. Marse Joe was too smart for that, but he got fired in 1930, while Wilson was rebounding with an awe-inspiring 56 homers, 190 runs batted in, and .723 slugging percentage. Unfortunately, the next year Rogers Hornsby, a great player and a mean man, shattered Wilson's confidence and chased the phenomenal hitter and legendary drinker out of town after Hack hit only 13 homers.

It's too bad Cub president William Veeck didn't have the same tolerance for baseball characters that became the trademark of his son, Bill. The elder Veeck put together a magnificent Cub team in 1929, and McCarthy should have been around to manage it for years. Instead, Marse Joe became the "push-button" manager of the mighty Yankees, bringing them back to Wrigley Field to humiliate the 1932 Cubs during a 4–0 World Series sweep. McCarthy's Bronx Bombers went on to win eight more AL pennants, shutting out the Cubs again in the '38 Series.

Without Hartnett in the lineup in '32, '35, and '38, the Cubs wouldn't even have had the chance to lose the World Series. Gabby's 1938 "homer in the gloamin' " off the Pirates' Mace Brown still ranks as one of the top three moments in Cub history.

The Cubs squeezed out another flag in 1945, the last year of World War II. Just about anybody who could totter to first base was away that season, wielding a rifle in the trenches or a wrench in a shipyard. The '45 World Series between the creaking Cubs and toothless Tigers ("I don't think either team can win it," said Chicago sportswriter Warren Brown) was one for the aged, not for the ages. One longtime diamond scribe asserted that if Ty Cobb could round up eight more living survivors of the 1907–08 seasons, they could take the combined 1945 Cubs-Tigers in six games. That may have been a slight exaggeration, though nothing that took place in the '45 Series disproved it.

1959 White Sox: They Finally Go-Go

It takes something special to gain one of the storied nicknames in sports: Seven Blocks of Granite (Fordham's line in
the mid-'30s anchored by guard Vince Lombardi); The
Fargo Express (boxer Billy Petrolle); The Go-Go White Sox.

No explanation is needed for that last one, especially on
the South Side of Chicago. They were Nellie Fox, Little
Looie, Jungle Jim, Billy Pierce. They were stolen bases,
bunts, one-run games, tactical baseball, sensational catches
by center fielder Jim Landis, the leadership of catcher
Sherm Lollar. It was the second-longest era of sustained
excellence in White Sox annals, right behind the 1917–20
powerhouse.

It also produced, sad to say, just one American League
pennant. That came in 1959, the only time this entertaining
group of Sox stalwarts could outfinish those pin-striped
finks from New York. No wonder baseball fans with long
memories from every other AL city reveled in the Yankee
demise of the late 1960s and early '70s.

The Pale Hose had been struggling to escape the long
shadow of the 1919 Black Sox for 30 years, but it didn't
happen until Frank Lane and Paul Richards teamed up in
the early '50s. The wheeler-dealer known as Trader Lane
and Frantic Frank ushered in a new South Side era when he
became Sox general manager in 1949. Two years later, when
Richards took over as field boss, the Go-Go Sox were born.

Lane had already supplied Richards with the man who
was to be the coiled mainspring of the Go-Go guys. He was
a tobacco-chewing second baseman named Jacob Nelson
Fox, pried loose from the Philadelphia Athletics by Lane for
catcher Joe Tipton. Fox was smaller than his listed 5'10" and
160 pounds, but his heart was bigger than Bridgeport. For
14 years, Nellie lit the fuse for the second Chicago fire.

When Fox was 16 his father delivered him from a Pennsylvania farm to Connie Mack and the Philadelphia A's in a
pickup truck. Canny Connie, operating on a shoestring ever
since breaking up his 1929–31 dynasty, liked the kid's spunk.
Fox came up from the minors to begin a 19-year big-league
career, and in 1950, his permanent address shifted from
Philadelphia to Chicago.

Whoa, Nellie! There was no stopping mound ace Billy Pierce (left), Manager Al Lopez (center) and Nellie Fox while the Go-Go White Sox stormed to the 1959 AL flag, their first one in 40 years.

That was the last of Luke Appling's 20 seasons at short-stop. Lane landed Chico Carresquel to replace Luke and went with Richards instead of the hometown favorite, Appling, as manager.

The Sox had always put a premium on base stealing, mainly because they had little else on offense, but now they ran wild. Thefts soared from 19 in '50 to an AL high 99 in '51, and the fans loved it. Newcomer Minnie Minoso led in stolen bases with 31. Comiskey fans responded, roaring "Go! Go!" at every baserunner.

Attendance soared to 1,328,234 in 1951, dipping under a million just once in the next 14 years. Lane's motion was perpetual as well, bringing in people such as double no-hitter pitcher Virgil "Fire" Trucks, Dick Donovan, and even ex-Cub Phil Cavaretta.

But Lane couldn't quell constant upheaval among the Comiskey heirs. He made an emotional exit in 1955, a year after Richards left to manage Baltimore. By unofficial count (nobody could figure how many times Willie Miranda had been shipped out or brought back), Lane traded more than 350 players in his nonstop tenure.

Another piece of the 1959 pennant-winning team fell into place in 1956, when Luis Aparicio took over at shortstop and became AL Rookie of the Year. With Little Looie and Nellie, the Sox soon had one of the best keystone combinations in the majors, on a par with Pittsburgh's Dick Groat and Bill Mazeroski or Tony Kubek and Bobby Richardson of the Yankees. Still, the same depressing scenario was played out yearly on the South Side. The Sox would challenge, the Yankees would come in to sweep a brawl-filled Comiskey Park series, and it was "wait till next year" time again.

Finally, in 1959, when Barnum Bill Veeck's group bought out Dorothy Comiskey Rigney, the stage was set for the drama of that year. With an infield of Bubba Phillips, Aparicio, Fox, and Earl Torgeson from third to first; Al Smith, Jim Landis, and Jim McAnany in the outfield from left to right; Lollar catching and starters Early Wynn, Bob Shaw, Pierce, and Donovan getting bailed out by relievers Gerry Staley and Turk Lown, the Go-Go Sox went for it at last.

Minoso had been traded away to get Wynn, but Jungle Jim Rivera, Ted Kluszewski, Billy Goodman, Norm Cash, Johnny Callison, and John Romano came off the bench to provide extra punch. Manager Al Lopez blended defense and speed for victory in 35 of 50 one-run decisions. That was enough to bring Veeck's Sox home five lengths in front of Cleveland for the first South Side pennant in 40 years. Who could blame Mayor Richard J. Daley, Sox fan No. 1 and Fire Commissioner Quinn for terrifying old ladies by setting off Chicago air-raid sirens in salute?

The disappointment of a World Series loss to the Los Angeles Dodgers, whoever they were, was offset by the exhilaration of that long-overdue pennant. At least Sox fans could take comfort in the knowledge that all of their heroes were trying in this Series, something their fathers hadn't been too sure about in 1919.

The 1947 Chicago Cardinals: A Dream Comes True

The Chicago Cardinals tasted a lot of despair in 39 years as the South Side's National Football League entry. At least before they flew to St. Louis in 1960 they could look back on two things the Bears never had: a coach with a sense of humor and the Dream Backfield.

Jimmy Conzleman was the coach. Quarterback Paul Christman, halfbacks Charlie Trippi and Elmer Angsman (who replaced Marshall Goldberg), and fullback Pat Harder were the backfield. They produced a memorable season in 1947, when the Cards went all the way to their second NFL championship. It was a sweet moment in Chicago sports history, a chronicle that has not been replete with such success.

Conzleman was a character, raconteur, man about town, and connoisseur of fine beverages. He played with George Halas on the Decatur Staleys, but genial Jimmy never took football, or life, as seriously as Papa Bear did. So 1947 was a fitting reward for Conzleman and the Cards, disproving for one season Leo Durocher's adage about nice guys finishing last.

Not that the Cards couldn't play rough when they had to. Despite the Bears' huge 45–19–6 edge in head-to-head battles over the years, the Cards had the knack of scaring Halas to death in close games. Their two meetings in 1947 were different because the Cards had the horses.

It came down to the final game of the season in Wrigley Field. The Chicago rivals shared the Western Conference lead with 8–3 records, but the Cards had trounced the Bears 31–7 in their Comiskey Park meeting on October 5. With everything on the line, relaxed Jimmy Conzleman and his Dream Backfield turned this showdown into a nightmare for the Bears.

But even Conzleman's savoir faire was ruffled by the pandemonium that marked his preparation for the rematch. The Cards' coach wanted to use his team's edge in speed for an early strike, designing a bomb from Christman to reserve Babe Dimancheff. It was almost as hard for Conzleman to locate Dimancheff to tell him about it as it was for the Bear secondary to cover the fleet receiver. After missing practice all week, Dimancheff phoned to tell Conzleman that he'd been at the hospital, where his wife had presented him with a daughter. She was named Victoria to celebrate the victory over the Bears that was not yet in the bag. Fortunately for Conzleman, Halas played into his hands.

With the Bear defense set to contain the slashing runs of Trippi and Angsman, end Mal Kutner went deep as a decoy on the first play from scrimmage. The secondary took the bait, and Dimancheff was all alone, turning Christman's pass into an 80-yard scoring play. The Bears never caught up and the Cards were conference champs, 30–21.

It was justice of a sort. Cards' owner Charles Bidwell died in 1947, shortly after outbidding the All-America Football Conference for Trippi by paying the Georgia All-American an unheard-of $100,000. Trippi proved he was worth it in the 1947 NFL title game on the frozen turf of Comiskey Park. So did Christman, the soft-spoken quarterback from Missouri, and Angsman, the Notre Dame product who made the big plays in the dramatic 28–21 victory over the Philadelphia Eagles. Angsman broke through the skidding Eagle defense for a pair of 70-yard touchdown scampers on identical plays. Trippi's magnificent 75-yard punt return in the third quarter enabled Coach Greasy Neale of Philadelphia to coin a gem. While would-be tacklers sprawled in Trippi's wake as he galloped from sideline to sideline, Neale bellowed at a fallen defender: "Get up! He'll be back again in a minute!"

Alas, that wonderful year and a tainted 1925 NFL title that really belonged to the Pottsville Maroons were all Card fans got out of the team's lengthy tenure in Chicago. The Cards reached the NFL title game again in 1948, but this time the weather in Philadelphia worked against them. Players on both teams had to help pull the tarp off snow-covered Shibe Park before the home team recovered a fumble, then punched over the only touchdown in a 7–0 Eagle triumph.

After that it was all downhill for the Cards. The team that had started as the Racine Cardinals in 1920 chased the Chicago Tigers out of town, but could not survive against the Bears. The Cards played their farewell 1959 schedule in Soldier Field, then departed for St. Louis, leaving behind a small, hardy band of mourners and some happy memories.

FOUR

HOW BAD WERE THEY?

Chicago's 10 Worst Teams

Picking mediocre Chicago teams is easy. We've had tons of them. Really bad teams? That's another story, and here it is.

The 1919 Black Sox: The Great Dumpers

Hey, wait a minute. Isn't that the same team listed in the last chapter as the best in Chicago history? How can it also be the worst?

It not only can be and might be, sports fans. It is. The 1919 Chicago White Sox, who were our best ever when all they played was baseball, hit bottom in a hurry when they started playing other games. Great as they were on the field, eight of these guys were crooks. Some of the blame can be dumped in other laps, notably the ample one possessed by Sox owner Charles A. Comiskey, but the Black Sox did themselves in.

Like a lot of other people caught red-handed in a clumsy criminal act, they paid the penalty. Because of his magnificent ability, Shoeless Joe Jackson is the one name among the eight Black Sox that outlived his death, but this unlettered country boy was not the ringleader. He simply went along with the botched-up caper at the urging of Charles (Chick) Gandil, the Sox first baseman. Other members of the Gang of Eight were shortstop Charles (Swede) Risberg, a man so tough that Jackson feared the Swede would kill him for talking; outfielder Oscar (Happy) Felsch; third baseman George (Buck) Weaver; reserve infielder Fred McMullin; and pitchers Eddie Cicotte and Claud (Lefty) Williams.

Over the years, the incident has been blurred by some of those legends fans like to believe. Jackson did not make a habit of playing the outfield in bare feet, as one legend holds. What really happened was that he played just one game in stockinged feet for his hometown mill team, the Greenville, South Carolina, Spinners. All Joe wanted to do was ease the pain of a blister, not become immortal. When Jackson hit a homer against archrival Anderson, a neighboring town, an unhappy fan bellowed, "Hey, Joe, how come you shoeless?" while the young slugger circled the bases. From then on, the legend of Shoeless Joe Jackson grew until it was shattered by another voice; "Say it ain't so, Joe."

Another baseball myth holds that a tearful newsboy made that plea outside the Criminal Courts Building in 1920, after

---

Black Sox Try to Fix Fixers

Years after he was banned from baseball with seven other Black Sox teammates for throwing the 1919 World Series to Cincinnati, Shoeless Joe Jackson told the inside story to *Tribune* columnist Dave Condon. Jackson revealed that the fix had been agreed on months before the Series.

He insisted that there were only seven Black Sox, but third baseman Buck Weaver knew about it and didn't squeal, so he got the boot, too. When Sox ace Ed Cicotte plunked Reds' leadoff man Maurice Rath with a pitch in the Series opener, it was a signal to insiders that the fix was in. But after Cicotte got short-changed on his end of a promised $100,000 payoff that never arrived, he tried to double-cross the gamblers. It was too late to save the Sox.

Extra! Extra! Read all about it! Back in the days when newspapers put out extras to stay on top the news, this Tribune front page tells the sad story of the 1919 Black Sox.

Jackson had just blown the whistle on the Black Sox to a Cook County grand jury. In sportswriter Hughie Fullerton's version, Jackson also choked back a sob before replying, "I'm afraid it is, kid."

Comiskey finally suspended the Infamous Eight near the end of the 1920 season. The word was out about dumping the 1919 World Series, and it looked like the Black Sox were ready to strike again, going into a suspicious seven-game swoon that enabled Cleveland to win the AL Pennant. The Sox had four 20-game winners that year—Red Faber (23), Williams (22), Dickie Kerr, and Cicotte (both 21)—but the gamblers were betting on the Indians.

Comiskey publicly denied the 1919 Series had been dumped. Privately, he hired gumshoes, begged newspapermen, and grilled fellow owners to find out what was happening. The truth was that Comiskey's nickel-nursing had almost ruined not only his franchise but baseball itself. Sullen and mutinous over the Old Roman's penurious wages, the Black Sox were easy marks for con artists who told them they could get rich by "taking it easy" on Cincinnati in the Series.

The promised jackpot was $100,000, supplied by New York gambler Arnold Rothstein. Known as "A.R.," he was a shady operator who got rich by cashing in on the greed of simple-minded victims like the Black Sox. At the time, $100,000 was worth a lot more than a million is now, but the dumpers actually got less than half of that. Jackson ended up with $5,000, not much to show for a shattered reputation.

Rothstein and his cronies made plenty, although the bungled deal almost backfired on them. Jackson testified he had been promised $20,000, payable in installments after each fixed game. Cicotte was shelled for four runs in the fourth inning of the opener, and Williams's control somehow deserted him the next day, enabling the Reds to grab a 2–0 lead in the best-of-nine set. The nine-game format, requiring the champion to win five, was used only in 1903, 1919, 1920, and 1921.

After that second loss, Jackson was asking, "What the hell's the matter?" because the promised payoff wasn't coming through. When Shoeless Joe got $5,000 instead of the promised $20,000 after the fourth game, he growled, "What's coming off here?" By then the Unfortunate Eight finally began to figure out what suckers they had been. Cincinnati had a 3–1 lead, so some brave talk about "We'll show those gamblers" was mere whistling past the graveyard. The Black Sox had been tarred for life.

They deserved the banishment from baseball that Commissioner Kenesaw Mountain Landis soon slapped on all eight. Even now some misguided meatballs insist Jackson belongs in the Hall of Fame because he was just an illiterate country boy. That's pure bull. Shoeless Joe and his fellow fixers could have been the heart of a White Sox Dynasty— maybe the best team to play in any era. What they chose to become was the worst ever. Sox fans have been paying for their folly ever since.

The 1969 Bears: An Unlucky 13

Maybe there were worse years for Chicago teams than 1969, though not too many. When the Misfits of the Midway gratefully tottered to the end of their NFL slate on December 21 with a 20–3 loss to the Detroit Lions, Windy City fans cheered. The year had wrung them out emotionally from start to finish.

Fans had suffered through miserable seasons by the Blackhawks and Bulls, with neither team even good enough to make the playoffs. The spring gloom was replaced by summer euphoria, when that peerless leader, Leo Durocher, steered the Cubs on a direct course to the NL playoffs and from there to the first World Series in Wrigley Field since 1945. Until September, few people on the North Side doubted for a millisecond that the New York Mets, not the Cubs, would fold in the stretch.

The reward for that faithful, fanatical flock, of course, was the Colossal Cub Chokeup of '69. It was a tough act for the Bears to follow, but they were equal to the task. Under Coach Jim Dooley they turned into the Milquetoasts of the Midway, sinking to the bottom of the NFL standings with a 1–13 record.

Never before, through 49 seasons of franchise history—as the Decatur Staley AC in 1920, the Chicago Staleys in 1921, and the Bears ever since—had a George Halas–owned team lost 10 games. This foldup was doubly disastrous because the Bears and their fans had expected a winning season.

It was a bitter comedown for Dooley. As a Bear end, assistant coach, and Halas's hand-picked successor in 1968, Dooley had a father-son relationship with Papa Bear. Suddenly, with the Bears in that '69 tailspin, Dooley was no longer a favorite son. The Bears had gone from a team that lost the

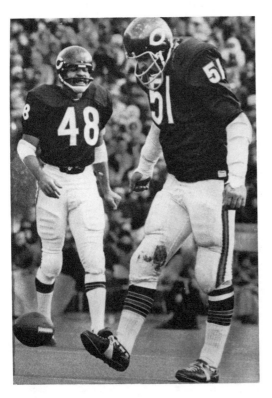

Aw, rats! No, Dick Butkus wasn't rehearsing for a jump to the Chicago Sting. The Hall of Fame linebacker is just showing defensive back Ron Smith (48) how he feels about another un-Bearable loss.

1968 Western Division title to bitter rival Green Bay, 28–27, in the last game, to a total loss in 1969. Nobody, least of all Dooley, could understand why the collapse happened so fast.

"Halas didn't want to hear me say we had to spend more money to draft better players," Dooley recalled. "We stopped communicating. He wouldn't draft a player in the first round if the guy had a lawyer or an agent. Those poor drafts hurt the Bears for 10 years. George Allen built the 1963 championship team by wheeling and dealing, but he left two years later."

Allen's ambition to take over when Halas decided to end his four-decade coaching reign had been obvious for years. Halas used that hunger to sharpen the rivalry between Bears' assistants, just as the crafty coach liked to pit his defensive unit against the offense. Since the defense carried the Bears through good years and bad, it was a one-sided skirmish, though Halas enjoyed the fireworks. The mean, combative side of the old man's nature led him until the day he died to do anything that might help the Bears win, short of spending money.

When they didn't win under Dooley, the bewildered coach was thrown to the lions, and not just in Detroit. Dooley had to cope with the November 10, 1968, injury that turned Gale Sayers from an all-time great into a mere mortal.

Before the 49ers' Kermit Alexander tore Sayers's knee ligaments with a clean tackle, the Bear superstar had rushed for 100 or more yards 16 times in less than four seasons. Only the week before the injury, he had set a Bear record of 205 yards that stood until Walter Payton tied it in 1977, then smashed it three games later with 275 yards against Minnesota.

Sayers came back to lead NFL rushers with 1,032 yards in '69, an incredible display of grit since the Kansas Comet was running on a wrecked right knee that took away speed and open-field elusiveness. Although Galloping Gale topped the 100-yard barrier four times in 1969, he never got there afterward and the knee limited his pro career to just seven years. Still, Sayers was almost the whole show in '69, when the Bears were limited to one touchdown or less in six of their 14 games. With a knee injury also bothering all-world linebacker Dick Butkus, the Bear defense limped along without the usual ferocity.

Irish Jack Concannon and Mormon Virgil Carter were supposed to share the quarterback role in that dreadful season. Cocky Concannon's talent never caught up with his confidence, but it was mild-mannered Carter who provided comedy relief with the famous "chicken-bleep" incident. Carter simmered when Concannon started—and lost—the first four games, then really boiled at Dooley's decision to go with strong-armed rookie Bobby Douglass, another Kansas product. Douglass, who was to become Bear Fans' favorite whipping boy, wowed them at first by hurling 70-yard strikes in a 38–7 Wrigley Field rout of Pittsburgh. Then his inexperience began to show, forcing Dooley to turn in desperation to Carter. Just one and a half games later, Carter was benched at halftime after riddling the Packers with two completions in 17 attempts. "That's the last game I'll play for the Bears," Carter fumed. "I hope Halas isn't chicken-bleep enough to keep from trading me." At least "Chicken-bleep" was the way it came out in the papers. Halas got the message, fining Carter $1,000 while secretly chuckling at his chutzpah.

Dooley wasn't laughing. He suffered through two more seasons at the helm before Halas sentenced the Bears to three years of the same mediocrity under Abe Gibron. The pain inflicted on Dooley by his bitter tenure led to reports of his drinking and carousing, almost breaking up his family. His courageous wife, Elaine, helped put the pieces together until Halas summoned Dooley back to the fold in 1981. Both Cub and Bear fans keep trying to forget 1969, but Jim Dooley never will.

The 1961–65 Cubs Flunk Out of P. K. Wrigley's College

Philip K. Wrigley was born to be a craftsman and a tinkerer. Fooling around with machinery, autos, engines, and whatever was the most fun this decent, sad-eyed man ever had. Getting to do just that at the Great Lakes Naval Training

Center during World War I made him happier than owning the Cubs.

Unfortunately for P.K., fate decreed that he should be born a multimillionaire, the heir to his father's and grandfather's chewing gum empire. Even worse for Cub fans, the Chicago National League baseball club was the most visible, if far from the most profitable, part of that empire.

Philip K. Wrigley was a good guy, a plain and simple man endowed with all the old-fashioned virtues and few vices, old or new. He answered his phone himself, speaking strictly off the cuff to all callers, newspapermen or simply irate Cub fans. Wrigley would answer their questions as truthfully as he could.

The intricacies of baseball, especially the successful operation of a major-league franchise, never were quite clear to Mr. Wrigley. He ran his business strictly on the up-and-up and tried to conduct baseball affairs the same way. In the cutthroat world of sports, where successful operators always had aces up their sleeves, straight-arrow P.K. was outmatched. No wonder the Cubs wallowed in the NL wilderness for so many seasons under his benevolent stewardship. What happened to Wrigley's team was living proof that Leo Durocher's most famous pronouncement had the hard edge of truth: nice guys do finish last.

P.K. took over when his dad, William Jr., died in 1932. At the time, the Cubs were loaded with talent, in the midst of a semidynasty that captured four NL pennants between 1929 and 1938. When the winners began to slip away because of age or misguided trades, fewer real prospects came up from the minors to replace them. The Cubs kept parading platoons of players through Wrigley Field, each of them heralded as the superstar who would turn things around. Instead, they turned Cub fans around for 40 years, sending them home in disgust.

The real superstar of the P. K. Wrigley era was Ernie Banks, signed from the Kansas City Monarchs of the Negro American League. The reason the Cubs paid $35,000 in 1953 for this unknown 22-year-old revealed the organization's incompetence with startling clarity. They wanted him as a roommate for second baseman Gene Baker who was slated to become the first black player in a Cub uniform.

Their colossal luck in blundering across the all-time Cub—and Banks is still recognized as Mr. Cub by fans born after he retired in 1971—couldn't overcome so much mismanagement. Wrigley was such a nice fellow that he was given a pass by most of the media and fans. How could you rip an owner who stressed family entertainment (albeit lousy baseball) in that irresistible Wrigley Field sunshine and who genuinely tried to make the Cubs a winner, spending his millions freely?

All P.K. got for his megabucks was the likes of Lou ("The Mad Russian") Novikoff, Chuck ("The Rifleman") Connors, Roy Smalley, Harry Chiti, Bob Speake, Glen Hobbie, Paul Toth, John Boccabella, Aldolfo Phillips, Boots Day, Pete La-Cock, and on and on. Wrigley's general managers simply couldn't swim in the same pond with the sharks running other teams.

The irony of this long-running hope opera was that Wrigley's virtues proved the Cubs' undoing. His loyalty to faithful employees was legendary. Instead of firing them, P.K. just kept recycling the same people in an endless front-office shuffle. Like the Cubs on the field, management was on a treadmill to oblivion.

The fatal flaw that led Wrigley to the ultimate folly was his passion for tinkering. All else had failed, so the owner revealed on January 12, 1961, that henceforth the Cubs would be led to glory, or wherever, by a revolving "College of Coaches." It never occurred to mild-mannered P.K. that 99 percent of the team's ferocity from then on would consist of behind-the-scenes back-stabbing by Cub coaches jockeying to upstage their rivals.

The results of this crack-brained experiment were predictable. The Cubs' five-year record under the Quarrelsome Coaches was 353–449; for the five preceding years it had been 328–442. But the change didn't really result in any more wins: in 1962, the schedule went to 162 games a season from the traditional 154.

Officially, the College of Coaches is supposed to have lasted only two years—the dismal 64–90 of 1961, followed by a disastrous 59–103. The coaches took their turn at the helm, with each coach hoping his fellow coaches would fall on their face. Some recipe for success. Wrigley should have listened to scrappy Don Zimmer, who said, "These guys and their conflicting orders are driving the young players crazy."

Like a bad hangover, however, coaching collegiality stuck around until the end of 1965, when disgusted "head coach" Bob Kennedy walked away. When it was mercifully over, Kennedy (182–198), Lou Klein (65–83), Elvin Tappe (46–69), Charlie Metro (43–69), Vedie Himsl (10–21), and Harry Craft (7–9) had losing managerial records. The other deans of Wrigley U—Bobby Adams, Rip Collins, Charlie Grimm, Goldie Holt, Rube Walker, Alvin Dark, Fred Martin, Buck O'Neil, Mel Wright, Walt Dixon, George Freese, Alex Grammas, Joe Macko, Stan Hack, Mel Harder, Whitey Lockman, and Les Peden—were all convinced they could have done better. Wrigley added still another comic twist in 1963, signing on Air Force Colonel Bob Whitlow as the Cubs' "athletic director." Whitlow hung on for years, contributing nothing but more acrimony.

As for Cub fans, their heads revolved in bewilderment as the revolving coaches slugged it out and the players went around in circles. The only unrevolving things in Wrigley Field were the turnstiles. Attendance dropped drastically, finally convincing P.K. things were far from okay.

The 1967-68 Bulls: Fans Won't Horn In

Now that Michael Jordan and high hopes for the future guarantee the Bulls nightly Chicago Stadium sellouts, it's hard for most fans to remember when this franchise hung on tenderhooks. It was a lot closer call than people think. The Bulls were a couple of errant jump shots or a few more empty seats away from joining the Bruins, Gears, Stags, Majors, and Packers/Zephyrs in the pro basketball graveyard. Chicago, the smart money said, simply wasn't a basketball town. Papa Bull Dick Klein proved them wrong, but he paid a high price.

Before the franchise turned the corner, Klein found himself on the sidewalk, dumped by Dick Motta, the unknown he'd brought in from Utah to coach the floundering Bulls. Motta arrived with the right formula for survival, but it was strong medicine: sheer guts, coaching skill, and hunger to succeed, blended with combativeness and paranoia.

Motta's formula didn't produce an instant winner. After the 1967–68 season, however, a near miracle was needed to save the Bulls for Chicago.

Motta took over in the Bulls' third season. What had happened in the first two years sounds like the plot of a Mel Brooks movie. The hero was Coach John (Red) Kerr, a local boy who made good. From the South Side, a product of Tilden Technical High School and the University of Illinois, Kerr was everybody's buddy, the quintessential good guy. The villain, undeservedly so, was Klein. Considering what Klein had gone through just to get the Chicago franchise, the fans should have cheered him.

The NBA had jacked up the price for granting a Chicago franchise to an unheard-of $1.6 million and then had refused to let Klein take Carver High's Cazzie Russell, a natural drawing card for his new team, in the 1966 draft because the New York Knicks wanted him. Despite everything, the unsinkable Klein plowed ahead, determined to put his Bulls over in Chicago. "They won't win 10 games," sneered St. Louis Hawks' coach Richie Guerin at first glimpse of the newcomers. But the Bulls surprised everybody the first time around by becoming the most successful expansion team in any sport.

Working with a motley crew of cast-off players and the defensive brilliance of a guard named Jerry Sloan, Kerr coached the 1966–67 Baby Bulls to a respectable 33–48 record. Kerr was rewarded with NBA Coach of the Year laurels. Klein got mostly headaches from not enough paying customers (the "official" average of 4,772 was sheer fiction) in the creaky old Amphitheater and the threat of payroll escalation from impending war with the upstart American Basketball Association.

The Bulls opened their second season in Chicago Stadium, saddled with a stiff rent tariff from benevolent landlord Arthur Wirtz. With up to 15 percent of gate revenue going to Wirtz right off the top, drawing more people was imperative. Instead, the Bulls lost four straight and Klein groped for the panic button, trading crowd-pleasing playmaker Guy Rodgers to Cincinnati for Flynn Robinson. "Rodgers is so popular, we've drawn less than 7,000 in three home games," Klein said, defending the move. "Last year we were the NBA's

John (Red) Kerr (right), first coach of the Bulls, explains a basketball's shape to another bewildered hoop scribe.

Cinderella team. This year we're the pumpkin."

Things got steadily worse as Klein interfered nightly with Kerr's coaching decisions. That did nothing for the Bulls' morale. Neither did supergunner Robinson's habit of taking 30 shots a game, some from the Stadium parking lot. The fans liked Flingin' Flynn, but he was not exactly a team player.

After the Bulls dropped 15 of their first 16 games, nothing could salvage 1967–68. Fans were staying away in droves, rumors of a move to Kansas City or elsewhere were rampant, and dissension split the dressing room and front office. If Klein's clowns had bowed out of the NBA following that disastrous campaign, Chicago would have barely noticed.

With the heat on him from fellow investors, a depressed Klein released an honest Stadium gate count after the Bulls had lost at home to the expansion Seattle SuperSonics. Next morning, there was this banner headline in the *Tribune*: "Only 891 See Bulls Lose." The ink was barely dry on the page before Klein got a telegram from NBA commissioner J. Walter Kennedy, fining him for telling the truth. "Don't ever announce an NBA attendance figure under 1,000," was the message. The second season's attendance average of 3,975, bad as it sounds, also was inflated.

Both Kerr and Klein knew their escalating feud could only end with the coach's departure. When the same thing happened between Klein and Motta a year later, it was the coach who stayed. Right to the end, Klein refused to give up hope for the franchise he had brought to life. "We're losing a slug of dough, but the Bulls are in no danger," he insisted.

They weren't, thanks to Motta, but Klein was, also thanks to Motta. The Bulls finished 1967–68 with a dismal 29–53 record. They still made the playoffs, getting hammered by Los Angeles in five games, the first of four postseason wipe-outs the Lakers were to pin on the Bulls. The only question seemed to be whether—or when—some unsuspecting city would take the moribund franchise off Chicago's hands.

The 1927–28 Blackhawks: Cold Feet on Ice

The trouble with this terrible season was timing. The Black-hawks were still a novelty in Chicago after a respectable 19–22–3 National Hockey League debut in 1926. The second time around, the Hawks drowned optimistic rooters in a frigid bath of ice-cold scoring, quickly freezing themselves into the NHL basement.

It was good training for the first wave of Hawk fans, enabling them to warn their kids and even their grandchildren about the perils of getting hooked on this exasperating team. Not that warnings help. Something about hockey turns those who play the violent game into a different breed. Its effect on hockey fans is even more strange, as anyone within earshot of Chicago Stadium can attest on game nights. More action takes place in the stands than on the ice.

But hockey was still something of an oddity in Chicago when the 1927–28 Hawks skated out for their second season. Their home then was the old Coliseum, a gloomy pile of stone at 15th Street and Wabash Avenue. The place had seen much more history than hockey. A prison for Confederate soldiers during the Civil War, it also was the setting for a dramatic slice of American politics. William Jennings Bryan won the 1894 Democratic presidential nomination in this stone fort with his famous "Cross of Gold" speech. When Major Frederick McLaughlin, another spellbinding orator, bought the Portland Rosebuds for a staggering $200,000 in 1926, Chicago Stadium was still in the blueprint stage. The Major had to park his transplanted team in the Coliseum for three years, something that didn't make the coffee tycoon very happy.

McLaughlin's hunger for quick success in the NHL succeeded only in creating the Curse of Muldoon, a hex that
hung around the Hawks' necks like an albatross for 40
years. McLaughlin axed coach Pete Muldoon after his respectable record in the Hawks' first season. McLaughlin's
reasoning was hard to fathom because the new team finished third in the NHL's American Division. They lost their
first playoff series to the Boston Bruins 10–5 in the two-
game, total-goal set. That was no disgrace, but McLaughlin
thought so, firing his first of many coaches in a stormy
scene. The outraged Muldoon declared the Hawks would
never win a regular-season championship, before stomping
off into hockey legend.

The woes that befell the Hawks the next season should
have convinced McLaughlin about the potency of Muldoon's curse. The 1927–28 Hawks surprised the Bruins in
their opener by earning a 1–1 tie in Boston, then sank like a
stone. In the remaining 43 games, they salvaged two more
ties and just seven victories, losing 34 times. Mysteriously,
the top goal-getters of the previous year developed holes in
their sticks. Dick Irvin, the captain and leading scorer of the
Hawks' debut was riddled by injuries this time, contributing
only five goals in 14 games. Another standout, winger Babe
Dye, had his career cut short by a broken leg. Their anemic
total of 17 points was the lowest in team history. Now that
the NHL schedule has inflated to 82 games, even abysmal
Hawk squads of the future will have trouble equaling such
futility.

McLaughlin went through two coaches in 1927–28, can-
ning Barney Stanley midway through the season and replacing him with retired goalie Hugh Lehman. Even though
Lehman's move made way for brilliant netminder Charlie
Gardiner, nothing seemed to help the jinxed, inept Hawks.
They finished dead last in the league, two weeks' distance
by dogsled from the playoffs. Was Pete Muldoon sitting
somewhere in a Yukon saloon, digesting all this bad news
and laughing uproariously?

The 1980 Bears Fold on the Road

It all fell apart on December 16, 1979, the day Mugs Halas died. The son and namesake of George Halas, known as "Mugs" ever since his early years as the Bears' water boy, keeled over with a massive heart attack. The Bears honored his memory by routing the St. Louis Cards 42–6 to clinch a playoff berth, but the fallout from Mugs's death had far-reaching effects on the team.

Even though the Bears fell apart in the second half to lose their 1979 playoff game in Philadelphia 27–17, fans were hopeful. Coming off a 10–6 season, Coach Neill Armstrong was convinced the 1980 Bears had the right stuff to challenge for their first National Football League title. So did grief-stricken George Halas, Sr., General Manager Jim Finks, and the players.

Nobody could explain why the classy Armstrong was unable to take the Bears back to the playoffs. He failed in 1980 and again the following year, the soft-spoken coach's last in Chicago. With veteran Mike Phipps and promising Vince Evans at quarterback, a Buddy Ryan defense showing flashes of how good it could be, and peerless Walter Payton rushing for 1,460 yards, the 1980 Bears had all the pieces. They just never fit together throughout a puzzling, frustrating season.

Most of the media people covering the Bears liked and respected Armstrong. Some of them rooted for the coach more or less openly. He seemed incapable of egomania, paranoia, or nursing a grudge, common afflictions in his pressure-packed profession. Even after being second-guessed by a writer or ripped by a columnist, Neill never lost his temper in public.

With all that benevolence piled atop the optimism from the fast finish of '79, the Bears radiated confidence when they invaded Green Bay to open their 61st season. The way the Packers stole an incredible overtime heart-stopper set the tone for a dismal 1980. Missing one chance after another to score with Phipps at the controls, the Bears found themselves deadlocked 6–6 in overtime. Green Bay's Chester Marcol got ready to end it on a chip-shot field goal. Both teams were reeling from exhaustion by then, but old pro Alan Page

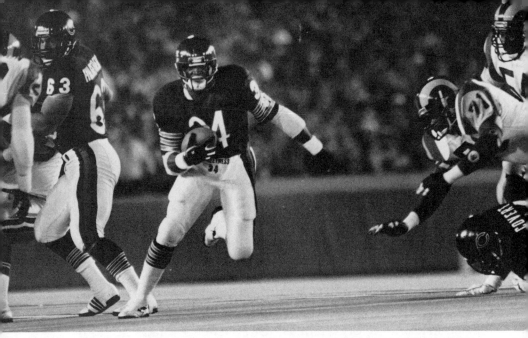

It didn't work like this when the 1980 Bears hit the road. Walter Payton roars through a gaping hole to daylight against the Rams in Soldier Field.

got through to block the kick. Amazingly, it rebounded right into the startled Marcol's hands and he scurried around the left side, into the end zone for a shattering 12–6 Packer triumph.

The Bears never got up from that early knockdown, losing six straight road games to kill any chance for the NFC Central title. The faces of the beaten Bears as they trudged to the dressing room after that split second of season-opening bewilderment told the story of the game—and the season.

Whenever Armstrong's Army tried to regroup and attack in enemy territory, another twist of fate intervened. They were crushed 38–3 in Pittsburgh, Terry Bradshaw ambushing them with three TD passes to unheralded Jim Smith. Evans replaced Phipps at quarterback too late to save a 13–7 loss at Minnesota. A borderline offensive interference call on James Scott erased a 66-yard scoring pass in Philadelphia, saving the Eagles' bacon 17–14.

A Monday night rally in Cleveland fizzled, followed by two more that stamped out the frustrated Bears' last playoff hopes. The first was a 10–6 Soldier Field surprise by Houston. Then in Atlanta, Payton dove to the Falcons' one-yard line in the third quarter and put the ball on the ground, confident the play was over. Cornerback Rolland Lawrence reached into the pileup and pilfered the football, along with the game. The enraged Payton was tossed out for the first time in his career, but the Bears were down and out, 28–17.

Not even Dave Williams's 95-yard kickoff return to open and close overtime in the Silverdome could salvage anything but pride. The 23–17 comeback over the Lions was a nice Thanksgiving present near the end of this turkey season. A 61–7 Soldier Field slaughter of the Packers provided only revenge, not relief. Armstrong, Finks's hand-picked coach, was on his way out after the 7–9 disaster was followed by a 6–10 record in 1981.

So was Finks, swept aside by Papa Bear himself to make way for the Mike Ditka era. Nice Neill couldn't win; it took Motormouth Mike to show the Bears how.

The 1969 Cubs: Bleacher Bombs

Maybe those Schlitz commercials were the tipoff. There was irascible Leo Durocher, transformed by the magic of TV into a simpering sociable sort. Surrounded by adoring sportswriters, Lippy Leo would spellbind them by relating

Ron Santo's famous heel-clicking bit salutes another 1969 Cub victory. Santo's exuberance backfired when the Cubs started their late-season collapse.

another page from his own baseball legend, then bark, "Let's have another Slitz, fellas."

But it wasn't Durocher's garbled syntax that bothered Cub fans who had a sense of history. What troubled these realists was the aura of unreality that adoring Cub fans were spreading over their heroes. The National League's resident losers had been magnified into Hall of Famers by vote of the left-field Bleacher Bums and other worshipers who packed Wrigley Field in 1969. The skeptics let themselves be convinced because they needed it and because everybody was convinced that everybody else was convinced.

It added up to a case of citywide mass hysteria that provided one of the most enjoyable summers ever. Chicago was a gigantic outdoor carnival from April to September 1969. When the true believers descended on the Wrigley shrine for services presided over by St. Leo, shepherd of the Cub flock, the scene resembled some kind of religious revival.

A Greek chorus in the bleachers wore hard hats (I could never figure out why they were painted yellow instead of Cubbie blue) and arose en masse at a signal from choirmaster Dick Selma to utter this non-Gregorian chant: "Gimme that old-time Durocher, gimme that old-time Durocher. . . ."

Alas, Leo Durocher, old or new, was the same self-centered egomaniac he had always been. The Cubs' manager regarded it as natural, normal, and inevitable that the fans made him rather than the players the center of attention. His jealousy of Ernie Banks's unshakable grip on number one status in Wrigley Field was kept submerged while the '69 party lasted, but it resurfaced as soon as the Cubs started losing. Ernie's bad knees would serve as one of many designated Durocher scapegoats for the September swoon.

But pinning all the blame for the '69 Cub demise on Durocher would be both wrong and unfair. Leo the Lion can be faulted for playing his regulars until their tongues dragged on the sun-baked Wrigley Field turf, for failing to be patient with young prospects like Adolfo Phillips, Joe Niekro, and Oscar Gamble, or for questioning the desire of pitchers like Ken Holtzman and others who became big winners elsewhere.

But Lippy Leo couldn't pitch, hit, or field for the team that was the best in the 1969 debut of the NL East. The Cubs folded again the next two years and couldn't win the division title under Durocher. The hard-bitten manager finally became a target for the team's frustration, and they staged a 1971 clubhouse revolt. The magic was gone by then. The number of hard hats in the bleachers gradually dwindled, signaling the end of this Cubmania epidemic.

The front-runners went back into hibernation. There was room once more for the Wrigley Field loyalists to witness the Cubs fading away with depressing regularity in 1970, '71, and '72. Leo the Lion uttered his final roar of defiance on July 25, 1972, stepping aside for Whitey Lockman. Leo insisted on pinning the 1969 collapse on his players. "I coulda dressed up nine broads as ballplayers and they woulda beat the Cubs," Durocher fumed. Years later, Lippy Leo took a different tack. "It was as much my fault as theirs," he said. "I should have rested the starting lineup more."

Long after Durocher departed to join Howard Cosell in the I-Me Hall of Fame, the 1969 Cubs occupied a special place in their fans' hearts. That was a never-ending source of amazement to Dallas Green and other non-Chicagoans, baffled at how fans treasured the memory of these losers. You have to understand the infinite capacity of Chicago fans to tolerate mediocrity before it starts to make sense. Let's face it, there have been one hell of a lot of mediocre teams for them to practice on.

The 1975-76 Bulls; Dead Last

When these Bulls lost their horns, there was anger and bewilderment in Chicago. Fans wanted to know when the 1975–76 bunch of impostors would cut the bull and start playing like the Bulls. A Dick Motta team loafing on defense, making dumb plays, shooting an abysmal 41 percent from the floor?

The unrest in the second balcony of Chicago Stadium, lair of the hard-core Bull fans, was considerable. Unlike the swells in the courtside ego-trip seats that now cost $100 a game, the people upstairs had a clear view of what was going on the season after the Bulls' 1975 NBA title bid.

"Take away [retired] Chet Walker, the glue man of this team," a Bulls diehard lamented early in the 1975–76 season. "Look at Jerry Sloan, playing on one leg and still bouncing off the floor after every loose ball. Get a load of Bob Love, sulking and glaring at Motta. Watch Norm Van Lier shooting too much and not making many [37 percent on the year], trying to be a rebounder, playmaker and intimidator all rolled into one. No wonder he gets frustrated and screams at the refs all night. Nate Thurmond just stands around, drawing his pay. Somebody please convince me Cliff Pondexter and John Laskowski are NBA players. They're the worst-looking rookies I've seen since Howard Porter."

There was little else to say, except that Motta was aware of every fault the unhappy rooter had pinpointed. The emotional coach also knew 75–76 would be his last year in Chicago. He was tired of wrangling with the players, the media, and the front office, notably Managing Partner Jonathan Kovler, a longtime Motta antagonist. After seven years of Motta-vating the Bulls with his volcanic us-against-the-world approach, the little coach had no eruptions left.

Well, almost none. When the Bulls kept sliding downhill in 1975–76, he reacted to media criticism with predictable hostility. He blasted Tim Weigel, then covering the Bulls for the *Chicago Daily News*, because Weigel wrote a strongly worded story headlined "Go Motta—Anywhere." He complained bitterly about Bob Love's sour-grapes lament in the *Tribune* that "Motta is a racist."

When the uproar grew louder about the Bulls' nosedive in just a few months from a team that fell one game short of the NBA finals to a disaster area, Motta sprang into action. He engineered a "spontaneous" press conference by the young players to parrot their confidence in him and plead with Chicago for patience. Laskowski was the logical spokesman, because Laz had learned under Bobby Knight at Indiana that coaches are infallible.

But not even that transparent ploy fooled fans. The Bulls denied the *Tribune's* Thanksgiving week story that Nate Thurmond was headed for Cleveland, then dealt Nate the Great to the Cavaliers for couple of gobblers named Eric Fernsten and Steve Patterson. The final blow was Jerry Sloan's departure for good after just 22 games. The battle-scarred knees that had taken the Evansville Hustler through 11 rugged NBA seasons simply had no more to give.

The Bulls finishing dead last was a fitting epitaph for Motta's reign. They finished in 1975–76 with a 24–58 record, the worst in their history. Motta coached the Bulls to a 356–300 mark in eight years, also going 18–29 in six straight trips to the playoffs. Then he went to the Washington Bullets and masterminded them to an NBA championship in 1978. It should have happened in Chicago three years before that.

The 1970 White Sox; Run Up the White Flag

Covering losing teams is an experience any Chicago sportswriter can tell you about. Since World War II, with rare exceptions, they have been the rule. Even so, the 1970 Sox were something special.

Before manager Jim Fregosi straightened them out, the 1987 South Siders started out at a pace that mounted a serious challenge to 1970's futility. All season, the 1970 gang showed such a consistent lack of ability to pitch, hit, or field that its place in Chicago sports history is secure. They were the first White Sox team to lose 106 games in a season, with or without an asterisk. Back in the days of nickel phone calls, train travel, and cellophane, the 1932 Sox dropped 102 for Manager Lew Fonseca. In 1948, Grandpappy Ted Lyons proved that popularity can't take the place of managerial skill by steering his longtime team to a dismal 51–101 log. After a half century of such punishment, interrupted only by a lone American League pennant in 1959, Sox fans had learned to live with adversity. Still, even their worst expectations were surpassed in 1970, the year everything fell apart.

The Sox were managed by Don Gutteridge, who had taken over when Al Lopez stepped down in 1969. Lopez's departure signaled a year of crisis for Arthur and John Allyn, the brothers with controlling interest in the team. Arthur made a good move in selling the Sox to his brother instead of accepting a higher bid from Milwaukee. Pipe-smoking John made a bad move in sticking with Gutteridge and General Manager Ed Short instead of bringing in Chuck Tanner and Roland Hemond right away. Failure to do so condemned the Sox and their fans to a season of folly that almost brought the ailing franchise to its knees.

Walter "No-Neck" Williams directs traffic while Luis Aparicio (11) slides home in County Stadium, beating a tag by Brewers' catcher Gerry McNertney, an exteammate. This was one of the few bright Sox moments in the disastrous 1970 campaign.

Only 495,355 fans, the lowest total since 1938, paid their way into Comiskey Park. If those Depression-era fans of 1938 thought they had problems, they should have seen the depression that settled over the venerable ballpark at first glimpse of the 1970 Sox attempting to impersonate major-league talent. The masquerade fooled nobody, not even Gutteridge. A nice man, Don didn't deserve the punishment he absorbed in the dugout. Before he got fired in September, his players were sneering at Gutteridge while sitting behind him on the team bus or in the clubhouse. The former St. Louis Brown and Cardinal infielder was too easygoing to suit the castoffs wearing Sox uniforms, so he was a scapegoat for their futility. Gutteridge accepted his fate, stepping out with a touch of class.

That was an element sorely lacking on the '70 Sox, especially when it came to performance. There were exceptions, notably shortstop Luis Aparicio and pitchers Tommy John, Joe Horlen, and Wilbur Wood. Young third baseman Bill Melton set a Sox record with 33 homers, but decent hitting was more than offset by a horrendous 4.54 staff earned-run average. Things got better when Johnny Sain arrived to tutor the pitchers, but it took time for the lingering odor of 1970 to blow away in the Windy City breeze.

The 1953–54 Blackhawks; Not Abel Enough

Not even the fabulous Fred Saskamoose could prevent the Blackhawks from having their worst National Hockey League season in 1953–54. Their goalie got chicken pox, the rest of the NHL almost chickened out on the future of the Chicago franchise, and Arthur Wirtz finally had to whip out his bottomless checkbook, never a favorite pastime of the Chicago Stadium owner, to assure the team's survival.

Saskamoose, a 19-year-old winger from Debeden, Saskatchewan, couldn't light up the Stadium the way Bobby Hull would four years later. Saskamoose gave it his best shot, but he failed to score in 11 games and vanished from the NHL. The rest of the hapless Hawks were not far behind, disappearing from the 1953–54 playoff chase after an 0–7–1 start. Things would have been even worse, if possible, without splendid netminding by Al Rollins. In the 1953 playoffs, Rollins's brilliance had enabled the underdog Hawks to take a 3–2 series lead before the Canadiens pulled it out by putting rookie Jacques Plante in goal. Plante would frustrate the Hawks often in the years to come.

The defenseless Hawks virtually forced Rollins to play with a bull's-eye on his chest when the 1953–54 season began, but the goalie gamely batted back a rain of pucks until stricken by chicken pox in mid-November. Two replacements were summoned, only to be beaten 29–8 in the next four Chicago losses. By this time, Rollins should have been cast in bronze for direct shipment to the Hall of Fame, but he donned the pads again to absorb more punishment. It was not a pleasant way for Hawks' player-coach Sid Abel to end a fine career on the ice. Abel made a few token appearances, then surfaced four years later to begin a noteworthy stint as coach of the Detroit Red Wings.

Neither Abel nor the front office could do anything to salvage the sinking Blackhawks. Stadium attendance matched their plummet in the standings, and rumors about pulling out of Chicago began to float around the league. It took Wirtz's pledge to spend whatever was necessary to stem the tide. Wirtz met with NHL commissioner Clarence Campbell and emerged to offer Chicago's anxious fans a Christmas present: the Hawks would not be going anywhere.

They certainly were motionless at the bottom of the six-team league, hobbling to the end of 1953–54 with a horrendous 12–51–7 record, 57 points behind first-place Detroit.

It was the only 50-plus loss season in Hawk history, but help was on the way. Instead of Saskamoose, the likes of Moose Vasko, Bobby Hull, and Stan Mikita would be there before the end of the decade to turn the team around.

FIVE

OUR GUYS PLAY SPACEBALL, TOO

Screwballs

S ome of the all-time eccentrics have worn Chicago uniforms. Most of them make winning more fun and losing
more bearable. Naturally, losing is always un-Bearable if
you're coaching the Bears, but even Iron Mike has mellowed
into one of our most endearing characters.

A couple of other Chicago characters may lack character,
a fact that doesn't detract from their entertainment value. A
sports writer seldom runs out of material around these basketball, baseball, and football personalities.

A Bull Market for Bull-Headed Coaches

There's a plentiful supply of delightful ding-dongs wherever
you look in sports, but this is one league where Chicago wins
its share of pennants.

Take the Bulls, for example. Sometimes the Bulls played
basketball, sometimes other games. Since they came to town
in 1966, it has occasionally been perplexing or even frustrating to keep tabs on the ever-changing cast of characters in
Bull suits. Still, sportswriters on the pro basketball beat
didn't suffer from terminal ennui. Exhaustion? Frequently.
Boredom? Never.

The tipoff to the kind of roller-coaster ride pro basketball would provide came from former White Sox boss Frank Lane, of all people. Frantic Frankie was the sort of man who just couldn't loll around on the beach, so when he wore out his welcome in baseball front offices, he had to find something else. In 1962 Lane somehow popped up as general manager of the Chicago Zephyrs, an alleged basketball team. The Zephyrs' real mission in life was to serve as punching bag for the rest of the league. They had debuted as the Chicago Packers in the 1961–62 NBA season, stinking up the Amphitheater with an 18–62 record.

Now the Packers-Zephyrs were in their second—and last—Chicago campaign, sending such court immortals as Bill (The Hill) McGill and Barney Cable out to get slaughtered nightly by real players like Wilt Chamberlain. Despite a hey-hey selling job by Jack Brickhouse on WGN telecasts, Chicago fans were sensibly ignoring these bums, under any alias.

So owner Dave Trager, in sheer desperation, tapped Lane to hype the operation and lure some unwary cash customers. If he had empowered the new G.M. to wheel and deal the way Trader Lane had done in building the Go-Go Sox, the Zephyrs would have gotten plenty of ink. Lane knew how to ship bodies in and out fast enough to turn the Zephyrs into Hurricanes.

All Frantic Frankie's job entailed was roaming around and thanking the few fans who showed up for games in the 9,000-seat Amphitheater. That didn't take long, so Lane had plenty of time to perch in the open-air press box and bellow his disdain at the referees.

Lane had lost none of his competitive juices, as he proved during a Zephyrs–Boston Celtics mismatch. At first glimpse of towering Clyde Lovellette wearing a green Celtic jersey, Lane erupted. He informed the press box that Lovellette allegedly had been spotted taking liberties with children. Lane's booming voice could be heard all over the building, and just in case Lovellette wasn't paying attention, Frankie roared, "Hey, Clyde! You pervert!" when the big guy lumbered downcourt.

Lane was a good tuneup for some of the NBA executive

types around the league. They ranged from screamers and intimidators like the Celtics' Red Auerbach; to sly types like the Bulls' Dick Klein, who kept ushers hopping with notes to the bench dictating strategy during games; to the cloak-and-dagger mentality personified by Seattle's Sam Schulman, who suspected the rest of the NBA was out to get him. Sometimes Sam was right.

The percentage of characters among owners in the NBA, I soon discovered, was even higher than in the players' ranks. And NBA coaches were the most interesting characters of all.

The first coach of the Bulls was John (Red) Kerr. He fit the role so well, he must have been sent over by central casting. No one doesn't like Johnny Kerr. To this day, wherever he goes, Kerr runs into a welcoming posse. The Old Redhead wears well because he's still the same uncomplicated, friendly guy he was while pumping in hook shots for Coach Harry Combes at Illinois or signing his first pro contract with the Syracuse Nats in 1954 for a whopping $5,500.

You had to be ready at all times for flashes of the Old Redhead's lightning wit. Red never met a one-liner he didn't like, regaling sportswriters with stories like the one about the day he broke the NBA endurance record by playing in his 844th consecutive game. "I was really feeling pretty proud of the record," he admitted. "Then I got a telegram from a fan: 'Congratulations, you're only 1,286 behind Lou Gehrig.' " Asked to sum up a no-talent rookie, Kerr took the diplomatic route: "He's ambidextrous—can't shoot with either hand."

Red was often his own favorite target, the sure sign of a man without an overinflated ego. Klein gave him the ax after two years with the Bulls, so Kerr moseyed on to Phoenix in 1968 as coach of another expansion team, the Suns. When the Suns won their NBA opener, he told Phoenix scribe Joe Gilmartin what a relief it was. "Last night I dreamed we'd go 0–82 this season," Kerr said. "So tonight you'll sleep better," Gilmartin predicted. "I doubt it," Kerr shot back. "I'll probably dream we'll finish 1–81."

Kerr's style and humor came in handy during the Bulls' first season, when a rookie crop of hoop scribes was trying to figure out what to write about in their daily stories. Red would entertain them with ad-libbed excerpts from his fictional autobiography: "15 years in the Pivot Without the Ball." When asked about the prospects of a reserve guard the Bulls had fished out of the expansion pool, he'd reply: "This guy is the most dangerous substitute since cyclamates."

And for those writers who had closed a gin mill or two the night before and had to scratch around for Sunday features, Kerr would trot out a real winner. It was a routine worthy of Casey Stengel. The best part was that a few new wrinkles would be added whenever a fresh wave of gullible media marvels invaded camp in search of the real Chicago Bulls. Kerr would dazzle them with the tale of the overnight train ride from Syracuse to Fort Wayne, Indiana, when the coach with the players—and presumably the Nats' coach, as well— was uncoupled on a siding a few miles outside Fort Wayne.

Kerr had to struggle with quite a crop of characters adorning the Bulls' roster in that unforgettable 1966–67 debut. There was center Erwin (Wolfgang) Mueller, who played better with a six-pack under his belt, although he couldn't see too well even when his eyes weren't bloodshot. There was Craig Spitzer, a seven-footer who had to settle for a job as a Rush Street cabaret bouncer when it became painfully apparent that he couldn't Spitz a ball into the basket. Then there was Bill Buntin, a tubby 6'6" refugee from Michigan. Kerr had his usual ready reply when Klein inquired if he could teach Buntin to play center: "Yes, but I can't teach him to grow."

The most tragic figure ever to wear a Bulls' uniform was seven-footer Reggie Harding, who once wore a mask while sticking up a gas station in his Detroit neighborhood. Reggie couldn't stay away from drugs or guns. Predictably, he was shot to death on his front porch just a few years after cocaine ended his promising NBA career.

When Bulls' fans recall "Nate the Great," they think of Nate Thurmond, who was far from great in his short, unhappy sentence here. But the original Nate the Great was Nate Bowman—not exactly great, either. Still, at 6'11", he was the only man in that first training camp to remotely resemble an NBA center. Alas, he chipped an anklebone and was dealt to the Knicks, where he somehow became a Madison Square Garden cult figure as Willis Reed's caddie.

Columbia Dave Newmark, a certified Greenwich Village–style hippie, didn't show up until Kerr made his getaway. That was only fair. With the likes of Wolfgang Mueller, Spitzer, Buntin, Harding, and Jim Washington risking arrest for impersonating pivotmen, Kerr had enough trouble in the middle.

The strain that coaching such amiable misfits was taking on the Old Redhead showed one night when the Bulls lost again because Wolfgang blew a last-second lay-up. Kerr grabbed the trademark towel he kept slung over one shoulder to dry the sweat off his hands and slammed it down on the press table.

We all missed Kerr's dry wit more than his wet towels, but the Bulls attracted a fresh crew of entertaining newcomers every year. Take Jim (Bad News) Barnes, a big strong guy, so easy going that he was good news to opponents. Maybe the Bulls got more than their share of such dudes because founder Dick Klein was a character himself. More likely, it simply was due to the abundance of offbeat inmates populating the NBA squirrel cage.

Dave Newmark has to be the backup center on the all-flake Bull team. He was a kid in tune with the times, reflecting the turn-off, drop-out, antiwar, off-the-pigs attitude of that hippie generation—sort of a seven-foot flower child, complete with T-shirt, sandals, and shaggy hair. Predictably, getting rid of Newmark soon became a high priority for Dick Motta, who became the coach in 1968.

But the sight and sound of this combative coach feuding with his players was commonplace. Right up to the end, the ones who did things Motta's way stayed, and the others got shipped out.

The love-hate relationship between Motta and Norm Van Lier was another of Chicago's most durable and entertaining shows. Motta unloaded one-way guys like Flingin' Flynn Robinson and Shaler (Super Shay) Halimon, but Van Lier was a force at both ends of the court. He and Motta were a matched set, two bantam roosters in search of trouble. More often than not, it found them.

Stormin' Norman, a slender 6'1", refused to pick on people

his size. He specialized in punching out tough targets, the bigger the better. Perhaps his most memorable bout was with 6'9" Sidney Wicks of Portland in Chicago Stadium on March 20, 1973. Wicks was one of the rare rebels to roll off the assembly line at John Wooden's UCLA basketball factory. He had a history of pulling off strange stunts, like the time in Chicago when he broke away and sank a lay-up—in the wrong basket. This night, Wicks and Van Lier collided, exchanged insults, and started grappling. When they separated, Moving Van darted to the Bulls' bench and grabbed a metal folding chair to use in folding, spindling, and mutilating Wicks. Fortunately, peacemakers intervened. "When Van Lier went for that chair, I knew he wasn't going to sit down on it," chuckled Motta.

With all the yelling and screaming these twin minipackages of dynamite aimed at each other, it's a wonder they never went at it. Van Lier sometimes accused Motta of playing favorites and failing to protect him in his frequent rhubarbs with referees. In 1975, the year the Bulls should have won it all—and didn't—Van Lier and Bob Love held out, promptly making the Top 10 on Motta's lengthy enemies list.

That rejection by his coach rankled Van Lier into blowing his top late in the season, kicking the scorer's table and getting thrown out. Stormin' Norman stormed right home to phone Brent Musburger, then the sports anchor on WBBM-TV, to lament that "Motta doesn't fight for me the way he does for Jerry Sloan."

After the shattering playoff loss to Golden State that killed hopes of an NBA championship for Chicago, everybody went off an emotional cliff, including Motta. The coach said, "I fear for Van Lier, and I'd hate to trade him to a good friend."

With Van Lier and Sloan in the backcourt and Dennis Awtrey at center during the '70s, fans saw a trio that ranked as the baddest Bulls of them all. Driving through the lane in those days proved hazardous to a lot of opponents' health and/or teeth, and if somebody arrived at the hoop still in possession of life, limb, and the ball, Awtrey took over.

A droll fellow, Dennis once summed up the Phoenix Suns as "your average white NBA team." But get the 6'10", 240-pounder mad and you were in trouble, as Kareem Abdul-Jabbar discovered. Awtrey's nationally televised TKO of the

Reggie Theus, one of the Bulls' all-time crowd-pleasers, limbers up in Chicago Stadium. Colorful Reggie cut a swath through Rush Street night spots after doing the same to NBA defenses.

superstar in a March 17, 1974, Bulls–Bucks war probably was seen live by a bigger audience than the total gate for every Joe Louis fight. "He was hitting me on the neck with his elbow when we lined up for free throws," Awtrey said. "I went after him, grabbed his shirt to spin him around, and popped him a good one."

When Reggie Theus came aboard in 1978 from Nevada–Las Vegas—where else?—the Bulls had their first real greyhound guard. Reggie was an event, playing frequent doubleheaders, first in the Stadium and then on Rush Street until daybreak. His whirling-dervish moves to the basket and Hollywood looks had the Windy City in a spin, especially the ladies. Reggie's cool-cat brand of sophistication and style provided some welcome diversion in a decade of futility for the Bulls.

They made the playoffs just once in his six-season guest shot, but Reggie went to all of Chicago's cafe-society charity affairs, dressed to kill in everything from a tux to tennis togs. It was a dull day when his picture didn't appear somewhere in the Chicago papers. Naturally, the rest of the Bulls resented Reggie's celebrity status, venting their spleen with snide comments about the "pretty boy with pretty awful defense."

Theus kept doing his thing, aware that the raps were aimed at his popularity, not his ability. He provided a touch of class sadly lacking in most aspects of the Bulls' operation. They hit bottom with the incredible 1982 first-round draft pick of guard Quintin Dailey. That inspired move made the selection of such biggies as Kennedy McIntosh and Tate Armstrong in previous years look good by comparison.

Of all the daffy things the Bulls have done, drafting Dailey took the fur-lined hoop. Their timing was even more bizarre, making it appear that the owners and General Manager Rod Thorne had been living on another planet while the Dailey furor was splashed across the nation's newspapers, radio, and TV.

Dailey had been convicted of assault against Vicki Brick, a female student at the University of San Francisco, where he was the hotshot guard. So when did the Bulls decide to stage a press conference to parade their number one pick before Chicago's media? Believe it or not, just a few days after the Equal Rights Amendment had been voted down by the Illinois legislature. Dailey, Thorne, and the Bulls reeled under a barrage of brickbats, with acerbic *Sun-Times* columnist John Schulian's angry words riddling the franchise like machine-gun bullets.

Thorne, the NBA's prototype good ol' boy, was actually bewildered by the uproar. Schulian expressed the outrage Chicagoans felt after hearing Dailey say he felt no remorse and just wanted to get on with his life. The fallout from that disastrous press conference haunted the Bulls until Arthur Wirtz and the other owners sold the team in 1985 to Jerry Reinsdorf, White Sox board chairman.

Thorne drifted off to work for the NBA, but Dailey's career never recovered from the heat put on him wherever he went by the National Organization for Women and other feminist groups. He soon spent time in a drug-treatment center, relapsed after being clean for a time, then resurfaced with the lowly Los Angeles Clippers.

It's a wonder Q stuck around at all after putting his foot in his mouth at that ill-timed Chicago debut. A ridiculous attempt to hide Dailey from the media by smuggling the Bulls' training camp into Peoria was doomed to fail. The front office blundering didn't play in Peoria with any more sincerity than it had in Chicago. N.O.W. pickets and speakers hurled their barbs just as effectively downstate.

The Dailey disaster was only one among many brouhahas that beset the Bulls from the end of the Dick Motta dictatorship until the beginning of the Michael Jordan era. Motta left in a four-door, eight-cylinder 1976 huff and Jordan arrived in a solid-gold 1984 Rolls-Royce.

Motta virtually raised a dying Chicago franchise from the dead. It relapsed without him, so Jordan got here just in time to repair the team's terminally ill image.

Unbeatable Parks, Beatable Teams

Chicago baseball teams haven't given us many winners. But both the winning and losing White Sox and Cubs teams have had their share of players who make covering the game more fun than working.

When Chuck Tanner walked in to take over as Sox manager in the dying days of the long-dead 1970 season, he enlivened a lifeless clubhouse. Just a glimpse at Tanner's 3–13 record over the last 16 games might have started a bringback Gutteridge movement, but this is one case where figures do lie. All it took was a few optimistic words from the new skipper and the gloom vanished from the Sox dugout. The man had—and still has—some gift (his critics call it con) that makes his players feel better. Robin Monsky, the former publicist for the Atlanta Braves, claims she was hounded out of baseball by Tanner's harassment, but in his six-year tenure on the South Side, Chuck Tanner did not appear to be that kind of man.

Charles William Tanner could be tough, but his image when he left Chicago was that of a creampuff who let Richie Dick Allen get away with murder. It's true that Allen was a prime suspect in the mysterious death of Pale Hose pennant hopes for three straight years. Still, blaming Tanner for handing Richie the smoking gun was ridiculous.

Allen was a guy much like Cubs' slugger Dave Kingman, simply unable to handle fame. He would start off with the best of intentions, then visibly wilt as the season went on. No pitcher or charging baserunner could intimidate this magnificent athlete. The demons were somewhere in Allen's head and when they took control, Hall of Fame talent evaporated, along with his concentration, desire, and all those promises to behave.

If Tanner had tried to crack down on him Richie would have had an excuse to flake off even earlier. There was a quality about this strong man that was likable, vulnerable, and genuine. The manager and the star related well.

In 1972, Allen played the role of the gracious superstar to the hilt. Smiling, winking, telling stories of basketball heroics with his brothers back in Wampum, Pennsylvania, Allen was a changed man from the way he had responded to the press two years earlier when he helped the Cards beat the Cubs in Wrigley Field. His bat seemed the only thing still menacing. Richie batted .308 in 1972 with a club-record 37 homers and 113 RBI.

When the Sox finished second, $5\frac{1}{2}$ games behind the A's, their fans really believed they were bellowing "Wait till next year!" for the last time. No such luck. Allen's numbers were big in the next two seasons, despite a broken kneecap in '73 but his problems were bigger. It was almost a relief to frustrated rooters when Richie quit on September 14, 1973, with a dramatic clubhouse speech.

The vacumm was soon filled by the return of Bill Veeck, who put together his "Rent-a-Star Revue" of 1977 with glue, old shoestrings, $1.98 in cash, and sheer chutzpah. This hit show also had its share of characters—third baseman Eric Soderholm, a poet; catcher Jim Essian, a philosopher, and designated hitter Lamar Johnson an all-around good guy. The team chemistry was good, mellow Bob Lemon was the right man to manage, and Veeck was at his conversational best in the Bards Room. This was Barnum Bill's happiest season since the Sox last won the pennant in 1959.

In 1979, though, the Sox went from the peak to the pits of Disco Demolition Night and Claudell (Washington Slept Here) Washington, a steep enough plunge to discourage even the unsinkable Veeck. An untested manager, Tony LaRussa, a mere 35, was summoned from the farm system to lower the lifeboats. LaRussa never forgot that Veeck opened the door, but he did his best work for the new owners, Fast Eddie Einhorn and Genial Jerry Reinsdorf.

Ron Kittle politely explains to Tribune diamond scribe Bob Logan how he swings that wood stick at the round ball to deposit it on the Comiskey Park roof. Kittle and Bull Luzinski played Babe Roof for the Sox in 1983.

Before long, the Sunshine Boys were Sox-cessful, but win or lose, LaRussa got the blues from all those boos. It wasn't a lyrical situation for the complex Sox manager, who was rejected by the South Side old guard. They scorned Tony because he was a handsome, computer-oriented, New Wave manager instead of the gnarled, seat-of-the-pants field bosses (Jimmy Dykes, Paul Richards, et. al.) they recalled with beer-soaked sentiment.

LaRussa hung on and won converts, though his stay in Chicago was marred by hostility until the day he left in 1986. Despite his yuppie credentials and law degree, Tony tolerated all kinds of characters, blending them well with humorless types like Steve Kemp, Harold Baines, and Tom Seaver.

Julio Cruz was another on the long list of misfit second basemen since Nellie Fox departed in 1963. Cruz had ability, though "Juice" couldn't squeeze it out consistently, ending up in the discard pile with such forgettable second sackers as Wayne Causey, Jack Brohammer, and Sandy Alomar. Cruz's hot-dogging made him a fan favorite in the 1983 stampede that won the West, but Juice then squeezed Reinsdorf and Einhorn for long-term megabucks and promptly flopped.

Ron Kittle, from nearby Gary, Indiana, got equal ink in '83 with his quips and radar blips caused by rooftop homers. A folksy, down-home type, parked two atop Comiskey's upper story, besides belting many more one-liners out of the park, to the media's delight. With Carlton Fisk's bat also smoking, one Comiskey Park bleacher poster was inevitable: "A Fine Kittle of Fisk."

Kittle's best line of the season was delivered after the AL Rookie of the Year to be learned he was on the All-Star squad for the 1983 Golden Anniversary gala in Comiskey Park: "When I walk out on the field and see all those great players, I better be wearing rubber pants."

The unfunny unraveling of the Sox in the 1983 AL playoff put an end to all the horseplay. No longer could Marc (Booter) Hill be detected loading up cigarettes so they'd explode when lit by unsuspecting victims. The comedy capers shifted to the executive suite, where Ken (Hawk) Harrelson proved in a totally unreal sequence of 1986 events that he was a much better TV spieler than a general manager.

Not even Woody Allen could have written the script for the Harrelson fiasco. The saddest part, aside from the damage this episode caused the Sox, was that good people ended up as the victims—LaRussa and the Hawk himself.

Now when fans think of high times and hilarity at Comiskey Park, memories drift back to the irrepressible Bill Veeck. After he sold the Sox because soaring salaries knocked him out of the box, Bill agreed he'd rather lose his shirt than his sense of humor.

"I sit in the bleachers at Wrigley Field and watch these millionaires play," he said. "When one of them drops a fly ball, I'm glad it's not me paying him the million."

A Cub Fan's Lament;
Keep the Players and Trade the GMs.

Just suppose Rick Reuschel had been ready to start the third game in San Diego. Or the fourth game. Or to come out of the bullpen and confront the Padres when Rick Sutcliffe ran out of gas in that agonizing fifth game.

No Cub fan needs an explanation. We still wince at the

Mild-mannered Cub Manager Herman Franks shows umpire Doug Harvey how the Bears missed a game-winning field goal. Herman sent the fans home chuckling, even though the Cubs lost again.

memory of that Lost Weekend, when three crushing losses to the Padres detonated the dream castle the Cubs had been building throughout 1984. Even the mere sight of a Padres uniform can still trigger nausea.

What kind of a way is that, you ask, to lead off a trip down memory lane with Cub characters? Straight-arrow Reuschel was the consummate Cub noncharacter. All you got from this Camp Point, Illinois, plowboy was honest effort and good pitching, not hotfoots and hijinx.

It was Dallas Green's horrible mistake that put Warren Brusstar and George Frazier on the playoff roster and stiffed Reuschel. And it's clear that most of the burlesque in Cub history since 1969 has taken place in the front office, not on the hallowed greensward of Wrigley Field.

Flash back to the wreckage of the Leo Durocher regime. While Leo's tirades were shredding the confidence of promising pitchers such as Ken Holtzman and Larry Gura, genial general manager John Holland was practicing looking the other way. In fairness to Holland, Leo was owner P. K. Wrigley's fair-haired boy (despite Durocher's billiard-ball dome), so what could he have done?

Fans who fancy real characters have Holland to thank for foisting the one and only Joe Pepitone on them in 1970. The timing was perfect. Like the Cub team he was joining, Pepi gave the impression he would make something wonderful

Gentleman Jim Defends Durocher

A Leo Durocher loyalist ever since the Cub manager interceded to get him a $6,000 raise, Jim Hick-
man still refused to blame Durocher for the 1969
foldup. "It wasn't his fault," insists Hickman, now a
gentleman farmer down home in Henning, Tennessee. "We just played bad baseball."

After all these years, third baseman Ron Santo is
still searching for an answer. "When people ask how
we lost in 1969, I tell them I don't know," he said. "All I
know is the Mets kept on coming."

happen any minute now. Cub fans are still waiting. Those
who were entranced by Pepi's early heroics got the idea that
life was all ball for this fun guy, one of the trend-setting
swingers. His clubhouse takeoff on Marlon Brando's "I
cudda been a contenduh" routine was hilarious, and the
swath he cut through the bright lights of Rush Street was
worthy of Harry Caray. Few suspected that Pepitone was a
troubled, tormented man, struggling with the seeds of failure planted in his boyhood by a tyrannical father.

Whenever things got too good, Joe had to find a way to
louse them up. The perpetual kid made the fans love him,
then tore their hearts out. Before he blew town in 1973, the
wreckage of "Joe Pepitone's Thing," a with-it night spot, and
Pepi's chain of hair salons went down the drain, along with
Cub pennant hopes.

Holland still hung around, slapping Band-Aids on gaping
wounds in the Cub roster until 1975. Cub fans were discovering that promising young players like shortstop Roger
Metzger were vanishing from the farm system in exchange
for such bizarre additions as Pepitone. When the rest of
1969's heroes followed Ernie Banks into limbo, they were
replaced by Oscar Zamora, Joe Wallis, Carmen Fanzone,
Steve Swisher, Billy Grabarkewitz, Pete LaCock, and others
of that ilk.

The entertainment value of that motley crew far exceeded
its talent, especially Fanzone, who played a mean trumpet

Leo Durocher had his detractors, but Herman Franks (left) wasn't one of them. Neither was Jim Hickman, a productive Cub in Durocher's lineup.

and a mediocre third base. Zamora, sporting a gold earring when not pitching, became a sort of cult figure, the spiritual heir of Harry Chiti and Bill Faul, the pitching hypnotist. So did "Tarzan" Wallis, a genuine flake who had the same kind of death wish that impels people like Indianapolis 500 drivers and Jim McMahon to keep tempting fate.

The fans loved Tarzan. They had to, because Holland had dealt Bill North, a genuine big-league centerfielder, leadoff hitter, and base stealer, to Oakland. His successor in center, Rick Monday, at least drew comparable worth when the Cubs used him to land Bill Buckner in 1976.

Durocher's heavy hand was visible in the 1971 trade of Holtzman, who had pitched two no-hitters for the Cubs, and the departure of Gura, who became a big winner in Kansas City. But Leo was gone when Holland shipped Cub great Billy Williams to Oakland in 1974 for Manny Trillo and two burned-out relievers, Bob Locker and Darold Knowles.

There was not much talent and even less hope when Holland departed near the end of a disastrous 1975 season. The Cubs' traveling secretary, Blake Cullen, pleaded for a chance to take over, and it's hard to see how he could have done a worse job. Instead, Wrigley shocked the fans again by handing the GM portfolio to a trusted retainer, E. R. (Salty) Saltwell, the director of park operations.

"Salty has gone from counting hot dogs to signing them," zapped *Tribune* columnist Bob Verdi.

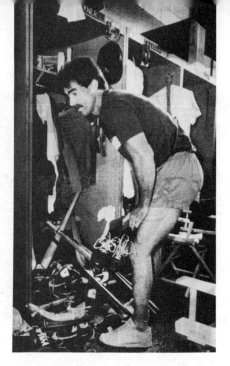

It's hit-the-road time for exCub Bill Buckner after the Red Sox released him in 1987. Billy Buck couldn't seem to shake off the goat horns from his crucial World Series error.

Saltwell promptly slammed the door on an unforgettable chapter in Cub annals by sending shortstop Don Kessinger, last of the '69 survivors, to St. Louis for Mike Garman, another of many relief pitchers who provided no relief. At least the Cubs had continuity in the operation. Saltwell kept right on mortgaging the future in 1976 by giving away slugging first baseman Andre Thornton for journeyman pitcher Steve Renko and utility man Larry Biittner. A decent hitter and a good guy, Biittner played the outfield like too many Cub outfielders before and since. He left his footprint in the sands of Wrigley Field one unforgettable day by missing a shoestring catch, then searching frantically for the ball. It was right there on the grass—underneath his cap.

Fanzone's hot trumpet and warm smile upstaged his chilly bat, making the early 1970s more bearable for Cub fans. Biittner did the same thing from 1976 through 1980, easing the strain of the post-Durocher transition years in Wrigley Field. They were two of the most easygoing players in an era when the Cubs' clubhouse needed a revolving door.

Not even the arrival of rookie standouts Burt Hooton and Rick Reuschel could save Durocher from being tossed overboard midway through 1972, another Cub campaign in vain. For those who still refuse to believe Durocher's colossal ego

Passing the Buck for Series Flop

The Red Sox invited Bill Buckner to leave Boston and take his goat horns with him. Buckner didn't mind, because he was tired of hearing about his disastrous error in Game 6 of the 1986 World Series. That blunder looms as large in Red Sox history as the grounder Cub first baseman Leon Durham muffed in the final game of the 1984 NL playoffs.

The California Angels picked him up, but Boston had to eat most of the veteran's $800,000 salary. "All the media and fan reaction after that error," said the ex-Cub. "Everybody in Boston holds that against me. I guess I was the easiest guy to take it out on."

Buckner was a Wrigley Field hero in his stormy, eight-year Chicago tenure, but he hated to play there. He made headlines by feuding with managers, calling Herman Franks "a fat clown," and scuffling with Lee Elia.

was the villain, just look at what happened to Ken Holtzman, one of baseball's premier left-handed pitchers, under Leo the Lion's kindly tutelage. The embittered Holtzman's 1971 record plummeted to 9–15 while his ERA skyrocketed to 4.48. In the next three years, after being dealt to Oakland, the lefty won 59 games, and the A's took three straight World Series. So much for "Gimme that old-time Durocher."

In his return as GM, former "head coach" Bob Kennedy couldn't end the Cubs' grand tradition of losing when it counted, while winning just enough to whet the appetites of gullible fans. A decent man, Kennedy refused to make a deal with the Cards for his son Terry, because he just couldn't bring himself to subject the young catcher to all that pressure. The Cubs desperately needed a receiver when injuries shortened Randy Hundley's career, but they had to operate with the likes of Steve Swisher and Barry Foote until Jody Davis arrived in 1981.

Herman Franks was another double-barreled bust as manager and general manager. A gruff, wily, self-made millionaire, Franks parlayed mediocre catching skills into membership in the Good Ol' Boys union that played musical chairs with managerial and front-office jobs. White, amiable, and well-connected, they rotated from team to team for years. Prominent members included Alvin Dark, Bill Rigney, Gene Mauch, Billy Martin, John McNamara, Charlie Fox, Chuck Tanner, Dick Williams (who, like Martin, is not that amiable), and all that gang.

The Franks tenure lapsed into comic-opera feuds with some of his players, notably Jose Cardenal and Bill Buckner. When Frank's candid assessment of Billy Buck ("He thinks of himself, not the team") hit print, the enraged Buckner retorted by calling Herman "a fat clown." After a brief stint of playing cards and swapping lies at his Salt Lake City men's club, guess who was recycled as general manager in 1980?

"Am I crazy for taking this job?" Herman asked his old sparring partners, the Chicago writers, at the comeback press conference. He probably was. As Cub manager from 1977 through the final week of '79, Franks had to deal with the tantrums of Ding-Dong Dave Kingman. Dim Dom Dell Dallessandro may have had the most mellifluous nickname in Cub history, but Kingman's was the most accurate.

Not until the 6'6" slugger hit 36 homers for the Mets in 1975 did he discover that fame was too much for him. Kingman's problems escalated faster than his home-run total, pursuing him coast-to-coast in 1977, a season he divided among four teams.

By the time the well-traveled Kingman showed up in a Cub uniform the following year, his pattern was predictable: a brief honeymoon with the media, then righteous indignation over some trivial incident, quickly escalating into all-out war. Through it all, the fans loved big Dave, especially after Ding Dong's 48 dingers in '79, tops in the NL.

Kingman was so unstrung by the adulation Chicago lavished on him that he assured his own demise next spring, dousing mild-mannered *Daily Herald* reporter Don Friske with ice water. The Cubs refused to extend Kong Kingman's contract, ending his checkered career as a part-time *Tribune* columnist, ice cream parlor owner (Kingman's Landing), and hero of all antiestablishment rebels, with or without a cause.

Compared to Kingman's peculiarities, Manager Lee Elia's storied clubhouse blast at Cub fans on April 29, 1983 ("They oughta go out and get a bleepin' job. . . ."), was understandable. An emotional man, Elia saw his boiling point exceeded by a 5–14 Cub start. This indicated to Cub fans that the Dallas Green regime would become a rerun of all the "rebuilding" episodes from the dim and distant past. Somehow, 1984 turned out to be the most fun for Cub fans since Jolly Cholly Grimm strummed his left-handed banjo to celebrate a string of pennants. To paraphrase the Ol' Perfesser, Charles Dillon Stengel, can't anybody here play this game?

When a Bear's Down, It's Hard to Bear Up

Losing was never a laughing matter to George Halas, the man who dragged the National Football League, kicking and screaming, into the big time, Bear fans looked at things differently. They sometimes had to laugh at the antics of Halas' hirelings to keep from sobbing softly into their suds.

Now the Bears and their fans have it better than ever. They can laugh like winners and chuckle at each other's antics, as well. After years of cowering under their blankets to watch the likes of Bobby Douglass and Bob Avellini complete rifle-armed passes to enemy defensive backs, Bear fans are also out of hibernation.

They paint their faces orange and blue, daub sheets with those "Hi Mom" banners for TV, whoop it up bare-chested (at least some of the men do) despite icy Lake Michigan wind

---

Throw a Net on Those Nuts

Dan Hampton fell out of a tree when he was a sixth grader, so maybe that explains his theory on defensive football: "If I was a coach, I'd grab all the wild and crazy guys and put them on defense. How many keepers does it take to hold down one insane man?"

gusts, and gulp down a little snakebite remedy to ward off the chill. Every city's wounds are healed by winners, especially Chicago. Windy City fans know there's nothing like a winning team after living so long with nothing like a winning team.

Let's face it, Jim McMahon could be an Ollie North clone and they'd still love him madly around these parts. The fact that the Bears' leader sometimes lives just as dangerously off the field only enhances his superhero status. He's an exception to the rules, the rare guy who can thumb his nose at convention and get away with it. Even McMahon's agent, Steve Zucker, still can't believe all the people who line up, waving $10,000 checks to lure the spike-haired quarterback to their club, lodge, sports night, bowling banquet, or whatever.

Lately, he has done more talking than quarterbacking. They all hope Jim jabs Ditka, hurls brickbats at Mike McCaskey, or brews a fresh batch of controversy with a new eruption, the more outrageous the better.

In Chicago, McMahon can do no wrong. He's becoming the all-time Bear character, eclipsing a parade of oddballs that strutted and fretted across the Halas stage for 60 plus years. Such certified space cadets as George Trafton, Doug Atkins, Hatchetman Ed Sprinkle and rotund Abe Gibron, the best all-round coach in the NFL, have been relegated to obscurity by today's bumper crop of Bear characters.

There's Refrigerator Perry ("I've been big ever since I was little"), Mongo McMichael, and Danimal Hampton. Ringmaster Ditka now makes enough on the side to guarantee free psychiatric care for Bears afflicted by an inferiority complex because they don't have their own restaurant, radio and/or TV show, and fan club.

What with standup comedy routines, singing, dancing, and motivational videotapes, pushing those quarter-ton Ditka pork chops over at City Lights or beaming from the cover of his bestselling book, or guesting on every talk show from "Tonight" to eternity, the coach has little time left to coach. What Bears fans hope most nowadays is (1) McMahon stays healthy and (2) Ditka stays put. Ditka and Chicago are now synonymous.

Clemson's William "The Refrigerator" Perry measures up as an Outland Trophy & Lombardi Award Candidate

Obviously, William "Refrigerator" Perry didn't miss any meals even before cashing in on his fame as a Bear rookie. The 360-pound Clemson star already had his own poster in college.

When Ditka goes berserk on the sidelines, grabbing jerseys, chewing tail, shredding clipboards, the whole nation tunes in, not just Chicago. No wonder the coach breaks the tension by polishing his offseason comedy act and taking it on the road. Now he knows how to motivate an audience with routines just a trifle less abrasive than he uses on his players.

"I'm not the best football player ever to come from Aliquippa, Pennsylvania," Ditka insists. "But at least we're both Ukranians. The other guy's name is Tony Dorsettski.

"I went a little too far after a game in Baltimore [1983, a 22–19 overtime crusher] and figured I'd get their attention by banging my hand on this trunk. As soon as I did, I knew it was broken. That was the last time my players laughed after they lost a game.

"People ask what kind of relationship I have with Jim McMahon and I tell them it's strange and wonderful. He's strange and I'm wonderful.

"I just tell jokes. I don't sing or dance, unless the band plays a polka."

The one name still guaranteed to make Ditka stop dancing—and laughing—is Buddy Ryan. Their rivalry is just as deep and personal as ever. Ditka resented Ryan's camarade-

Mike T. Won't Second-Guess Mike D.

Mike Tomczak didn't agree with Coach Mike Ditka's decision to start Doug Flutie at quarterback in the Bears' 1987 playoff loss to the Redskins. Instead of whining about it in print the way Jim McMahon did, Tomczak earned respect by buttoning his lip, and accepting his role as caddie for the fragile McMahon.

"I made mistakes, but I never lost confidence in myself," said the former Ohio State standout.

rie with the media, especially when the new head coach was trying to survive in those first few rocky years. Ditka chewed his cud and swallowed his tongue while the defensive coordinator helped the Bears win Super Bowl XX. When Ryan left to coach the Eagles, their parting language was XXX-rated.

"He's talking about a Super Bowl in Philadelphia in three years," Ditka snapped. "He'll be lucky if he's still in Philadelphia in three years."

The old master, George Halas, probably would have kept Ditka and Ryan together unless and until they killed each other. Halas loved such animosity on his coaching staff, well aware that complacency foments mediocrity. Halas, a man who always had his priorities straight, told this story with a straight face:

"Get together with your girl friend and it lasts 20 minutes. Go out for a drink with the guys and it's over in a few hours. But when you win a game in the NFL—that lasts a whole week!"

The closing story belongs to another old-time Bear character, No. 51, Dick Butkus, the linebacker supreme who closed holes with violent finality for nine years in a Bear jersey. Asked why Butkus didn't get a game ball after bottling up Baltimore almost single-handed, Colt quarterback Johnny Unitas had the answer:

"They had to stop awarding game balls to Butkus. When they give him one, he eats it."

SIX

TEN GAMES WE'LL NEVER FORGET

Chicago's Best Games

A lot of spectacular Chicago games and players have disappeared into the murky mist of pre-TV. Face it, the tube gives fans a live look at magnificent moments that years ago, only a few thousand lucky spectators could have seen. Maybe that compensates for fans having to put up with Howard Cosell.

December 12, 1940: Bears 73, Redskins 0, No!

To this day, it's *the* ultimate pro football game. The numbers are even more awesome now than they were then, because they've stood the test of time.

Consider this: in 68 years of Bear history, almost 900 regular-season and playoff games, only twice have they come within a dozen points of that incredible 73. The Bears crushed the Packers 61–7 in Soldier Field on December 7, 1980, causing tight-lipped rage in the Green Bay dressing room. The Packers accused Bear coach Neill Armstrong of running up the score and vowed revenge. Sure enough, the Pack sacked the Bears 16–9 on the same field in the 1981 opener, greasing the skids for Armstrong to get sent packing.

The other regular-season Bear rampage was a 61–20 mauling of the 49ers on December 12, 1965—Gale Sayers's six-touchdown day.

The Spree of '73

At Griffith Stadium, Washington, D.C., December 12, 1940.

Bears (73)	Position	Redskins (0)
Nowaskey	LE	Masterson
Stydahar	LT	Wilkin
Fortmann	LG	Farman
Turner	C	Titchenal
Musso	RG	Slivinski
Artoe	RT	Barber
Wilson	RE	Malone
Luckman	QB	Krause
Nolting	LH	Baugh
McAfee	RH	Justice
Osmanski	FB	Johnson

Bears	21	7	26	19 —	73
Redskins	0	0	0	0 —	0

Osmanski, 68-yard run (Manders, kick).
Luckman, 1-yard plunge (Snyder, kick).
Maniaci, 42-yard run (Martinovich, kick).
Kavanaugh, 30-yard pass from Luckman (Snyder, kick).
Pool, 19-yard interception return (Plasman, kick).
Nolting, 23-yard run (kick failed).
McAfee, 34-yard interception return (Stydahar, kick).
Turner, 21-yard interception return (kick failed).
Clark, 44-yard run (kick failed).
Famiglietti, 2-yard plunge (Maniaci, pass from Sherman).
Clark, 1-yard plunge (pass failed).
Attendance-36,034.

Mastermind George Halas (right) and quarterback Sid Luckman relish the Bears' 73–0 slaughter of Washington in the 1940 NFL title game. Their success made T-formation football the rage, dooming the old single wing.

The Redskins had to wait two years to avenge their 1940 humiliation. They got it by snapping the Bears' 18-game winning streak with a 14–6 upset in the 1942 NFL title game.

Upsets come and go. The Bears' dynasty ended eventually, to be replaced by Paul Brown's Cleveland Browns, Vince Lombardi's Packers, and Chuck Noll's Pittsburgh Steelers. Now the Bears are dipping into the NFL honeypot again with the spin of another sports cycle. And the Redskins are on top of the League as Super Bowl champs. But that 73–0 still towers over the NFL record book and the imagination of football fans, gaining stature with the passing years.

It makes the 29–6 White Sox slaughter of Kansas City in 1955 seem like a squeaker. In all of sports history, it probably ranks right next to Joe DiMaggio's 56-game hitting streak. Curiously enough, DiMag did it in 1941, within months of the Bears' feat.

How can one team pulverize another so totally in a championship game? It's a well-known fact that the Redskins had skinned the Bears 7–3 on the same Griffith Stadium turf just three weeks earlier. Instead of assuring another cliff-hanger in their rematch for the NFL crown, the last play of that game turned the Bears into grizzlies. Halas insisted that interference by defensive back Frank Filchock caused Sid Luckman's potential winning TD pass to bounce off Bill

Osmanski's chest in the end zone. While the Bears screamed, the gun sounded, the officials fled, and the Redskins celebrated their 7–3 triumph.

Because their defense had held the mighty Bears without a touchdown in November, the Skins figured there was no need to change it in December. Washington's windbag owner, George Preston Marshall, added more incentive by labeling the Bears "crybabies." The Halas-Marshall feud boosted interest in the December 8 showdown. Not even Halas dreamed that his Bears would put on such a devastating show for the sellout crowd of 36,034. About 1,500 Bear fans came to Washington by train, and midway through the second half, their jubilant shrieks could be heard clearly amid the stunned silence that hung over Griffith Stadium.

The second play from scrimmage opened the floodgates. Osmanski took a Luckman pitch-out, burst through the line, and went 68 yards for the first of 11 Bear touchdowns. A block by George Wilson wiped out both Ed Justice and Jimmy Johnston, informing their goggle-eyed Redskin teammates that the Bears meant business. In less than 13 minutes the Bears had 21 points. The first half was 28–0, the second half 45–0.

If pictures of this devastating Bear blitz had been flashed back to Chicago as it was happening, the way they were in Super Bowl XX, fans would have been dancing in the streets. It was an antidote for the Depression that had blanketed America throughout the 1930s. From a technical standpoint, it also validated Clark Shaugnessy's T formation.

Skinhead Marshall was out of footballs–and words–when the slaughter ended. The Bears had intercepted eight of Slingin' Sammy Baugh's passes, only one less than he completed before stumbling to the sidelines to sob on the losers' bench. For 43 years, Papa Bear looked back on this 60-minute massacre as one of the happiest hours of his long, battle-scarred life.

May 12, 1970: Money in the Banks

Phil Regan, after two productive seasons as the Cub relief ace, mysteriously lost the hop on his Vaseline ball in 1970.

Two of the best ever, Ernie Banks and Billy Williams, accept Wrigley Field plaudits on May 30, 1970. Banks was honored for his 500 homers and Williams for his consecutive game streak.

The 33-year-old right-hander was sitting in the left-field bullpen on a Tuesday afternoon, watching Ernie Banks dig in for his first try against Atlanta right-hander Pat Jarvis.

Morning rain kept the Wrigley Field crowd down to 5,264, but the sun was shining when Banks stepped up with two out, bases empty, and the Braves leading 2–0. It wasn't the ideal setting for the warclub of Mr. Cub. Weekend crowds had turned out a few days earlier, hoping to watch a slice of Chicago history—homer number 500 for Banks. Ernie had tripled against Cincinnati both Saturday and Sunday. At 40, with 80-year-old knees, getting to third base was almost as hard on Ernie as it was on the fans, who were yearning to see him touch 'em all on one swing.

They especially wanted it on Mother's Day, because Ernie dedicated the big blast to the moms of all those Cub fans. Coming from somebody else, such sentiment would have triggered eyeball rolling, throat clutching, and cynical comebacks in the pressbox. From Ernie Banks, it was a different matter. In a world where not much can be taken at face value, Ernie had credibility. People loved him. His hold on Chicago fans has seldom been duplicated. Bobby Hull was idolized. Jerry Sloan, Dick Butkus, Billy Williams, Fergie Jenkins, Gale Sayers, Carlton Fisk, Alan Page were liked and respected. Ernie Banks was loved.

Michael Jordan of the Bulls, Walter Payton of the Bears, Nellie Fox of the White Sox, Randy Hundley of the Cubs, and Stan Mikita of the Blackhawks all approached Banks's level of acceptance, both personally and professionally. But Ernie surpassed them all, touching a chord in everybody, except perhaps the lunatic fringe of racists or militants, both black and white. The man's innate goodness was transmitted by his voice, his smile, and his actions on and off the field.

Even Leo Durocher, Banks's severest critic, found something nice to say at the end of this magical afternoon, when Williams's ninth-inning homer pulled the Cubs even, enabling them to win 4–3 in the 11th.

Hard-throwing right-hander Wayne Simpson was the Reds' hot rookie in 1970, going 14–3. Arm trouble cut his career short, but before that he had a blazing fastball and confidence bordering on cockiness.

"Banks is not going to hit it off me," Simpson said, looking ahead to his Sunday start against the Cubs. He was right. First time up, Banks unloaded on him, rifling a liner that hit the left-field wall so hard it caromed into the corner while Banks limped into third. Welcome to the bigs, rookie.

So Ernie was still at 499 and holding when Pat Jarvis threw him a 1-and-1 fastball on the inside part of the plate. "The pitch was right where I wanted it," Jarvis said. A couple of million Chicagoans agreed with him when Banks parked it in the bleachers for the long-awaited homer. The ball hit concrete underneath a bench and rebounded to the turf.

"When he hit it, I didn't think it was going in," Regan said.

"I saw Rico Carty [Braves' leftfielder] turn toward the stands and then I knew," Banks said, a week of tension draining from his body.

"What a relief," Regan added after turning the historic ball, retrieved by Carty, over to Fergie Jenkins for safekeeping. "I touched a milestone," chuckled Jenkins, who will eventually join Banks and Williams in the Hall of Fame. "We should have some champagne to pour over him," suggested Ron Santo while the Cubs waited for Ernie to extricate himself from the media mob.

The last word was reserved for Banks. As always it was a cheerful one. "Hey, an old guy like me couldn't pick a better time than Senior Citizens' Day," he said. "What a moment to remember."

July 6, 1983: An All-American Night.

It was 50 years in the making. Even dour Bowie Kuhn, the embattled commissioner of baseball, agreed that Jerry Reinsdorf and Eddie Einhorn had written a punchy script for the Golden Anniversary All-Star game.

Back in Comiskey Park, where it all started, American League bats painted a golden glow on the festivities by providing the same happy ending. The AL's 13-3 romp in—where else?—Comiskey Park erased a bit of the humiliation the Senior Circuit had dished out since 1950.

Babe Ruth, naturally, hit the first All-Star home run on July 6, 1933, when the National League went down to defeat, 4-2, in the inaugural game. Even without the Sultan of Swat, the AL was ruthless in piling up a 12-4 lead in the first 16 All-Star shows. The drama began turning into burlesque when Ralph Kiner's ninth-inning homer sent the 1950 clash into overtime. Red Schoendienst hit another to win 4-3 for the NL in the 14th. That triggered one of the most amazing streaks of dominance in sports history. Somehow, the AL blew 30—count 'em 30—of 37 ensuing clashes before the players assembled in Chicago for the 1983 return to All-Star roots. The players and owners contributed to the sorry situation, cheapening the All-Star concept with two games each year from 1959 through 1962. Pure greed was the only reason for doing so. The players sought to load up their pension fund quickly, and the owners didn't want to get stuck with the bill.

So who got mugged? Don't be silly. The fans, who else? What began as a one-of-a-kind spectacle was tarnished by such unashamed avarice. Commissioner Ford Frick said in 1959 that "as long as the fans [he meant suckers] will support this entertaining spectacle we feel it's our right" and on and on and on.

Not even that could quench the fans' thirst for the All-Star concept, even if the AL couldn't put it into practice. Baseball lives, thrives, and survives on the tradition that's passed along from grandparents to kids.

So when the Sox owners Einhorn and Reinsdorf brought the '83 biggie back to where it all began, the scramble for tickets was ferocious. The owners put the game on with style, especially in assembling living members of early All-Star teams to appear in an old-timers' game the day before. It was like a living Hall of Fame.

The spectacle recalled the first game in 1933, meant to be a one-shot spectacular for Chicago's Century of Progress fair. With Connie Mack managing the AL and John McGraw coming out of retirement to handle the NL, how could it miss? Then Ruth hit a two-run homer off Wild Bill Hallahan on his second trip to the plate and put the stamp of permanence on the All-Star game.

George Herman Ruth was the man who had saved baseball from the Black Sox disaster, revolutionized the game, and made it come alive in every American city, town, village, and country crossroads. Now 38, fat, and at the end of the line, the Sultan of Swat visited Chicago one last time to rekindle past greatness.

Only nine months earlier, the Babe had stepped up to the plate in Wrigley Field and provided another unforgettable moment with his "called-shot" homer off the Cubs' Charlie Root. It was typical of Ruth to top that North Side drama with double heroics on the South Side: the homer that won the first All-Star game and the eighth-inning catch of Chick Hafey's blast that saved it. What a way for the Bambino to go out—back on top. Even so, he was dumped a year later by the arrogant Yankees and retired early in 1935.

The 1983 All-Star game was satisfying revenge for victory-starved AL buffs. Fred Lynn capped a 13–3 cakewalk with the first grand slam ever (off Giants' southpaw Atlee Hammaker) stroked in 54 of these "Dream Games." That the dream had become a nightmare for the NL didn't matter to the majority of Sox fans among the jam-packed 47,595 in Comiskey Park. For one night, at least, not only the AL but all of baseball was safe at home.

January 26, 1986: One for Papa Bear

If this game had been a movie, it would be good for remakes. Chicago fans would be lining up to buy videotapes of "Super-McMahon: The Super Bear's Super Bowl" as fast as the studio could grind them out. Even without new dialogue, actors, or plot, it would be guaranteed four stars from Siskel, Ebert, Grabowski, and every other ecstatic Bear fan.

This story is the best Midwest football yarn since Pat O'Brien played Rockne and George Gipp was portrayed by that young actor—what was his name again?

Anyway, Super-McMahon's exploits are well known in Chicago. Bear fans believe he'll bounce back from shoulder surgery and other assorted ailments to lead the Bears into another Super Bowl for a new version of their smash 1940 hit, "73-0."

The supercool youngster portrayed a great quarterback in Super Bowl XX. His go-for-it flint, striking the steel of Coach Mike Ditka, produced the sparks that turned the 1985 Bears into a blowtorch. They knew that without McMahon they wouldn't even have been in the Superdome on this supercharged Sunday, facing the New England Patriots for National Football League supremacy.

Sure, the defense was great. It had been for years, even before Buddy Ryan installed his peculiar blend of spit and vinegar and called it the 46 defense. Mean, tough, head-bashing defensive teams had been a George Halas trademark ever since his Staley Starchmakers knocked the starch out of opponents.

Walter Payton and Willie Gault were a matched set of offensive A-bombs, ready to detonate on any play. Motivator Ditka, the yeller and screamer, and father-figure Ryan knew how to meld all those aces, showing them the way to win Chicago's first NFL championship since 1963. And McMahon was the mystic figure who made them believe they would do it.

By the time the Bears finished a 15-1 regular season, they knew their fearless QB was right. Back-to-back playoff shutouts over the Giants and Rams confirmed their confidence. It didn't really matter which American Football Conference team drew the Super Bowl short straw. The Bears would have preferred their favorite villains, the Raiders, or perhaps Miami to avenge their only defeat, but no foe could beat them this day. The first half was 23-3, the second half 23-10. In an unplanned farewell tribute to Ryan and his 46 defense, it ended up a 46-10 massacre.

The Patriots, who barked and snarled at the Bears early,

turned into patsies almost as soon as McMahon clicked with Gault for a 43-yard pass on the Bears' second play from scrimmage. They were bottled up, bewildered, and humiliated by Richard Dent's flip-flops that shredded the New England plan to zone-block against the Bear blitz. Dent deservedly got most valuable player laurels as the leader of the defensive mugging that draped seven sacks over hapless quarterbacks Tony Eason and Steve Grogan. New England was frisked for six turnovers—four fumbles and a pair of interceptions. Eason was helpless, getting the hook after failing to hit on any of his six passes. McMahon completed 12 of 20 passes for a whopping 256 yards and scored two touchdowns. William (Refrigerator) Perry belly-whomped a yard for his TD. The losers were triple-stomped 408–123 yards in total offense.

By halftime, Chicago fans in the Superdome were already planning French Quarter victory parties. In the third period, gaps began to appear in the Superdome stands. The crowd of 73,818 melted away while Merlin Olsen and Dick Enberg tried to keep NBC's national telecast from disintegrating like the Patriots, who now played in sullen silence. "You wish the NFL would put in an 'Uncle' rule to avoid playing those last few minutes," Olsen commented.

In Chicago, sideline shots of their heroes counting down the final minutes were all that mattered. The rout was complete, the prophecy on a pregame banner totally fulfilled: "Papa Bear, This One's For You."

March 12, 1966: Golden Jet Flight 51

The tension was growing in Chicago. Not only were Blackhawk fans getting edgy and irritable. So was Bobby Hull after 10 days in vain pursuit of his record-breaking 51st goal.

Only two other men in National Hockey League history had scored 50 times in a single season. Maurice (Rocket) Richard, legendary power plant of the Montreal Canadiens' dynasty, did it first in 1944–45, 50-game season. Bernie (Boom-Boom) Geoffrion of the Canadiens Lite Beer fame, equaled that in 1960–61.

When Hull cracked the magic 50 barrier in 1961–62, the

schedule had been hiked to 70 games, but the talent level was a lot higher as well. Hull was a marked man from the second he swung his skates over the dasher to take his turn on the ice. Every team in the league assigned a shadow to harass the Hawks' superstar—hooking, holding, tripping, or trying to provoke him into fights. Opponents figured the penalty box was the one place where Hull couldn't demolish their goalie with his blistering slap shot.

Bobby still scored on them all in the 1965–66 season. He slammed into a Chicago Stadium goalpost, narrowly escaping serious knee damage, then rebounded quickly to keep pouring in the pucks. The Golden Jet went into orbit in pursuit of the Rocket record with three hat tricks and 15 goals in his first 11 games. He kept the heat on, hanging up a pair of four-goal midseason games just over a month apart.

Only 14 other Hawks ever tallied four times in a game. Denis Savard got his in a 1986 playoff loss to Toronto. Stan Mikita did it twice, but Hull pulled off four four-goal games. Both of this remarkable athlete's four-baggers in 1965–66 came on home ice. No wonder Chicago was Anticipation City as the record drew closer. Hull had 44 goals in 45 games, giving him plenty of time.

But it wasn't until the Hawks' 57th game that Hull made the shot that gave him another 50-goal season. It was a bumpy trip to his next stop, the all-time record. Nobody wanted to yield the historic score, so Hull was pursued by a nightly posse of hatchetmen. With their netbuster cordoned off, the Hawks were shut out three straight times while the pressure mounted.

The Hawks trailed the New York Rangers 2–0 in the third period on March 12. A Stadium mob of more than 20,000— this was before Chicago fire marshals cracked down on standing-room fans blocking the aisles—gnawed its nails while Hull fired 17 shots at Ranger goalie Cesar Maniago, the same victim who had admitted Geoffrion to the 50-goal club in 1961.

Mikita snapped the Hawks' scoreless string of 228 minutes, 56 seconds with a goal at 2:57 of the final period, cutting the gap to 2–1. The stage was set.

At 5:35 of the third period, Hull unleashed a 50-foot slap shot from center ice. Bingo! Chicago Stadium went bananas.

The game was delayed almost 10 minutes for the hat-toss-ing, foot-stomping, rafter-rattling demonstration, proving that Robert Marvin Hull, the kid from Point Anne, Ontario, population 1,000 or so, was the biggest man in his adopted hometown of Chicago.

"The ice was sticky," Hull said after the Hawks had rallied to win 4–2. "It wasn't my best shot, but our forwards were moving in and their defense dropped back, so I let it go."

Maniago claimed Eric Nesterenko should have gotten the assist instead of Lou Angotti and Red Hay. "Nester got the blade of his stick under mine and pushed it aside," the Ranger goalie said. "It was far from Hull's hardest shot. The puck just slid past on my left side."

What mattered was that it went into the net. The Golden Jet became the first man in NHL history to tally 51 goals in one season.

"The greatest scoring feat since Frank (One-Eye) McGee got 14 goals in a 1905 Stanley Cup game," gushed *Tribune* hockey writer Ted Damata, who ate up the Hull show.

Scoring 50 goals may be routine now, though that in no way dims Hull's luster. The fans cheered until he skated a victory lap, wearing a top hat tossed onto the ice. Afterward, Hawk Captain Pierre Pilote had the perfect punch line.

"What's all the excitement?" Pierre asked innocently. "You'd think nobody had scored 51 goals before."

April 20, 1986: The Jordan Rolls On

Chicago fans already knew that Michael Jordan was some-thing else, one of those players who comes along every 25 years or so. When he finished writing a hoop symphony on the fabled parquet floor of Boston Garden, the Bulls' guard was a 23-year-old legend in his own time.

Jordan's 63-point effort couldn't win a playoff game for the Bulls, but it won the admiration and respect of the whole country, including the victorious Boston Celtics. Jordan, the one-man team, came close to being the equal of a five-man team that went on to hoist its 16th National Basketball Asso-ciation championship pennant into the Garden rafters.

Some Bull fans got mad at Larry Bird when the Celtic superstar noted that Jordan had taken 41 shots in his 53-

Ship this picture—and both players—to the basketball Hall of Fame right away. Mr. Bull, Michael Jordan, swipes a rebound from Mr. Celtic, Larry Bird, in another of their classic duels.

minute assault on the playoff record book. The smart ones realized Bird was paying Jordan a compliment. Like Bird, Air Jordan flies as much as it has to. At playoff time, especially against the Celtics, if Jordan isn't superb, the Bulls get blown out. They were swept 3–0 in that 1986 series and again in their 1987 first-round matchup with Boston.

Discouraging? Yes, unless you look at the future. Jordan is two or three years from his peak. If the Bulls put enough second fiddles around him, he won't always have to be a one-man band.

Never was that more evident than on the April Sunday in 1986 when Jordan broke Elgin Baylor's playoff record of 61 points. It took Miracle Michael two overtimes to do it, but the Bulls still lost, 135–131.

Jordan had bagged 49 in the best-of-three series opener at Boston. A late Bull surge failed and they were routed 123–106. Jordan knew he had to play two feet higher than his usual above-the-rim space station to keep his team alive in Game 2, with America looking in on CBS-TV. The superstar was at his best from the opening tipoff, sparking the underdogs to an early 27–16 lead.

The rest of the afternoon was first-rate theater, as greyhound Jordan was pursued all over the court by Bird's fox-and-hounds posse. In the end, it was only the constant roar of support from 14,890 home fans, the 262nd straight

Garden sellout, that enabled the Celtics to snare their prey. If they could have heard the rest of the nation's basketball fans urging Jordan on while glued to TV sets in coast-to-coast saloons, ghetto houses, and lakeside condos, the outcome might have been different.

This was the day when the Jordan phenomenon took off like Air Jordan himself. Fans around the NBA had been coming out to see this kind of brilliance for two years, and Tar Heel zealots knew all about it in North Carolina. Now even football and baseball buffs, who normally prefer the hay-fever season to basketball, watched him go. The Jordan spectacular had everything except a happy ending.

It's impossible to tell how many dollars were generated for the NBA by that single telecast. Season tickets, souvenirs, items Jordan endorsed—especially Air Jordan shoes—soon were selling like hotcakes for big bucks, as was anything associated with this hottest of all sports properties. The Refrigerator Perry craze had been like this for a few months, though along with the same likable sincerity that had made the Bears' rookie a big name, Jordan had staying power.

His feats are unreal, but he's real. In Chicago, the touted Olympic hero and Carolina rookie got the kind of instant acceptance fans give to only a select few.

Jordan has had other big games since, but the 63-pointer in Boston was the breakthrough. The automatic scoring machine shot 22 for 41 from the floor and missed only two of 21 free throws, adding six assists, five rebounds, and three steals. The only thing he failed to do for the Bulls on this unforgettable afternoon was grab a broom and sweep the dressing room—or teach the rest of them how to play like him.

October 2, 1984: Cubs 13, Frustration 0

Cub fans had waited 39 years for this day. The lucky 36,282 in Wrigley Field and the millions who were there in spirit figured it was worth waiting for.

This was the climax to a sizzling Chicago summer. Cub fans finally believed—no, they *knew*—their long-overdue heroes wouldn't blow the National League East crown that had eluded them in 1969. The fans were right.

It'll look just as pretty with lights, but Cub fans are still in the dark on when—or if—this scene will be repeated. It's 1984 playoff action, with the Cubs mauling San Diego 13-0.

Now all that stood between the Cubs and the World Series was three victories over the San Diego Padres. "What, me worry?" Cub believers asked each other, trying to conceal the tremor in their voices and the tremble in their hands. This was not just another sunny, beautiful, meaningless afternoon in Wrigley Field, like so many we've sat through for four decades. One pitch, one baserunning blunder, one bloop single could make the difference in the whole ever-lovin' season.

To make it perfect, the Tigers had run away from the American League East and were about to triumph over the West division kingpin Kansas City Royals. The 1984 World Series would be a rematch of that nonclassic 1945 collision between two of baseball's hotbeds, Chicago and Detroit. Except this time, Cub backers vowed, the outcome would be different. The Cubs would erase the sting of the '45 setback by replaying their 1907–08 tail-twisting of the Bengals. What tradition of Cub failure? The "Men in Blue" would bury it to the tune of their hit song ("... Now's the time and here's the place we even up the score ... the pennant will fly over Wrigley in '84...."), their booming bats, and Red Baron Rick Sutcliffe's rifle arm.

It sure looked that way as soon as Sutcliffe set down the Padres in the first inning of the first-ever Wrigley Field playoff game. There was a sense of anticipation in the Wrigley pews on this gorgeous October afternoon. Leadoff man

Bob Dernier, first half of the 1984 Cubs' Daily Double, promptly turned hope into hysteria.

"Things seem to happen for my ball club when the wind is blowing out," said Cub manager Jim Frey. If only Frey's decisions later in the playoffs had been as sound as that observation. . . .

With the regular umpires out on strike, a salesman named Dick Cavanaugh found himself calling balls and strikes for this historic game. Padre starter Eric Show's first pitch to Dernier was high. Cavanaugh called it a ball. The second serve was high, as well. Dernier swung, lofting a fly ball that soared with the wind and kept going into the left-center bleachers. The rout was on.

One out later, Gary (Sarge) Matthews lined a rocket for another homer into the ranks of his bleacher army. From then on, Wrigley Field was an outdoor loony bin, Cub fans exorcising decades of frustration with a joyous, two-hour primal scream. Even Sutcliffe put on a show with Show, launching a moon shot over the right-field screen to open the third inning. The Cubs added two more runs in that frame, then bombed reliever Greg Harris with a six-spot in the fifth. Their last two runs should have been saved for the lost weekend in San Diego, although the 13–0 final seemed like an evil omen only for the Padres on this triumphal day.

Good-hit, slow-field Keith Moreland put the frosting on the cake, preserving Sutcliffe's shutout with a diving, bases-loaded catch in right field. If any faint hearts still harbored doubts, that play convinced them God must be a Cub fan.

Padre catcher Terry Kennedy escaped the debacle with his sense of humor intact. "The turning point was Show's second pitch," he said.

December 12, 1965: Gale Force 36, 49ers 20

What really went through the mind of George Halas in the closing minutes of Gale's tornado? Rookie Sayers came into the National Football League with a reputation and a nick-name, the Kansas Comet. Veterans enjoy knocking the cock-iness, and the stuffing, out of such phenoms.

So maybe, as he claimed, Halas really did fear that one of the frustrated, humiliated 49ers would try to hurt the

Bears' new superstar if he was permitted to go for a record-shattering seventh touchdown. Wrigley Field fans could smell it when the Bears reached the San Francisco 2-yard line with the final seconds ticking away. "We want Sayers!" was the roar from the crowd of 45,814.

Instead, Halas gave them Jon Arnett to punch across the meaningless TD that ran the final score to 61–20. Sure, the 49ers defense would have zeroed in on Sayers in that spot, but they had been trying in vain all afternoon to stop the brilliant halfback. What would-be tacklers got for their effort was a faceful of mud from Sayers' flying cleats in the rain, mist, and slop. The only man who stopped this Gale force was his coach, George Halas.

"I took Gale out because it flashed through my mind that he would get hurt if he carried the ball again," Halas said. "I've been kicking myself ever since for not letting him try."

In a way, maybe Halas made the right choice. Bear fans never will stop providing their own scenario for that last scoring thrust. If Sayers had been injured, or just stopped short of the goal line, it might have rubbed some luster from a truly great performance. And one touchdown more or less didn't mean much in comparison with Sayers's awesome display of broken-field running.

The goo from two days of rain made the Wrigley turf treacherous enough to give the Comet a split-second edge on defenders. Wet or dry, Sayers could break loose on any surface if not surrounded by a gang of tacklers. On this sloppy Sunday he wore shoes with nylon cleats instead of rubber. Along with his blazing speed and shifty, change-of-pace style, Sayers became unstoppable.

After taking a short flip from Bear quarterback Rudy Bukich in the first quarter, he didn't stop until he crossed the goal line, 80 yards away. Before halftime, the fleet rookie tallied twice more on dashes of 21 and 7 yards. Then Sayers put the game out of reach by eluding the entire San Francisco defense on a 50-yard sprint to paydirt and capping the next march with a one-yard plunge.

The record-equaling sixth touchdown came on a punt return that many NFL observers rank right up there with Sayers's incredible kickoff runback two months earlier in Minnesota. When young fans at pro football's Hall of Fame in Canton, Ohio, see those masterpieces on videotape, they know immediately why Sayers's plaque hangs in the Hall.

Gale took the punt on the Bears' 15-yard line, eluded tackler after tackler until he broke clear at midfield, then simply outran pursuers to the end zone. The game should have ended right there, with Sayers racking up 336 yards in total offense and running his TD total for the season to 21. Coach Halas, who had seen them all in his day, summed up the Sayers show with the ultimate compliment: "This was the greatest one-man performance I've ever seen on a football field."

October 1, 1959: Klu Sox Dodgers, 11–0

The Los Angeles Dodgers didn't have a Klu. In their first Comiskey Park World Series game since 1919, the Go-Go White Sox suddenly stopped scratching for one run and started socking for 11.

South Side fans were so happy to see a Series again after 40 years of futility, they would have settled for a lone tally to win the opener 1–0. Instead, the Sox Klued them in with a display of power that gladdened the heart of every Chicago Irishman from Mayor Richard J. Daley to that legendary saloonkeeper, Mr. Dooley. Ted Kluszewski was proclaimed an honorary Irishman after Big Klu belted two homers to pace an 11–0 Sox rout of the Hollywood Dodgers in only their second California dreamin' season after being transplanted from their ancestral home in Brooklyn.

They might have been budding stars in Tinseltown, but on this afternoon in Chicago, the Dodgers were merely extras. Before a seven-run Sox spree in the third inning was over, Dodger pitchers were getting kicked around like stuntmen. Kluszewski's third straight hit was his second homer of the game, this one off the forgettable Chuck Churn.

By then, starting pitcher Roger "the Dodger" Craig had been spared the ignominy of dodging more bullets and was soaking under the showers. With such a fat cushion, Sox ace Early Wynn breezed for seven innings, then let Gerry Staley share his shutout. With such unaccustomed thunder supporting him, Ol' Gus didn't have to betray the weariness in his sturdy arm. The right-hander got the Cy Young Award for his sparkling 22–10 log in 1959, but he was 39 and time had taken its toll on everything except Wynn's will to win.

In that golden moment, with the ecstatic Comiskey crowd of 48,013 bellowing with glee on every pitch, Wynn looked as invincible as ever. There was no indication that day that the veteran would have to struggle through four more twilight years of 29–29 pitching to reach the 300-victory club. He finally did it for Cleveland in 1963 and fled gratefully into retirement.

Five Dodger pitchers were raked for 11 hits in the slaughter, including an erratic 23-year-old lefty named Sandy Koufax. Once again, Bill Veeck looked like a genius after stealing Kluszewski from Pittsburgh on August 25 for outfielder Harry (Suitcase) Simpson and minor-league infielder Bob Sagers.

Klu's trademark sleeveless shirt and bulging biceps struck a discordant note in a Sox lineup powered by speed, defense, and the Mighty Midget keystone combination of Luis Aparicio and Nellie Fox. Still, the muscular first baseman batted a welcome .297 in 31 games down the stretch and earned a secure place in Chicago history by becoming the only Sox player to homer twice in a World Series game. Sox fans raised a glass to his memory when 63-year-old Klu's big heart gave out on March 29, 1988.

A Potpourri of Chicago Biggies

Some unforgettable moments in Windy City sports have already been forgotten. When fans look at the record of Chicago teams, they tend to forget how much magic is woven into all those decades of defeat. The occasional peaks helped us survive all those valleys, so some of them are worth recalling, if only in passing.

How about the other two storied homers in Wrigley Field history, ranking up there with Ernie Banks's 500th? They were Babe Ruth's "called shot" in Game 3 of the 1932 World Series and Gabby Hartnett's 1938 "Homer in the Gloaming." Amid fierce bench jockeying, Ruth took two strikes from Charlie Root, then either did or did not point to the center-field bleachers before smashing Root's next pitch there. Root swore the Babe's gesture never happened, and Yankee (also ex-Cub) manager Joe McCarthy, of all people, agreed. Everybody agrees the Yanks won 7–5 and finished sweeping the Series the next day.

Hartnett's ninth-inning blast, on September 28, 1938, broke up a 5–5 tie with Pittsburgh just before darkness closed in. "I knew it was gone right away," said Gabby after belting Mace Brown's 0–2 pitch over the fence in left. Some fans mistakenly believe that blast clinched the pennant. It knocked the Pirates out of first place, but the Cubs had to beat them again the next day—and they did—to wrap up the flag. Ironically, Hartnett had been the catcher when Ruth hit his called-shot homer six years earlier.

Bob Feller's Comiskey Park no-hitter on Opening Day in 1940, when the Indians' ace topped Edgar Smith 1–0 on a raw, chilly day, has never been matched.

Sox fans didn't get to see the 1959 pennant clincher—it happened in Cleveland on September 22—but the old ballpark rocked on September 17, 1983. Juice Cruz turned on the electricity, dashing home on Harold Baines's sacrifice fly for a 4–3 victory over Seattle. That wrapped up the first AL West title ever for the Sox, and a rain-soaked throng of 45,646 celebrated.

Or how about Luke Appling's Sox record hitting streak of 27 straight games in 1936, the year the Hall of Fame shortstop won the AL batting crown with a .388 average? Appling, the master of bat control, once fouled off 16 pitches in a row to wait for the one he wanted.

The most unbelievable Chicago one-man show of them all was staged in 1930 by Lewis (Hack) Wilson of the Cubs. A character Ring Lardner should have invented, Hack hacked 56 homers and 190 ribbies, batting .356 with an unreal .723 slugging percentage. And all that after being the goat of the 1929 World Series for losing a fly ball in the sun. "Old Hack will make 'em eat those boos," vowed the barrel-chested, 5'6" strongman. Boy, did he ever.

The Bears' 14–10 triumph over the New York Giants in the 1963 National Football League Championship game was another of Wrigley Field's all-time moments. As always, defense won it for the Monsters of Wrigleyville.

After they moved to Soldier Field in 1970, Walter Payton arrived to provide the top individual thrill. He came into the

Luke Appling, "Old Aches and Pains" of the Sox. He could foul off a pitch or spin a yarn with equal ease.

October 7, 1984, game against the New Orleans Saints need-ing 66 yards to break Jim Brown's all-time NFL rushing record of 12,312. It happened on a play called "Toss 28, Weak," the 2,794th time Sweetness had carried the mail for the Bears. He cut left for six yards, and the man who always played, in Dan Hampton's pithy phrase, "like he wants to be the best tailback on his 10th-grade team," was all alone at the top.

Although he skated for years in Bobby Hull's shadow, Stan Mikita gave Blackhawk fans as many Chicago Stadium thrills as anyone. Stash's retired No. 21 hangs in the Sta-dium rafters with Hull's No. 9. Denis Savard scored four goals for the Hawks in an April 10, 1986, playoff loss to Toronto, but the wildest scoring streak in Hawk history be-longs to Bill Mosienko, who played all of his 14 NHL seasons in Chicago. Nobody will recall that Mosienko won the 1945 Lady Byng Trophy as hockey's most gentlemanly player. The broken left ankle he got as a souvenir of the first NHL All-Star game in 1947 has faded from memory. But Mosienko became a permanent trivia question in Madison Square Garden on March 23, 1952, by scoring three goals in 21 seconds. Gus Bodnar assisted on all three scores at 6:09, 6:20, and 6:30 of the third period. That enabled the last-place Hawks to end their season by collecting a 7–6 victory over the Rangers and the fastest hat trick ever.

The most memorable Bulls game was the wild Milwaukee Arena finish on January 17, 1970. The Bulls trailed the Bucks and their new superstar, Lew Alcindor (now Kareem Abdul-Jabbar) by 13 points with just over two minutes to go. They were down by eight in the final minute and by four with one—that's right, one—second on the clock. Guess what? The Bulls won in overtime, 132–130. Super Shay Halimon hit a 25-foot shot, cutting the gap to two in the last second. Don Smith of the Bucks nicked the basket support wire with his inbounds pass, turning it over to Chicago. Bombs away! Halimon clicked with a corner jumper that would have been a winning three-pointer under today's rules. Instead, the teams struggled into overtime and the Bulls prevailed, even though center Tom Boerwinkle fouled out and Bob Kauffman had to play defense against Alcindor.

SEVEN

TEN GAMES WE'D LOVE TO FORGET

Chicago's 10 Worst Games

H ere are 10 more unforgettable games. Try as they will, Chicago fans just can't forget them. The TV set in their heads shows endless reruns of that accursed grounder rolling under Bull Durham's glove, or Jay Schroeder eluding the Bear blitz to toss the fatal TD pass.

In case those scenes are beginning to fade, tune in again to see how really frightful they were.

October 7, 1984: Padres 6, Cubs 3

Back in the safe, sane, and sensible Midwest, Cub fans in Soldier Field glued transistor radios to their ears while watching Walter Payton trample on the New Orleans Saints for 154 yards.

Although Sweetness dashed into the Hall of Fame by eclipsing Jim Brown's all-time NFL rushing record of 12,312 yards, he couldn't compete with the Cubs. They were running even faster—backward. Back, down, and out, into the obscure brand of immortality that America reserves for losers. Game 5 of the 1984 National League playoffs, a 6–3 loss to the Padres in Jack Murphy Stadium, not only prevented

the Cubs from ending a 39-year World Series boycott, it was
a capsule summary of the entire season, not to mention Cub
history since 1945.

After the Padres went down 2–0 in the best-of-five series,
even they had been ready to concede. "On the flight from
Chicago we were looking at travel magazines and talking
about where to go on vacation," said the Padres' Tim
Flannery. What cruel irony. Flannery's pinch-hit grounder to
first base turned out to be the blow that sent the Cubs on
vacation.

Actually, it was more of a tap, a routine bouncer—the kind
that sure-handed Cub first baseman Leon Durham gobbles
up. Go get it, Bull. Go . . . Bull? Oh, no!

Oh, yes. The floodgates were open and the Padres poured
through, to the delight of the 58,359 live spectators and the
despair of millions across the country who mourned the
panic-stricken Cubs. Thanks to WGN-TV's powerful signal,
Harry Caray's charisma, and 96 regular-season victories—
their highest total since 1945—the cuddly Cubbies were
America's darlings. Photogenic guys like Rick Sutcliffe, Jody
Davis, Gary Matthews, Ryne Sandberg, and yes, Durham,
too, lured the nation to daytime TV.

Only a colossal turnabout could turn the nondescript Padres into the first team in NL history to climb out of an 0–2
playoff pit. *Tribune* columnist Bernie Lincicome, already

Bull, Bull, Both Blue

Leon (Bull) Durham sympathized with Bill Buckner,
his predecessor at first base for the Cubs, over
Buckner's horrendous 1986 World Series error. Durham committed one just as costly in the 1984 NL
playoffs.

"After Buckner's error he still could look ahead to
the seventh game," Durham said. "All I could do was
pack up my bags and go home. I don't know if we
lost the pennant because I missed an easy ground
ball, but I still dream about that play."

fashioning a reputation as Chicago's resident sports cynic, called it a Cub chokeup. He was right.

First, the Cubs dented the Padres' Ed Whitson, who never faced arrest for impersonating Cy Young, then let him off the hook in Game 3, a 7–1 San Diego romp. Then Manager Jim Frey sat there and watched Steve Garvey destroy his pitching staff without ordering them to employ one of two time-tested coolants for hot bats: a knockdown pitch or an intentional walk. Leo Durocher would have been bellowing "Stick it in his ear!" when Garvey came up in the ninth inning of Game 4 with the score tied 5–5.

Instead, ace reliever Lee Smith stuck it over the plate, and Garvey struck it over the right-field fence. Maybe the Cubs knew then and there it was not their year. And maybe Cub fans should have started rehearsing their doleful, perennial chant: "Wait till next century!"

But Rick Sutcliffe was ready to start the decisive game, instead of the World Series opener in Detroit. When soon-to-be Chicago public enemy number one Eric Show yielded his fourth and fifth homers of the series to give Sutcliffe a quick 3–0 lead, Chicago fans mumbled through clenched jaws, "The Red Baron will get us there."

Through no fault of his, the Red Baron crashed in flames an agonizing few miles from the pennant landing. The Padres cut the gap to 3–2 in the sixth inning, when it was clear Sutcliffe was out of gas, but Frey sent his groggy ace back out for the seventh round. Instead of Padre punches, it was Cub chokes that landed the knockout punch on the game right-hander.

Ex-Cub Carmelo Martinez walked to begin last rites for his former team, a sure sign that Sutcliffe should get the hook. Steve Trout was ready in the bullpen, but Sutcliffe survived, and the Cubs died. Martinez was bunted along, scoring the tying run when Flannery's trickler trickled under Durham's glove.

Everybody in Chicago could have told Frey what would happen next. Alan Wiggins parachuted a pop fly single. Tony Gwynn's vicious grounder rocketed off Sandberg's shoulder for a two-run double. Garvey—who else?—singled home Gwynn to nail down the coffin lid on the Cubs. And *then,*

Frye summoned Trout to douse the fire. All those gallons of tears dripping into steins of suds in Chicago saloons could have quenched it, too.

Unfortunately, the came too late, just like Frey's move. Inevitably, the alibis flowed. Durham's glove had been doused when the Gatorade jug tipped over on the visitors' bench. Bill Buckner snickered publicly at Durham's boot, only to clone it himself two years later, enabling the Mets to steal the 1986 World Series from the Red Sox.

And so it goes for the Cubs.

May 18, 1971: Montreal 3, Blackhawks 2

Chicago Stadium was rocking and the Montreal Canadiens were reeling under a 2–0 deficit in the seventh game of their National Hockey League championship showdown to end the 1970-71 season. Fans crammed into every nook and cranny of the Madison Street ice palace were savoring their reward for a decade of frustration since the Hawks had last quaffed champagne from the Stanley Cup. Somehow the Hawks found a way to blow game, set, and match, sending their backers back to earth with a thud.

For out of the fog came the Pocket Rocket, Henri Richard, to hector the Hawks the same way his celebrated brother, Maurice (Rocket) Richard, had for years. Of the many demoralizing, disheartening, and disgusting playoff losses ever hung on the Hawks, this 3–2 stunner topped them all. That covers a lot of territory because Les Canadiens pounded 50—count 'em, 50—playoff lumps on Chicago in 17 series between 1930 and their last postseason collision in 1976.

But this time when the Stanley Cup slipped through their mitts they had a new excuse. Expansion and expanded schedules had been pushing the end of NHL schedules deeper and deeper into spring. Who could foresee that would cause a blanket of fog inside the Stadium to shroud the home club's demise?

The pattern for the series set in earlier, when the Hawks jumped off to a 2–0 lead at home, then lost twice in Montreal to even the best-of-seven showdown. The Hawks held service, 2–0, and with rookie Ken Dryden tending the Canadiens' net, the visitors' chances of ending it in the Forum looked good. They held a 2–0 lead in the third period when disaster struck. The puck hopped over Hawk defenseman Bill White's stick, setting up the goal that brought the Canadiens back to life. A frantic rally won it for them 4–3, and the Hawks flew home to be greeted by 3,000 fans.

The Hawks weren't the only unit that buckled under the pressure. The Stadium air-conditioning unit, overmatched by muggy mid-May weather, couldn't cool the place enough to prevent a pocket of fog from swirling around the rink. The players tried to disperse it by halting the game and skating in circles. But when play resumed, Jacques Lemaire fired a long shot that glanced off Hawk goalie Tony Esposito's arm and into the net, cutting the lead to 2–1. Esposito claimed he was blinded by the fog, a fog-gettable excuse. With Lemaire forechecking Eric Nesterenko, a pass intended for Bill White caromed off the Hawk net. Lemaire gobbled it up, found Richard open in front, and fed him for the tying goal.

At 2:34 of the third period, Richard broke away on the left boards, leaving young Keith Magnuson floundering in his wake. Richard beat Espo again, and that was that. Jim Pappin had the tying goal in his sights a few minutes later, but Dryden somehow kicked the puck away.

"This one hurt a lot worse than the 1965 Stanley Cup final we lost to Montreal," lamented Bobby Hull, who hit the crossbar with a shot early in the heartbreaker. "I don't know how many more chances I'll have to be on a Cup winner."

Prophetic words. Hull was gone to the World Hockey Association after one more Chicago season. With Hull, the Hawks might have ended the Montreal jinx in the 1973 final. Without him, they lost another Stanley Cup to the Canadiens. At least their fans had to suffer through only six games that time.

May 11, 1975: Warriors 86, Bulls 72

Mayor Richard J. Daley sent the Bulls a telegram just before they were eliminated from their first National Basketball Association playoff series in St. Louis on March 25, 1967.

"It took the Blackhawks 40 years to win—I am sure the

Bulls will do it in five," Hizzoner predicted.

Now, just over eight years later, the Bulls were ready to make Da Mare's forecast come true, at least by the elastic standards of political punditry. They had just whipped the Golden State Warriors in Oakland to take a 3–2 lead in the Western Conference finals. The Bulls were one game away from the World Series of pro basketball!

The setting for Game 6 was perfect. From the poor little basketball team that couldn't hit the floor with a dribble, the Bulls had undergone total metamorphosis, emerging as the NBA's Monsters of Madison Street. Their rock-and-sock style had created a bull market for Bull tickets, turning Chicago Stadium into the same ear-shattering echo chamber it had been for the Blackhawks just a few years earlier.

It was Mother's Day, a gorgeous Sunday afternoon in Chicago. All that stood between the Bulls and the NBA finals was one more victory over Golden State. Just one more to wipe out all the wipeouts Bull fans had endured from the Celtics, Lakers, 76ers, Hawks, and, yes, the Warriors. No way fire-breathing coach Dick Motta would let the Bulls be goats in their own pen, where they rolled up a 29–12 record in the 1974–75 regular season, then won five straight playoff tilts.

It started out fine. With the crowd of 19,594 roaring in confident anticipation, the Bulls sprinted to a 25–16 edge just before Rick Barry's 22-foot bomb trimmed it to seven at the first-quarter horn. Not to worry. The Bulls shot 55 percent from the floor in the initial 12 minutes, connecting on 11 of 20 field-goal tries.

When Bullshooters clicked like that, it was all over but the shouting. They had finished dead last in NBA offense during the season, shooting 45 percent and averaging 98.1 points a game. Motta's deliberate offense kept that figure down, and the Bulls won with hard-nosed defense, leading the league by limiting opponents to an average of 95 points. These Bulls hit opponents, not baskets.

Unfortunately for them, Coach Al Attles had the Warriors ready to live up to their nickname on this fateful afternoon, and he manipulated his bench like a chessmaster. He had picked up muscleman Bill Bridges, a 6'6" forward whose entire NBA playoff career had been spent ripping the horns off Bulls. As a St. Louis Hawk in 1967, an Atlanta Hawk in

1970, and a Los Angeles Laker in 1973, Burly Bill's Bull-bashing had played a key role. This time, he gave super-gunner Barry and the rest of the young, inexperienced Warriors just enough beef and savvy to pull them through. He did it in Game 6 simply by pounding on Bob Love, inflicting bonus bruises for each of the Chicago forward's 22 points.

That nullified the home-court advantage. "I got in his jock," Bridges said of his defensive crunch on Love. Bridges also intimidated forward Chet Walker and clogged the middle, slicing Motta's pattern offense into paper dolls. Then Barry sparked a 12–2 surge that put Golden State in command 46–38 at halftime.

The last 24 minutes was a Punch and Judy show. Bridges would slug a Bull forward at one end of the court, and Barry would burn a Bull forward at the other end. It was over long before the final bell tolled on an 86–72 Warrior triumph. That gave Barry and his supporting cast enough ammunition to beat the Bulls 83–79 in the seventh game, then take a nonstop cable car to the NBA throne room by sweeping the Washington Bullets four straight.

Bull fans are still wondering what was the Motta with the Bulls.

January 3, 1987: Redskins 27, Bears 13

In many ways, this game hurt more than its twin, the Bears' 21–17 first-round playoff loss to the same Washington Redskins on the same Soldier Field rug, just one year and one week later, on January 10, 1988. The disastrous walkout by the NFL Players Association during the 1988 regular season had drained a lot of fun out of the rest of that campaign.

It certainly took its toll on the Bears, perhaps more than on any team in the league. The relationship between Coach Mike Ditka and his players soured when the strike ended. They were mad at Ditka for praising the Spare Bear strike replacements, who won two of three "scab" games during the walkout. The love affair between the Bears and their adoring fans cooled as well. The players were shocked to learn how quickly Soldier Field crowds forgot them and cheered for Spare Bear retreads like quarterback Mike Hohensee.

Beer Down

Bear fans' despair after their 1987 playoff ouster by Washington was summed up by John Siebert: "Give me a beer, a shot of booze, anything. I just want a drink, and I don't want to talk about the Bears ever again."

With miracle quarterback Jim McMahon slowed by a hamstring pull, there was no playoff miracle in '88. The fans weren't as emotional before the game or as depressed afterwards as they had been in 1987. It seemed almost an anticlimax when Redskins' quarterback Doug Williams brought them back from a 14–0 deficit and Darrell Green returned a Bear punt 52 yards for the winning TD.

The 1987 playoff loss to Washington also hurt more than the 1934 "sneakers" game, when the New York Giants sneaked past the baffled Bears to win the National Football League championship 30–13 on frozen Polo Grounds turf by changing at halftime from football shoes to sneakers. It hurt more than the 23–0 whitewash in San Francisco that kept the Bears out of Super Bowl XIX.

The pain was deeper this time because it was so unexpected. Without often-injured Jim McMahon, most Bear fans conceded, they'd have a rough time beating the Giants in the NFC final or Denver in Super Bowl XXI. But giving up the title the Bears had earned in Super Bowl XX this easily caused a lot of XX-rated dialogue among shocked Soldier Field spectators.

The Bears figured the Redskins would be tough, but not this tough. Doug Flutie had been able to call down the thunder at Boston College whenever he needed a miracle. Not this time. Maybe Coach Mike Ditka was expecting too much too soon from the 5'9" quarterback. The Bears needed big plays from Flutie, and he gave them little numbers: 11 for 31, 134 yards.

Second-guessers had a field day pouncing on Flutie's errant passes and excoriating Ditka for starting the kid instead of experienced-but-immobile Steve Fuller or inexperienced-but-eager Mike Tomczak. Analysts who dealt in reality instead of emotion, however, pointed the finger of guilt in another direction: the Bear defense.

Suddenly, the invincible defense of Vince Tobin was vincible, punctured by a cool quarterback who performed like he had been tutored by Vince Lombardi. Coaches from every other NFL team, after years of being terrorized by the Bear blitz, ran this game film over and over with a glint in their eyes. They watched the Redskins' Jay Schroeder tease, taunt, and tantalize that murderous pass rush, rolling away from it, tossing two touchdown passes over it, and even running the old belly-series keeper that Sonny Jurgensen used at Duke 30 years ago.

Coach Joe Gibbs of Washington admitted that mixing up

Hey-Hey-Hey, Good-bye

Song parodies of the "Super Bowl Shuffle" sprang up like weeds when the Bears failed to repeat their 1986 triumph over New England. Brothers Al and Howard Fleishman dashed off this ditty, called "Super EmBEARassed":

We are the Bears and we are through,
Another Super Bowl was too good to be true.
Like all Chicago teams, you knew he could,
Blow the season like you knew we would.
We're not here to get harassed,
We're just here so say we're super embarrassed.

Individual players also got worked over:

Walter Payton
They call me Sweetness, but I just turned sour,
You saw me on TV, takin' a shower.
I had an ego, but now I'm humble,
Because inside the 20, I always fumble.

Jim McMahon
I'm Jim McMahon behind these sunglasses,
I drink lots of beer when I ain't throwin' passes.
I don't play much, 'cause I'm seldom healthy,
But Taco Bell sure has made me wealthy.

the pass offense left a bunch of mixed-up Bears pounding the turf in despair while Art Monk beat Vestee Jackson and then Mike Richardson on a pair of blitz-busting TD tosses. Gibbs found the right man for the job in Schroeder. Getting sacked twice and throwing an interception couldn't stop the Skins' signal caller from putting the Bears in the bag. Along with 134 yards from his rushers, Schroeder's 184 in the air were sufficient.

"We kept the Bears' defense off balance," Schroeder said. "I sprinted out, stayed in the pocket, threw quick to beat the blitz, or kept more people back to block."

It added up to a convincing beating from a team as good as any in the NFL and better than almost everybody on the Bears' powder-puff 1986 schedule. Schroeder noted that the Redskins came in "battle-tested" and ready to exploit Chicago weaknesses. If more incentive was needed, a *Tribune* headline proclaiming "Bears Ready—If Redskins Show Up" provided plenty.

"That was all we needed," grinned Skin stalwart Dexter Manley.

What the Bears needed was less confidence—and more defense.

October 8, 1983: Orioles 3, White Sox 0

"I was needed in the players' lounge to talk to the young guys," said Greg (Bull) Luzinski. "They were taking this loss pretty hard, so I wanted to explain that baseball is a game of ups and downs. If a kid doesn't bounce back from a tough defeat, it could affect his confidence for good.

"It was more important for me to be there talking about things like that instead of standing around answering the same questions from the press, over and over. They already knew all the answers anyway."

Bull, Luzinski. As phony as your Lite Beer commercial. The White Sox fadeout in their 1983 American League playoff with the Baltimore Orioles was excusable. Your disappearance from the dressing room after the hallucinogenic game that ended the Sox's fantasy season was inexcusable.

That's not to make the Bull the designated goat of this

four-game playoff knockout, despite the designated hitter's woeful 2 for 15, a .133 clip. Right out there, taking the media heat, was Jerry Dybzinski, the utility infielder whose base-running blunder had blunted the only real Sox chance to win this bitter struggle. Instead of following Luzinski's example by hiding, Dybzinski was manfully pinning the goat horns on himself.

"My instincts told me to keep running," he said. "I was hoping they'd throw to third to get me while the run scored. I can run bases and bunt, but I didn't do either when the team needed it."

Dybzinski's instinct betrayed him because the Orioles had been in such critical situations many times. With Vance Law at second, Dybzinski at first, and one out in the seventh inning of a scoreless duel, Julio Cruz lined a single to left. Vance obeyed Coach Jim Leyland's stop sign at third, but Dybzinski motored around second with his wheels in over-drive and his brain in neutral.

Baltimore leftfielder Gary Roenicke charged the ball and hit the cutoff man, just as a major leaguer should. The relay to Rich Dauer hung Dybzinski up, and Law broke for the plate during the rundown. Dauer's peg to catcher Rick Dempsey was waiting for him. At that point, the 45,477 Co-miskey Park faithful should have trudged out into the gathering twilight of the chilly October afternoon. The pattern of this playoff had been set, and nothing could change it. The Sox were wholly dead because of the holes in their bats.

The tipoff was Game 1 in Baltimore, three days earlier. Sox fans were so euphoric about LaMarr Hoyt's brilliance in the playoff opener that they failed to notice the Pale Hose offense getting paler and paler. In the last three innings, the Sox got nothing out of seven baserunners, a balk, and a wild pitch. With men in scoring position they went 1 for 13, somehow hanging on for a 2–1 nod. "You want ugly? We got ugly," summed up Dave Kindred of the *Washington Post*, citing the "Winning Ugly" label hung on the Sox by Texas manager Doug Rader.

It got uglier. Rudy Law accounted for 4 of the 11 Sox hits in the next two games. A mud-fence homely 4–0 shutout in Baltimore was topped by a truly grotesque 11–1 Oriole orgy in Chicago's first-ever playoff tilt. That left it up to lefty Britt

Burns to get the Sox even and take them to a decisive fifth game at home, with Hoyt rested and ready to tweak the Birds' beaks.

When you pitch a shutout and can't win, it's certainly not your fault. Burns dueled Baltimore rookie Storm Davis and bullpen bulwark Tippy Martinez to a standstill until Tito Landrum came up with one out in the visitors' 10th. Landrum spent most of 1983 in the minors, batting just 41 times in the big tent. He soothed his own ulcer by transferring the pain to Burns, drilling a fastball into the upper deck.

The season was over, though the Orioles scored two more unneeded runs before the losers went peacefully in their half of the 10th. "I would have been out there next inning if they needed me," Burns said.

That spoke volumes for Britt, but the silence of Sox swingers drowned out those fighting words: Harold Baines, .125; Carlton Fisk, .176; Luzinski .133. Too bad Burns couldn't have faced those three in the 10th inning instead of Landrum.

October 12, 1929: A's 10, Cubs 8

Nothing like this has happened before or since in the World Series. Naturally, it happened to the Cubs. And once the 10-run snowball started rolling down the hill to bury the Bruins, they were powerless to escape.

The Cubs had waltzed to the 1929 National League pennant by 10½ games over Pittsburgh, racking up a gaudy 98–54 record. Even with Hall of Fame catcher Charles (Gabby) Hartnett idled by a sore arm, the Cubs had a North Side galaxy of stars, notably second baseman Rogers Hornsby, whose .380 average and 229 hits are still one-season team records. A slugging outfield of Hack Wilson, Riggs Stephenson, and Kiki Cuyler also backed up pitchers Pat Malone (22–10), Charlie Root (19–6), and Guy Bush (18–7).

This could have been the best Cub team ever. Unfortunately, it wasn't the best team in the 1929 World Series. Even without the fabled 10-run inning, Connie Mack's Philadelphia Athletics had enough power, pitching, and balance to beat any team in baseball that year.

Hack Wilson was the goat of the A's 10-run 1929 World Series uprising against the Cubs, but he was a hero to this kid. It's young Bill Veeck, chatting with Hack in spring training.

The A's won 104 games, losing just 46, to steamroll the Babe Ruth–Lou Gehrig Yankees by 18 lengths. The New York media have rhapsodized about the 1927 Yankees for so long that many baseball fans, with no real basis for comparison, accept the questionable dogma that they were the all-time best. For my money, the greatest baseball team ever to plant 18 spiked shoes on a major-league diamond was the 1929–31 Philadelphia Athletics.

Those A's had Jimmie Foxx at first base, Al Simmons in left field, and Mickey Cochrane behind the plate, all Hall of Famers. Their trump card was Robert Moses Grove, the best left-handed pitcher ever. Grove won 31 games in 1931, but in '29, the first of three straight AL pennant years, the A's won 30 of the 37 games started by the supreme southpaw. Ol' Man Mose blended a mean temper with an unhittable fastball. They say that on a cloudy day, you couldn't even see Grove's hummer from the stands.

So, sad to say, the 1929 Cubs were overmatched in this Series. Crafty A's manager Connie Mack had the best pitcher in baseball on his staff and didn't even have to use him as a starter in the World Series. Grove hurled only 6⅓ innings of spotless relief, striking out 10, to earn saves in the second and fourth games. Mack outfoxed Cub manager Joe

McCarthy, no dummy himself, by starting Howard Ehmke
in the Wrigley Field opener. Supposedly washed up at 35,
Ehmke's off-speed junk and control drove the Cubs crazy.
The sidearm right-hander fanned 13, then a World Series
record, by delivering the ball out of a background of white
shirts worn by spectators in the center-field bleachers.

Now you know why those good seats are permanently
blocked off by the green "pool table" covering them. Why
the Cubs didn't use their home-field advantage by finding
some sidearmers to pitch in Wrigley Field is another of the
mysteries surrounding this inscrutable team. Ehmke's victory set the tone for this one-sided Series, with the fourth
game the one for the book because the Cubs were victimized
in such crushing fashion. It still seems incredible.

Trailing 2–0 when the Series shifted to Philadelphia, the
reeling Cubs needed a mound masterpiece in Game 3. They
got it from Guy Bush, the Mississippi right-hander who
learned how to pitch at Tupelo Military Academy. Bush out-
dueled George Ernshaw, a 24-game winner for the A's that
season, escaping frequent jams to preserve a tense 3–1 victory.

The mighty A's shrugged it off and another confident
crowd packed Shibe Park in bright sunshine for the fourth
game on October 12. Shibe Park, a cozy little bandbox that
resembled Comiskey Park in miniature, had only 29,921 capacity for the Series, with every seat filled and standees
crammed everywhere. Like Wrigley Field, Shibe Park wa sin
a working-class residential neighborhood. Owners of row
houses across the street piled ricketty wooden bleachers on
their roofs and sold tickets. Eventually, Connie Mack had to
build his right-field wall into a 30-foot "spite fence" to elimi-
nate the competition.

Inside or outside the park, A's fans felt a twinge of panic
when the visitors battered Jack Quinn, Rube Walberg, and
Eddie Rommel for eight runs. Cub ace Charlie Root was in
top form, blanking the A's on three hits through six frames.
Mack was preparing to concede defeat by benching his regulars after they batted in the seventh.

When Al Simmons' homer led off the bottom of the seventh, the fans grumbled "At least Root won't shut us out."
He sure wouldn't. Foxx singled and Bing Miller's fly to cen-

ter fooled Hack Wilson, the catchable ball dropping for a single. Disaster bekoned because Wilson had broken his regular sunglasses and wore new ones with lighter shades. They couldn't cope with the glare, directly in the stocky outfielder's eyes, and the Cubs couldn't cope with the deluge that followed.

In rapid-fire succession, Jimmy Dykes and Joe Boley lashed run-scoring singles. After pinch hitter George Burns popped out, Max (Camera Eye) Bishop TKO'd Root with a single, cutting the gap to 8–4. Art Nehf took over and Mule Haas lofted a deep fly to center. Again, the treacherous sun betrayed Wilson and ball landed behind him. Haas circled the bases for a three-run inside-the-park homer, the A's trailed by just one, and Shibe Park was an emotional cauldron, ready to erupt.

When Nehf walked Cochrane, putting the tying run on base, he got the hook. McCarthy summoned John (Sheriff) Blake, who tried to arrest the rally by serving a double-play grounder to Simmons, batting for the second time in the inning. Whoops! The ball hopped over third baseman Norm McMillan's glove for a single. Foxx brought down the house with his second single of the inning, sending Cochrane home for an 8–8 deadlock. Down to the last hole card, McCarthy played his ace, Pat Malone, and the A's trumped it. Malone nicked Miller with a pitch, loading the bases. Dykes then slammed a double to the wall in left, scoring Simmons and Foxx. The 10-run uprising was history, and so were the Cubs.

Even going into the ninth inning the next day with a 2–0 edge, the shell-shocked Bruins couldn't stop looking over their shoulders. Sure enough, the A's came on with a three-run blast to put the Cubs out of their misery. All the dazed losers could salvage from the debacle was McCarthy's classic retort when a kid asked him for ball.

"Young man," the Cub manger snapped. "Just go out to center field and stand behind Wilson. You'll get all the baseballs you want."

July 15, 1979: Disco Disaster

It sounded like another clever promotion by Bill Veeck, the man who raised hustling to an art form. Maybe it wasn't in a class with his midget pinch hitter stunt, but it was clever enough, in its own way. Why not blend music with baseball, luring a new generation of young fans to Comiskey Park at 99 cents a head for Disco Demolition Night?

The gimmick was reduced grandstand admission for kids who brought a disco record to add to a between-games bonfire. The '79 Sox were drooping with ex-Cub shortstop Don Kessinger at the helm. Attendance was down sharply from 1977, when the South Side Hit Men lured fans with window-breaking power and winning baseball. So Veeck was ready to listen when told that disc jockey Steve Dahl could plant young fannies in empty Comiskey seats with his antidisco routine.

Unaware that he was dealing with an explosive situation in more ways than one, Veeck agreed to let Dahl detonate the disco records via a fireworks blast in the outfield after the opener of a doubleheader with Detroit. When the stunt backfired and thousands of young people spilled out of the stands to mill around on the turf, the situation careened out of control. A foolish move, such as trying to drag some of the more obnoxious exhibitionists away, could have triggered a full-scale riot.

Veeck wisely declined to call in Chicago cops. "Using force in that situation would have been a terrible mistake," he said. He took to the field himself, pleading in vain for the kids to get back in their seats. but mob psychology had taken over, enhanced by some beer and a few joints here and there. Before they stormed the field, rowdies had been tossing firecrackers and disco records at players. "How'd you like to get hit in the eye with one of those things?" asked Sox outfielder Wayne Nordhagen.

Tribune columnist David Israel let fly with the first volley of criticism heaped on this ill-advised event: "Ten years after Woodstock, we have Veeckstock." Howard Cosell joined the attack, lamenting, ". . . too much carnival about the White Sox, from the front office to the on-air [no-holds-barred announcers Harry Caray and Jimmy Piersall] presence."

SOXOGRAM
GET
READY
FOR THE
DISCO
DEMOLI-
TION
BETWEEN
GAMES

Exploding disco records in the Comiskey Park outfield trigger the crowd and the place goes up for grabs on July 12, 1979. After the Sox forfeited to Detroit in the wake of a near-riot, owner Bill Veeck admitted he'd made a mistake in judgment.

Veeck bit his tongue and swallowed the local barbs, but barked back at Cosell.

"Who could be phonier than Howard?" he demanded. "Anyway, with a club as bad as ours, singing 'Take Me Out to the Ball Game' with Harry is the only entertainment our fans can look forward to."

The official attendance was more than 49,000, though some kids simply rushed the gates and others made a dangerous climb to find gaps in Comiskey Park's stone facade. Nobody knows how many were actually there. The shocking sight of thousands of Chicago and suburban kids running amok and tearing up the Comiskey turf was flashed on TV screens, giving the Veeck regime a black eye that contributed to his decision to sell the Sox to Jerry Reinsdorf and Eddie Einhorn in 1981.

"My investigation was inadequate," Veeck confessed. "The promotion worked far too well by drawing the wrong kind of people. As soon as I saw the obscene signs they brought in, I knew we were in for trouble. I never should have let

Dahl's people into the ballpark."

Veeck patiently outlasted the troublemakers. The kids eventually got bored and went home, leaving behind trampled turf that never fully recovered from the damage. "We just let 'em run until they got tired," Veeck said.

Veeck and his partners paid in money and credibility for this bizarre escapade. The Sox lost the first game. The night-cap was postponed and later forfeited to Detroit. And the most ridiculous comment on the whole sorry business came from Russ James, the production director of WLUP, Dahl's radio station: "Veeck asked for it and he got it. In a way, this is positive. It shows what power people have."

September 30, 1962: Packers 49, Bears Ouch!

Roger Leclerc is best remembered by Bear fans as a place-kicker. He converted 55 extra points without a miss in 1965 and kicked five field goals in a 16–15 loss to the Detroit Lions on December 3, 1961. But Leclerc also was a reserve line-backer during his Bear career, from 1960 through 1966. When he had to fill on for injured middle linebacker Bill George on this visit to Lambeau Field, Leclerc learned how the football felt when he kicked it.

Coach Vince Lombardi was busy in Green Bay, welding the whole state of Wisconsin into an adoring backdrop for the Packer dynasty that would win three straight National Football League titles and the first two Super Bowls. The sole survivor of the NFL's tank town era was preparing to transform itself into "Titletown, USA." Leclerc and the rest of the Bears turned into human tackling dummies under a Green Bay tidal wave that showed Lombardi's troops what heights they could scale under his leadership.

Astonishingly, two vital cogs in the Packer offense, run-ning backs Paul Hornung and Tom Moore, were knocked out of action by injuries early in the game. Lombardi simply summoned Elijah Pitts to team with bruising fullback Jim Taylor, and Packer power began to assert itself. Bart Starr, rapidly establishing himself as the NFL's premier quarter-back, had too much firepower for the Bears.

"Even when we knew where they were going, we couldn't

stop them," Leclerc noted after the slaughter. "And Starr is the best in the league at calling audibles if he sees a gap in the defense. I'd say he changed 60 percent of their plays at the line."

Still, it was only 7–0 late in the second quarter, when the crafty Starr reached into his trick bag. He tossed a 54-yard touchdown pass to Ron Kramer after confusing the defense by sending both running backs out on a crossing pattern, and the visitors were down 14–0 only 1:14 before halftime. The rout was on. Quarterback Bill Wade, harassed and hounded by the Green Bay pass rush, was sacked for 41 yards in losses. When he had time to throw, nobody was open.

Jesse Whittenton, one of the best defensive backs in pro football, was covering Bear spread ends Angelo Coia and John Farrington all by himself. No wonder Wade completed almost as many passes to the Packers (five) as he did to Bear receivers (seven). The veteran had a rocky 7 for 20 afternoon, for 132 yards. But it was on the ground that the Bears really got chewed up, getting outrushed 244–85. Taylor carried 17 times for 136 yards while Starr was connecting on 9 of 12 passes for 154 more.

A three-touchdown onslaught in the third quarter put the game away, but the Packers added anther pair in the closing minutes. Herb Adderly scampered 50 yards to score with another interception before the final gun barked mercifully. Lombardi's affection for Bear boss George Halas made the Green Bay genius almost apologetic in this postgame remarks.

"I'm sorry the score got that big," St. Vince said. "Once we got rolling, there was nothing we could do about it today."

This was not the worst margin of defeat in Bear history. The Baltimore Colts got revenge for a 57–0 walloping administered by Halas's horde in 1962 (less than two months after the Bears' whitewash in Green Bay), pounding them 52–0 on September 27, 1964. The Bears were also crushed 53–14 by the Chicago Cardinals in 1955, humiliated 47–0 by the Houston Oilers in 1977, and stomped 42–0 by the Cleveland Browns in 1960.

Even so, the 49–0 mugging by the Packers hurt more because it was uncharacteristic of this bitter rivalry. Since they met for the first time in 1921, the Bears and Packers more often than not have lived up to that colossal cliche, "hard-fought and evenly matched." How much more hard-fought can you get than the Packers' 2–0 triumph in 1932 or the Bears' 2–0 revenge in 1938?

The Bears left town feeling the same way the Packers did in 1980 after their series lowlight, a 61–7 Soldier Field shellacking. The Midway Monsters wanted to even the score for that 49–0 jolt, and they did it in 1963, sacking the Pack twice en route to Halas's last NFL championship as head coach.

April 15, 1973: Lakers 95, Bulls 92

Not until Chet Walker clicked with a corner jumper just 2:58 before the final horn did it appear that the Bulls actually could win this game. Until then, the capacity crowd in the Forum had been waiting for the Lakers to take command and draw clear in the stretch. They had done it so many times to the Bulls that the script—and game stories—just about wrote themselves.

Unlike the Bears, Cubs, and White Sox, the Bulls at least made the playoffs in the late 1960s and early 70s. Coach Dick Motta's firebrand tactics and will to win goaded his players into postseason action six straight times. When they got there, just like the Blackhawks, the Bulls had a depressing tendency to fall on their horns in the first round.

Chicago qualified for the playoffs in eight of its first nine NBA seasons, from 1967 through 1975, losing 18 straight playoff road games in the process. They suffered quick knockouts six times in a row, until Motta's merry men finally won on their 19th try away from home. It was a 108–103 decision over the Detroit Pistons in Cobo Arena, appropriately enough on April 1, 1974.

But the Lakers were too big a hurdle. The Bulls ended up in the slaughterhouse all 13 times they faced L.A. in their Forum playoff tilts. The Forum, an ornate edifice, was built in 1967 by Laker owner Jack Kent Cooke. Replete with California-style glitz, it's in suburban Inglewood, across the street from Hollywood Park racetrack and a few miles from L.A. International Airport. Inglewood is full of the stark contrasts California thrives on: a tacky, two-story doughnut atop a Manchester Boulevard snack shop near million-dollar yachts moored at Marina Del Rey. In a setting like that, you know strange things are going to happen.

Most of them have happened to the Bulls. After 12 playoff setbacks there, they were looking for a Lucky 13 streak buster on April 15, 1973. What they got was one of the top three gut-busting, nerve-shredding, heart-stopping losses in franchise history. It came in the seventh and deciding game of the Bulls-Lakers series. The winner would be heavily favored to knock off Golden State in the Western Conference finals and advance to the championship round.

Each team had won three times on its home court, leaving the deadlock to be broken in the Forum. Lakers' coach Bill Sharman had been croaking at the refs, despite an ulcerated vocal chord, about Chicago's "half-bump and shove" defense. His star, 7'2" Wilt Chamberlain also lamented their "fall-down play." "Hey, if Wilt hit you, you'd fall down, too," responded Jerry Sloan, middle linebacker of the tough Bull defense.

But it was the Lakers' defense that came to the fore when Walker put the visitors ahead 90–83 less than three minutes before the end. Somehow, no whistles greeted the home team's strong-arm tactics in a 12–2 rush that turned it around, bringing 17,505 Forum fans out of their chocked stupor. Even the Hollywood types like Jack Nicholson and Lorne Greene stopped trying to upstage each other long enough to gape at the drama unfolding on the court.

With the Bulls clinging to a 92–91 edge in the closing seconds, Chamberlain blocked Norm Van Lier's shot, grabbed the carom and hurled a floor-length pass to Gail (Stumpy) Goodrich. It looked like Wilt's moon shot would go into the balcony, but it came down barely inbounds, saved by Goodrich's fingernails. He deposited the winning lay-up and Sloan passed up a 15-foot jumper in the dying seconds. Towering Chamberlain bent down to give 6'1" Van Lier a consoling hug.

"A twist of fate," the Dipper said. No, not fate. Just the same old California Dreamin'.

December 4, 1987: Red Wings 12, Blackhawks 0.

The Blackhawks celebrated three days early, reenacting the December 7, 1941 raid on Pearl Harbor with a 12–0 loss to the Detroit Red Wings. The Wings were the bombers and the Hawks the bombees, taking the worst shellacking in the 62-year history of the Chicago NHL franchise. It had been a long time since things got this bad, a 12–1 Hawk fry in Montreal on January 9, 1954.

This Hawk team wasn't as bad as that one, because they rebounded from the one-dozen goal barrage to make the 1988 playoffs. It was still a depressing night for the visitors in Joe Louis Arena. Detroit scored in the opening 24 seconds, led 6–0 after one period, and fired 45 shots on goal at clay pigeons Bob Mason and Darren Pang.

"It could have been worse," said Hawk coach Bob Murdoch. "The way we played, it could have been 50–0."

October 14, 1906: White Sox 8, Cubs 3

For Cub fans, the World Series has been one agonizing, never-ending maiden voyage of the Titanic. Unlike the White Sox, the Cubs have tried to win all 10 Series they've played since 1906.

But that '06 inaugural against the Hitless Wonder Sox set the tone for decades of October outrage on the North Side. Under "Peerless Leader" Frank Chance, the 1906 Cubs had steamrolled the National League.

Franklin P. Adams was still a few years away from writing his famous ditty ("These are the saddest of possible words— Tinker to Evers to Chance"), but that "trio of Bearcubs, fleeter than birds" was in the thick of things. The Cubs won four NL pennants and two World Series in the five seasons from 1906 through 1910. Leading the way were manager– first baseman Chance, shortstop Joe Tinker, and second baseman Johnny (The Crab) Evers.

That cantankerous double-play combo was superb. And the Cubs had other stars, notably mound ace Mordecai (Three-Finger) Brown. When Brown lost most of his index finger in an accident on his family's Indiana farm, nobody

Could this be the greatest infield ever? It might be, it could be—it's (left to right) third baseman Harry Steinfeldt, shortstop Joe Tinker, second baseman Johnny Evers and manager-first baseman Frank Chance.

figured it would turn the tot into a Hall of Famer hurler. But with the "drop" that stub finger put on his pitches, the Cub right-hander went 26–6, 20–6, 29–9, 27–9, 25–14, and 21–11 in 1906–11. The only other Cub pitcher to string six 20-win years together was Fergie Jenkins—20–13, 20–15, 21–15, 22–16, 24–13, and 20–12 in 1967–72.

But Chance was outmanaged by Sox player-manager Fielder Jones, a centerfielder, to be precise. An intriguing man, Jones had the temerity to tell Sox owner Charles A. Comiskey to take a hike when the Old Roman's 1909 contract offer failed to meet the manager's demand for a chunk of stock in the club. Fielder didn't get it, but winning the 1906 American League flag with his team's batting average at .230, a full 32 points below the Cubs, was phenomenal. Third baseman Lee Tannehill stroked at a robust .183 clip, and Jones was the club leader in homers, hitting two of the six Sox four-baggers that season.

This was before spacious Comiskey Park opened in 1910 to put a premium on pitching. The 1906 world champs operated out of a bandbox at 39th Street and Princeton Avenue that had been abandoned by cricket players. In contrast, the Cubs' West Side park at Polk Street and Wolcott Avenue was a palace.

With the horses he had for the all-Chicago series, the su-

Sox Sack Cubs in City Series

The players don't get excited about resumption of the Cub-Sox City Series. They'd rather have the day off, but diehard fans still enjoy the crosstown matchup.

The Sox won 95 and lost 62 to the Cubs from 1903 through 1942, when they played a best-of-seven series almost every year. Only once—in 1906—was the City Series also the World Series. The "Hitless Wonder" Sox won that one in six games.

From 1949 through 1972, the Cubs reversed the trend with 13 victories and 10 defeats in their annual boys benefit game. On June 25, 1964, a series record throng of 52,712 packed Comiskey Park to see the Sox rout the Cubs 11-1. Mayor Jane Byrne's 1981 charity series brought them together again nine years later, at the end of the baseball strike. They played a 0-0 tie in Comiskey Park, followed by a 4-3 Cub win in Wrigley Field.

Lately, it's been all Sox again in the crosstown classic, promoted by a beer sponsor. They have won three straight, bringing the City Series count to 108-76 in favor of the South Siders. That does not include Cub-Sox spring training games, some forgotten in the mist of time.

perconfident Chance made an arrogant boast: "We'll win with our second-string pitchers." Only diehard Sox fans disagreed with that prediction and the 3 to 1 odds on the heavily favored NL champs. Chance had no chance after the Hot Sox turned tiger by winning 19 straight games to grab first place for good on August 12.

Imagine the Peerless Leader's shock when southpaw Nick Altrock matched Brown's four-hit pitching in the Series opener. An error and a passed ball set up the runs that gave the Sox a 2–1 triumph, just the way they'd been rehearsing all season. The chill of an early Chicago winter was forecast by snow flurries that pelted the crowd of 12,693 in West Side park.

Things seemed to return to normal the next day, when the Series shifted to thc South Side and victory went to the Cubs 7–1 on Ed Reulbach's one-hitter. Jones had the trump card, however, in Big Ed Walsh, once described as "the only man who can strut sitting down." The cocky right-hander won his two World Series starts, the pivotal third and fifth games, to put the underdogs in control, 3–2.

Chance brought Brown back with one day's rest, but Doc White, who had saved Game 5 for the Sox with three scoreless relief innings, was a match for him. Spotting their flustered rivals a run in the first frame, the Hitless Wonders became hitting fools, knocking out Brown in the second to roll up a fat lead. As he had throughout the Series, reserve infielder George Rohe delivered, and the White Sox coasted home 8–3. A frenzied crowd of 19,249 mobbed the Jones boys while the Cubs wandered off in a daze.

Exactly one week short of 78 years later, the same thing happened to the Cubs in San Diego. There really is nothing new under the North Side sun.

No, these aren't the Flying Nuns. They're cast members of a comedy titled *Nunsense*, on their way to see the Cubs perform.

EIGHT

NO LEERING IN THE PRESS BOX

Chicago Fans the Media Flames

Ben Bentley, the last of the old-time press agents, knew how to measure the potential of a sporting event.

"It's that daily ink," Benny used to say, between chomps on his ever-present cigar. "Everybody mugs for the TV camera at gametime, but unless fans can read about a team or a fight or a game every day in the paper, they know it's not for real."

Chicago fans may be blind in their loyalty, but they're not dumb. They don't buy the standard slump-ridden player's alibi: "Youse guys turned the fans against me by printing that negative stuff (i.e., his .110 batting average) in your crummy paper." Fans know that players, just like the rest of us, write their own reviews with day-in, day-out performance. A sportswriter who tried to make people believe Joe Mugwump played poorly when Mugwump actually played well would be laughed out of town.

Despite years of losing, Chicago fans stick with bad teams through thick and thin. In my book—and this is it—they're the best fans anywhere. Fans knew their sports, but they still have strange notions about what a newspaperman is and what he does. In this age of equality, I probably should call

myself a newspaperperson, but to heck with it. My criterion
for this business is competence, not race, sex, age, looks,
personality, charisma, karma or clout.

If you care about reporting accurately, honestly, and
fairly, you're okay with me. Some of the best newspaper
guys I know are claimers, not stakes horses. They plug along
every day, covering whatever comes their way with the same
energy and enthusiasm.

There's always more to write about nowadays, in less
space, because fans can't get enough of their teams, players,
and games. Even after being at the park and watching TV
replays, they still want to read about it the next day. Whenever the Bears make a first down or a Cub bloops a single,
newspaper circulation goes up. Fans went all the details, and
we better get it right. Doctors bury their mistakes, but when
a sportswriter blows one, it's reproduced a million times.

Players don't get the same kid-glove treatment in the papers that's heaped on them by TV and radio housemen. Understandably, that increases clubhouse tension, especially
during losing streaks. Most athletes are aware that fair and
unbiased coverage is the only way a beat writer can build
credibility. The Chicago manager who understood that best
was Tony LaRussa of the White Sox.

"This is the major leagues," Tony would tell rookies. "Your
performance will be scrutinized closely."

Mostly, clubhouse sulking and pouting is a game played
within well-defined rules. If the losing pitcher clams up, the
reporter talks to his catcher, who growls, "How the hell do I
know what kind of stuff he had? They hit every pitch before
it go to me."

When players don't like what they read, they'll find some
way to let you know. Most are more subtle than Bears' quarterback Bob Avellini, who grazed Sun-Times grid scribe Joe
LaPointe with a practice pass to make a point about a story
he considered pointless. "Slo-Mo wasn't throwing at you,
Joe," consoled columnist Rick Talley. "If he was, he'd have
missed."

If you don't take this sort of thing personally, sportswrit-
ing is still a good way to make a living.

TV or Net TV, It's a Radio-Active Town

Any fool, including a sportswriter, knows that television has changed the face of pro and college sports profoundly and permanently. For good or bad, TV exerts more influence on the games we play and watch than anything since Roman Legions invented soccer by kicking human skulls around. That's why a form of Russian roulette is played by promoters, hucksters and con men, wagering their bankrolls and sanity on the risky proposition that televised mounted water polo will take the country by storm.

TV moguls still talk about creating fans, but only winners can do that. Whenever the Cubs, New York Mets or Atlanta Braves win two in a row, count on their superstations to label them "America's Team." Like most fans, I ignore such hype, but when Chicago's TV sportscasters talk, I tune in. No question about the top tube talent in town—Tim Weigel of WLS-TV. Weigel's weiners are winners and his sports goofs are among the best bits of all, garnished with clever graphics and commentary. If you like your sports straight, catch newcomer Rich King on WBBM-TV.

On the radio side, Chet Coppock is my favorite. Most of his detractors are pompous types who think sports should be reported with solemn dullness. Lighten up, you mopes; it's entertainment.

Morris Knows How to Survive

Johnny Morris was disappointed when CBS took him off color commentary for Bears' games, but the WBBM-TV sportscaster has overcome more adversity than that. In 1982 he survived a ruptured blood vessel in his brain. Instead of undergoing brain surgery, Morris recovered after three weeks in the hospital. Miraculously, the damage repaired itself.

"I have a fear of failure," Morris said of the drive for success that made him a standout pass-catcher on the 1963 NFL champion Bears. His 93 receptions for 1,200 yards in 1964 are still team records.

Never known as shrinking violets, Sox fans urge the South Side Hitmen to take the opposing pitcher for a ride. They helped make the 1977 season a resounding success.

Still, a lot of fans prefer Chuck Swirksy's gee-whiz approach on WGN. For hard work, nobody can match the WLS guy, Les Grobstein. When I covered the Bulls, Cubs and Sox, Les was a kid you'd find in everybody's press box and clubhouse, taping anything that moved. He's a no-nonsense radio reporter, a refreshing touch in the throng of media marvels who specialize in softball questions.

When I was a rookie on the baseball beat in 1970, Chicago was loaded with old pros, but they already were an endangered species. Jim "Monsignor" Enright, who went out of his way to take greenhorns like me under his wing, was one of that vanishing breed, along with Wendell Smith, John Carmichael, Charlie Bartlett, Jack Griffin and Ed Muzzel. Two of the best at the Windy City tradition of hands-on aggressive reporting were Dave Condon and Bill Gleason.

Condon had a sense of humor, splendid writing ability and unmatched contacts. He wrote *Tribune* sports editor Arch Ward's "Wake of the News" column for years, leaving Arch free to dress up the baseball All-Star game and the College All-Star grid spectacular. When I worked on the *Trib's* neighborhood news desk in the early 60s, a chubby, agitated man charged out of the sports department next door.

"Stop the press!" he bellowed. "This is a real scoop! We just found a white Golden Glover!"

That was just Dave Condon's style of humor. There was not a racist bone in his body. Jackie Robinson, Larry Doby and other black athletes found a champion in him.

With his inexhaustible Irish wit, Bill Gleason wowed more fans on the rubber chicken circuit than any Chicgao toastmaster since Carmichael, another droll side-splitter. A lifelong South Sider, Sox fan, Notre Dame historian, first-rate newspaperman and World War II combat infantryman, he can still lower the boom like Claney. His *Sun-Times* columns, along with Condon's in the *Tribune*, were major-league.

All in the Family

There's no generation gap in the Sheehan family of White Sox fans. Sara Sheehan, her daughter, Sara, and granddaughter, Laura, go to Comiskey Park together to root for the South Siders.

Sara and her daughter, a floor trader in the Mid-American Commodity Exchange, live in Naperville, Mrs. Sheehan grew up on the South Side, and still has fond memories of the 1977 Sox Hit Men. Her daughter is active in the ChiSox Fan Club.

"Mom and Laura get bored with some of the bad games the Sox play now, but I stay and root to the bitter end," she said.

Time marches on and the old order passes. Just about the only old-time, seat-of-the-pants scribe left in Chicago is Joe Mooshil, Midwest sports editor for Associated Press. Joe is still there in Chicago press boxes, grinding out fast, accurate daily leads. Jerome Holtzman, the dean of Chicago baseball writers, is all by himself in that specialized area.

Women did not play a major role in Chicago sports coverage until a few years ago. Now they're emerging here and all around the country. Those who care about what they're doing enough to learn from their mistakes will get the same acceptance men had to earn. Two outstanding examples are Linda Kay of the *Tribune* and Toni Ginetti of the *Sun-Times*.

Shawon Tell

Young Cub shortstop Shawon Dunston had a tough summer in 1987, with a broken finger and a limping batting average. He weathered the storm with the aid of some advice given to him by Larry Bowa in 1982: "Don't read the papers."

Windy City Lament: Hot Fans, Cold Teams

Patience may be a virtue elsewhere in the sports world. In Chicago it's a necessity. For most of this century our teams have been threatening to win something with monotonous regularity. It happens once every decade, on the average, although the Bulls are a trifle sluggish—0 for the 60s, 70s, and 80s in the National Basketball Association.

No wonder Chicago fans develop patience. Sure, Wrigley Field is beautiful, Comiskey Park is historic, and Soldier Field is imposing. That may be enough to mollify architects in the crowd, but most fans would settle for watching their teams chisel some winning numbers on the scoreboard. And architecture doesn't help Blackhawk and Bull boosters; Chicago Stadium is a dump, any way you slice it.

Regardless, hockey fans flock there year after year, hoping to see the Hawks regain the Stanley Cup they last won in 1961. Then stop to consider that the atomic age was just dawning in 1945, the Cubs' last pennant-winning season. It took 19 Super Bowls before the Bears got into one, and the Fabulous Fifties were fading fast before the White Sox got a chance to blow a World Series. Only the Sting has won two championships so far in this decade, but few Chicagoans noticed.

So how come all it takes is one contending season, or in the Cubs' case a one-game winning streak, to start those turnstiles spinning merrily again in every Chicago playpen? The point is clear. Chicago fans have ancestors who survived the Fort Dearborn Massacre and the Great Chicago Fire of 1871, so they can take any degree of punishment their teams hand out.

It probably would be a lot more fun to win the World Series, Super Bowl, and Stanley Cup every other year. If Chicago did, we might turn into arrogant creeps, like Yankee fans. Even so, I suspect most Chicago fans would gladly gamble on such a possibility. Who else but a long-suffering Bear fan would use the prospect of a winning season to palm off a marriageable daughter, via this ad in the *Sun-Times* lonely-hearts section?

ATTENTION BEAR FANS
Take my daughter and you will have season tickets for life. My pleasingly plump, adorable offspring is 37, a caring person with a Master's degree and a great sense of humor.

That match can't last. The bride will never know if Prince Charming really lusted after her or the Bear ducats.

Bearmania hit such a fever pitch that there were 30—count 'em, 30—TV or radio shows blanketing Chicago airwaves. Just about everybody connected with the franchise grabbed a piece of the action, from Diana Ditka to Kevin Butler. Naturally, the scramble was fiercest for the services of the Bears' top talkers, Coach Mike Ditka and quarterback Jim McMahon.

Ditka pulled down only about $100,000 for two radio gigs and his Sunday night postmortem with Johnny Morris on Channel 2. He still leads the nightlife circuit, despite competition from McMahon's restaurant, because the coach's restaurant and adjoining City Lights saloon is doing boffo business. Not even George Halas, godfather of the NFL, ever was named Pork Restauranteur of the Year.

The Bear craze shows no signs of slackening. "The Bears have done the impossible," Chet Coppock said. "They're bigger than Hulk Hogan."

The long-standing enmity between Cub and Sox fans is summed up in "South Side Irish," a big hit in many saloons: "And when it comes to baseball, we have two favorite clubs: The Go-Go White Sox, and whoever plays the Cubs." The Cubs have been around since 1876, a quarter century before the White Sox, but no rooters have deeper roots than Pale Hose partisans. The fourth and fifth generation is growing up to stick with the Sox through thin and thin. Since Charles A. Comiskey brought an American League franchise to Chicago, the team has won two World Series (1906, 1917), lost one (1959), and thrown one (1919).

None of that adversity seems to discourage Sox fans. Not all of them are South Siders, though most are sons, daughters, or grandchildren of blue-collar working people who settled there. Thousands of immigrants made their living in South Side factories, slaughterhouses, and steel mills at the turn of the century, when the White Sox arrived to give them a common interest and shared pride in the Hitless Wonders' upset over the mighty Cubs in 1906.

As for the Cubs, those who lived and died with them in the summer of 1969 had to start feeling their age when a cluster of hard hats was spotted on the left-field pines in the summer of 1987. It was the 20th reunion of the Bleacher

Gone, but not forgotten, the Honey Bears were disbanded after the Bears won the Super Bowl. Since then, Soldier Field fans have been seeing a lot more of the game.

Bums, the raucous crew that sang, chanted, and drank beer with choreography by Dick Selma.

Not all Cub fans are that demonstrative, or that obnoxious, but they can compare their frustration or match their loyalty with backers of any team in any sport. They've been waiting since 1945 for the pennant that Jack Brickhouse predicted was just around the corner.

It's just as well he did. Without Brick's daily dose of optimism, chances are all save the hardiest Cub believers would have marched like lemmings to the Michigan Avenue bridge and taken the plunge.

For Cub fans, some things never seem to change.

"We're rebuilding," Manager Herman Franks told a writer in 1978. The scribe walked into the Cards' clubhouse and asked Lou Brock what it had been like when he was a Cub rookie in 1961.

"They were rebuilding," Brock replied.

This raucous demonstration outside Washington's RFK Stadium was the same kind the Bears saw in Philadelphia during the 1987 NFL players' strike. Things were a lot more peaceful in Chicago, to the players' dismay.

NINE

YOU CAN'T BEAT FUN AT THE OLD BALLPARKS

Chicago's Ballparks

Just say the words "Wrigley Field" to a Cub fan or "Comiskey Park" to a Sox fan. Watch his or her eyes light up, memory bank switch on, and the good times start to roll once again.

Maybe the best thing about sports is the endless supply of tall tales they provide. When you have a setting like these magnificent baseball museums to return to in memory whenever you want, it makes storytelling easier. Sometimes Wrigley Field or Comiskey Park is the story. Like aging but still beautiful dowagers, they are something special, not just for what they've been but for what they still are.

Soldier Field and Chicago Stadium are not in that class, either aesthetically or emotionally, but they played central roles in our sporting life for many years. If, as Bill Shakespeare said, life is a brief hour of strutting and fretting, Chicago sure has splendid sports stages to strut and fret on.

With or without lights, Wrigley Field is a Chicago landmark. And when Comiskey Park goes down, the South Side will mourn.

The Friendly Confines Can Be Fiendly, Too

Most fans' recollections of Wrigley Field contain sunshine. If the sun really shone as much as it does in Cub fans' memories, there'd never be another cold winter in Chicago. After a few years, even accounts of Gabby Hartnett's 1938 Homer in the Gloamin' began to sound suspiciously as if Old Sol had just darted behind a cloud minutes before the Cub catcher smashed the most dramatic clutch hit in the first century of this long-playing franchise's history.

Actually, the game should have been halted after eight innings because it was too dark to play the ninth. How dark was it? Well, Harnett always described that blur he'd belted into the gathering gloom as a letter-high fastball on the outside corner. Pirate right-hander Mace Brown, whose delivery was maced out of sight, insisted it was a curve, low and away. Catcher Al Todd claimed the pitch he never got to catch was a breaking ball inside.

That tells you something of the contradictory, confusing life and times of Wrigley Field, a living landmark nestled into its North Side neighborhood. You'll never get a consensus on whether Babe Ruth really pointed to the center-field bleachers before hitting Charlie Root's next serve into that exact spot. Cub fans still turn purple with rage trying to convince obstinate blockheads that day baseball (a) did or (b) did not kill the 1969 Cubs. And who can prove if Jose Cardenal's eyelid really was stuck shut the day he had to be scratched from the Cub lineup, pleading impaired vision? The thing they all agree on is Wrigley Field's charm.

The park was an unwitting gift to Chicago by Lucky Charlie Weeghman, who thought he was building a monument to himself for only $250,000. Weeghman wanted a modern park to house his Chicago Whales of the outlaw Federal League in 1914. His timing was four decades before the television age, and the quick-lunch restaurant operator's luck ran out.

Weeghman Park, designed by Zachary Taylor Davis, the architect of Comiskey Park, was ready in time to stage the Whales' April 23, 1914, home opener. Not even the managerial presence of Joe Tinker, shortstop on the Cubs' legendary Tinker-to-Evers-to-Chance double-play combination, could

Schmidt Not Easy to Please

Despite Mike Schmidt's career barrage of 47 Wrigley Field homers—third behind visiting player leaders Willie Mays (54) and Hank Aaron (50)—the Phillies' slugger is not crazy about the place.

"It's not a hitter's park," Schmidt insists. "The walls are closer, but the wind blows in."

That's not nearly as harsh as this verdict by Jeff Meyers of the *St. Louis Post-Dispatch*: "Wrigley Field looks like an ancient steel-and-concrete warehouse that somehow has escaped urban renewal."

save this Whales campaign. Both the team and the league were dead in the water two years later.

As part of the settlement with the NL, Weeghman was permitted to buy the Cubs. With the help of financial angel William Wrigley, Sr., he scratched up $500,000 to close the deal. Lucky Charlie moved them into his park in 1916, but soon had to sell out to Wrigley. The Cubs were on their way.

The park was remodeled in 1922, renamed Wrigley Field four years later, and expanded by the addition of the upper deck in 1927, hiking capacity to 40,000. Not until 1937 were the original wooden bleachers in center and right field replaced by a concrete structure, topped by the bleacher planks that have since been sat on by millions.

The guy who said "Victory has a thousand fathers, but defeat is an orphan" never sat in the Wrigley Field bleachers. Fans on those pines never stop blaming something besides bad play for Cub losses.

Cub fans are not as goody-goody as their stereotype would have you believe. Even before 1967, when the left-field Bleacher Bums were born, there were a few real bums in the bleachers. The evidence is in plain sight atop the bleacher walls. One of the few blemishes on Wrigley Field's appearance is the wire "basket," 42 inches high that juts out at a 45-degree angle to the wall. It stretches all the way around from left field to right, topping the 11-foot wall to keep unruly fans from invading the outfield. A horde of beer-soaked

youngsters went over the wall after the 1970 home opener, creating an ugly scene while battling ushers and cops in a mini riot.

When the Cubs returned from their next trip, the basket was in place, depressing proof that even Wrigley Field can't charm some rowdies and creeps into acting civilized. The percentage of such meatballs is low, but it's enough to keep Wrigley security forces ready for bleacher confrontations. For most people, the sheer enjoyment of an afternoon in the bleachers is not dampened by displays of mopery from spectators or players.

Wrigley Field is the true fan's shrine. The old ballpark has risen above rust and dust, defeat and disillusionment, to become a symbol. Not only in Chicago but anywhere baseball is played, a TV screen flashing pictures of Wrigley's ivy-covered walls somehow creates instant affection in viewers. Even those who have never been closer to Chicago than Cripple Creek, Colorado, wax nostalgic.

Although Chicagoans take many of their city's treasures for granted—Lake Michigan is the outstanding example—they do not fail to pay Wrigley Field the homage it deserves. Except for the most rabid fringe of Cub-hating Sox fans, this little patch of turf draws more worshipers than Holy Name Cathedral. The Water Tower, the Everleigh Sisters'

Let there be lights! Artist's sketch shows how new era of night baseball will alter Wrigley Field's traditional look.

sporting house, and many other Chicago landmarks are older than Wrigley Field. Despite sheltering losers most of the time, the baseball park at Clark and Addison streets remains hallowed ground. Bill Veeck, who understood this sort of thing, had a good explanation.

"It's a living thing, adapting to its environment," Veeck said a few months before his death in 1986. "When everybody got a car, Wrigley Field no longer was the ideal spot. It survived because people discovered how lovely it was to come and sit there in the sun and enjoy a game. There are only four real baseball parks left. Boston has one [Fenway Park], Detroit has one [Tiger Stadium], and we're very fortunate to have the other two in Chicago. Now you hear people saying Wrigley Field and Comiskey Park have to go to make room for progress. It's shameful when places that provide so much pleasure suddenly become inadequate because there's a few more bucks to be made elsewhere."

As usual, Barnum Bill was right. No amount of money could replace—or reproduce—the unique atmosphere of Wrigley Field. When asked why they feel so strongly about it, fans invariably respond by recalling a memory. Maybe it's the Cub dynasty that won five National League pennants in 16 years. Or maybe it's that day they came to the park when they played hookey from school. Whether it was their first game as a kid, or the day Ernie Banks hit number 500, or the Saturday afternoon when Ryne Sandberg capped an amazing Cub comeback for a spellbound national TV audience, they remember both the game and the park. A lot of these fans grew up listening to Hal Totten's balanced, knowledgeable play-by-play. Totten was the first Cub broadcaster. He chucked his job as a *Daily News* rewrite man in 1924 to see what life was like behind the WMAQ mike. Many of his listeners are still Cub fans, either in Chicago or scattered around the world.

All these factors play a part in the remarkable hold this ugly-duckling team and its beautiful ballpark have on the hearts and minds of so many people. The enthusiasm of fans rebounding from the 1984 playoff debacle indicates that there is a self-sustaining chain reaction of loyalty to pick fans off the deck no matter how many times the team KO's their hopes.

"The ballpark is the big thing," explained Chicago stockbroker Dick Karlov. "I can't imagine a nicer place to watch baseball. It's the one pleasant memory from my childhood that I never worry will change."

"It's a park that wears many faces," said Andy McKenna, the man who hired Dallas Green away from Philadelphia to steer the Cubs into uncharted waters. "Wrigley Field can be a completely different place in the spring or the fall. More than anywhere else, the weather and the park itself determine the outcome of a game. For smart pitchers like Fergie Jenkins or Rick Sutcliffe, Wrigley Field is always a pitchers' park. For spectators, no other setting can compare. It's intimate without being contained, giving the fans freedom of movement."

True enough. The customers move quickest when the wind shifts, sending biting chill to replace warm sunshine in a matter of minutes. During the time it takes a hitter to strike out, the temperature can drop 20 degrees. It's an eerie kind of baseball when fog creeps in off the lake, blotting out the high rises, shrouding the scoreboard and bleachers in mist, and hanging over the field like the Ghost of September 1969.

That can be more fun to watch than some 20-run batting practice orgies when a hot wind blows out. On those days, the batter stares northeast at the pitcher, his eyes shielded from the lowering sun, which glares fiercely at the outfielders, particularly in right and center. Many a game has been decided by Wrigley's most famous battery, Sun and Wind.

The park has 38,143 seats and a firmer grip on Chicago fans' hearts with every passing year. Will it last into the 21st century? Will the Cubs clinch a pennant here before the 22nd century? Will it look as beautiful at night? Their fans will be there to find out.

Comiskey Park: Will the South (Side) Rise Again?

For a park that's been pronounced dead so many times, Charles A. Comiskey's "Baseball Palace of the World" still makes a lively looking corpse. It has outlived all but a handful of the places where major-league baseball was played for so long: Ebbets Field, the Polo Grounds, Forbes Field, Crosley Field, Shibe Park, Sportsman's Park, Griffith Stadium, and Cleveland's League Park, an all but forgotten bandbox. League Park deserves to be remembered for October 10, 1920, if nothing else. That's the day the Indians' Elmer Smith hit the first grand slam in World Series history, and Cleveland second baseman Bill Wambsganss pulled off the only unassisted triple play in Series annals.

All right, so what if Comiskey Park's storied past can't quite match that one afternoon when it comes to World Series drama? The most exciting thing ever to happen in a South Side Series game was slow-footed Sherman Lollar getting thrown out at the plate by 10 lengths to kill a 1959 Sox rally—and the Sox. So what if the Series gave serious Sox fans more grief than joy, because the last two were 40 years apart? Even though some abysmal Sox teams resembled zombies in the years since 1910, Comiskey Park has never been mistaken for a graveyard. When Charles A. Comiskey brought the Sox to Chicago in 1900, his first thought was of the wooden park at 35th and Wentworth, where he had managed the Players League team 10 years earlier.

Nancy Can Play Slow or Faust

Nancy Faust's trademark still is "Na Na Na Na Na Na Na Na Hey-Hey-Hey, Good-bye," but her repertoire is much wider. Ever since she played a few bars of "Jesus Christ, Superstar" on the Comiskey Park organ whenever Richie Allen came to bat, Nancy has had a signature tune for most Sox players.

But "Hey-Hey Good-bye" has been the biggie ever since Nancy saluted the 1977 South Side Hit Men with it. Thanks to her, it's become popular in many other parks across the country. The song is still a gold mine for Dale Frashuer, Paul Laka, and Gary De-Carlo, who formed a group called Steam and recorded it in 1969.

That location was on a southbound streetcar line, but he couldn't buy the land. So Comiskey had to settle for band-box South Side Park. Somehow, he crammed 19,249 into the park to see the 1906 World Series clincher over the Cubs, but the Sox quickly outgrew that single-deck wooden structure.

Comiskey Park, only the fifth steel and concrete grandstand to be built, was the answer. "Charlie Comiskey built that park by himself, brick by brick, because his friends and the banks wouldn't come up with any loans," said John Phillips, a longtime Sox watcher who joined the Chicago chapter of the Baseball Writers Association of America in 1923. "They were convinced he'd go broke in a hurry, but he fooled them all."

The Old Roman shaved a few bucks off the cost by insisting on a plain exterior, rejecting the architect's plans for an elaborate Roman facade. So instead of resembling Shibe Park's distinctive tower entrance, Comiskey Park had its own look, featuring raised block C's at intervals.

In time, Comiskey's nickel-nursing turned out to be a smart move. His park survived to become a one-of-a-kind Chicago landmark. Comiskey ignored bankers and similar stuffy types who warned he was crazy to sink anywhere from $600,000 to $750,000 into this risky venture. He rushed it to completion in time for the July 1, 1910, opening, but the cost was high in more than dollars. Hours before the gates opened for the first time, Frank McDermott, a 46-year-old laborer, was killed when he fell from the grandstand roof.

Superstitious types thought Comiskey might have to have his new park exorcised after four Sox pitchers were hurt in the first few games. Instead of a poltergeist, the problem turned out to be loose turf, which soon settled. The Old Roman paid scant attention to such distractions. He was too busy taking bows, watching his critics eat crow, and presiding over civic testimonials to his "Baseball Palace of the World."

Comiskey had no trouble getting a $1 million loan when the time came in the 1920s to enlarge his park and replace the old wooden bleachers. With Babe Ruth's bat the magic wand that banished bitter memories of 1919, fans flocked by trolley, automobile, and on foot to the South Side showplace.

Three-quarters of a century-plus after it was built, Comiskey Park still provides solace for all those losing teams with the continuity and tradition that welds Sox fans together. Along the way, seating capacity rose to more than 50,000 (with a rather fanciful 55,555 on May 20, 1973, as the all-

time attendance peak), then dipped to its present 44,432.

Most of the millions who went there took away only memories. Just as he did with the Wrigley Field ivy he planted in 1938, Bill Veeck left his personal stamp on Comiskey Park. The picnic areas behind the outfield walls and the exploding scoreboard were Veeck innovations. Barnum Bill brought fun back to a ballpark that sorely needed some.

On the South Side they've learned to live with adversity. The Pale Hose sank into the depths of the American League after Shoeless Joe Jackson and seven other standouts were banned for throwing the 1919 World Series. The Go-Go White Sox, fueled by Mighty Mites Nellie Fox and Looie Aparicio, made the 1950s more exciting than the first Flexible Flyer sled for kids lucky enough to be growing up on the South Side during this eventful decade. Sadly, the Go-Go era was preceded by 30 years of stop-stop baseball and succeeded by another quarter century of futility.

Sox fans almost lost their charter AL franchise to Milwaukee, Seattle, Denver, or even Oakland not long ago. The last proposed deal would have been a long-shot switch of the Sox and the Oakland A's in 1977. Now St. Petersburg, Florida lusts for the Pale Hose.

Chicago insurance millionaire and baseball innovator Charles O. Finley once wanted to swap horses—and presumably his mule, Charlie O.—by bringing the A's here and shipping the Sox to the Bay Area. A brilliant, abrasive man, Finley had enemies on every baseball level from Commissioner Bowie Kuhn on down, so the imaginative gimmick never got off the ground.

Regardless of all the emotion involved, the stark, sobering fact Sox fans must contend with is the knowledge that there's not enough of them. The Sox have to be contenders every season, or at least moving in that direction, to prevent the inevitable franchise-switch rumors from resurfacing. Bad as the Cubs were in the 1950s and mid-'60s, and again in the late '70s and early '80s, the notion of leaving Chicago was unthinkable. Only the most rabid Sox fans would contend it's the same way for their team—and recent history invalidates those arguments.

With all the controversy, upheaval and turmoil that never seems to abate on the Sox scene, a single thread weaves through the confusing. Call it tradition, if you prefer. Call it loyalty, habit, a sense of history, affection, or love for Chicago's embattled AL entry. Whatever it is, the disease is contagious, spreading from fathers and mothers to sons, daughters, and grandchildren. The hard core of Sox fans probably shrinks a little every year, but it's still raucous and devoted. The role of perpetual underdog suits these tradition-minded people well. Their forebears came to America at the turn of the century with a battered suitcase and hope for a better life. The reasons they persist stubbornly in rooting for the White Sox through a seemingly endless parade of disappointments probably are the same reasons they strove to make it in America.

That blue-collar fan tradition of loyalty to their roots has served the Sox well. When the next few generations prospered enough to climb up the economic ladder, they shifted from Comiskey Park's bleachers to box seats and season tickets. Mayor Richard J. Daley, the South Sider who made Comiskey Park's Bridgeport neighborhood the capital of Chicago, represented thousands of upwardly mobile, life-long Sox fans. Without those fans Comiskey Park would have been torn down long ago, the franchise gone, and memories scattered on the wind.

The Sox drifted with the AL tide for decades, winning a few, losing a lot. In lieu of pennants, Comiskey Park became the fans' symbol. Aging gracefully and battling against the ravages of time, baseball's oldest park has grown in stature ever since it opened, four years before Wrigley Field.

Only Wrigley (1914) and Boston's Fenway Park and Detroit's Tiger Stadium, both debuting on April 20, 1912, are in the same class with this living monument. As sad as Sox fans are about the way their team has floundered since its one-shot AL West title in 1983, the prospect of seeing Comiskey Park torn down is more devastating.

"When Comiskey Park is all spruced up for the occasion, there's not a better setting for postseason baseball," remarked Sox manager Tony LaRussa before his 1983 team dropped two straight home playoff battles to Baltimore.

Comiskey Park never looked better than it did throughout the 1983 season. It was petted, pampered, manicured, fixed up, spruced up, whitewashed, and scrubbed into a dazzling state of readiness for the Golden Anniversary All-Star game, an authentic rerun of the original All-Star spectacular, staged on the South Side as a highlight of the 1933–34 Century of Progress exposition.

It was a memorable show. The Sox even talked other clubs into altering the schedule so the game could be played 50 years to the day from the All-Star inaugural, which took place July 6, 1933.

"Eddie Einhorn and Jerry Reinsdorf did a marvelous job getting support for the old-timers' reunion and all the other events," said Commissioner Bowie Kuhn. For once, the embattled Bowie got no argument from the rest of the major-league power structure.

Reinsdorf and Einhorn aroused hostility and suspicion among diehard Sox fans with their stand that Comiskey Park is simply too old and too costly to maintain. It was interpreted as a ploy to sell the Sox down the river after enough politicians had thrown cold water on new stadium proposals, first in suburban Addison and then next door to Comiskey Park.

When the old palace has to come tumbling down, a replacement park should be going up in the shadow of the grandstand. Let's hope it blends the tradition of Comiskey Park with less primitive conveniences such as escalators and abundant restrooms. On that opening day, it should be easier for Sox fans to transfer their memories and loyalties to the new stadium. And in case anybody asks me, it should be called Bill Veeck Park, in fitting tribute to a man who gave much to both the Cubs and Sox.

Chicago Stadium: A Real Steal on Ice

Too bad Paddy Harmon didn't live to see his dream come true. Chicago Stadium turned into everything he had promised it would, but long before that happened, Paddy was strumming a harp and trying to con the other angels on his cloud into backing a heaven-hell softball series.

Self-styled "Colonel" Harmon was the kind of character who gave Chicago its special character in the Roaring Twenties. He fit right in with Al Capone, Red Grange,

Charles Lindbergh, Babe Ruth, and all the larger-than-life types who Charlestoned their way through this carefree decade of roadsters, flappers, speakeasies, hip flasks, The Front Page, and all manner of killings, from Wall Street to gangster-style. America was in rebellion against its puritanical past, and sports played a prominent role in shaping new freedoms from old taboos.

So it made sense to Harmon that Chicago should have its own ultramodern indoor sports arena. Everything was bigger and better in this era of unbounded optimism, and Paddy certainly did his bit to keep fans' expectations soaring. On February 1, 1926, he announced the purchase of a square block, 544 by 266 feet, at Madison and Wood streets on the near West side. Paddy boasted that in less than a year, he would build an $8 million super arena with 39,000 seats, four elevators, and an 800-car garage beneath a ceiling soaring to 152 feet.

Because Harmon plunked down $1.5 million for the real estate parcel, Chicagoans took him at his word. The Stadium actually took three years to complete, with 25,000 seats and a $6 million construction tab, but without the elevators or garage. Fortunately, it was finished a few months before the stock-market crash of 1929 triggered worldwide depression. The Colonel was still scrambling to stay afloat on the gala opening night, when a disappointing turnout of 15,000 paid $21.60 for the top ticket to see Tommy Loughran keep his lightweight title by beating Mickey Walker.

A fire started on the roof that night, and a brisk wind could have touched off another Iroquois Theater disaster. Luckily, the fans were unaware until the danger was over, preventing a murderous stampede to the exits. The Blackhawks moved from the Coliseum to the Stadium on December 16, 1929, rewarding 14,000 fans with a 3–1 victory over the Pittsburgh Pirates.

The next big Stadium event was Harmon's wake. Trying to forget his troubles and elude his creditors, Paddy flipped his sports car on a suburban dirt road and died at 53. For the next few years, the Stadium was on the verge of bankruptcy, often paying bills with money fresh from the ticket windows.

This is the way we remember Chicago Stadium best. Slogging through icy wind and knee-deep snowdrifts to see the Blackhawks or Bulls play is a tradition winter can't overcome.

Young Stribling lured 15,179 boxing fans to witness his December 12, 1930, decision over Tuffy Griffith, and the $84,232.41 in gate receipts saved the day.

The Depression killed once popular events like six-day bike races, featuring the ever popular Torchy Peden. Even the Bears drew only 11,198 on December 18, 1932, for the first of their eight league championships, a 9–0 freezeout of the Portsmouth Spartans in the NFL's first indoor title game. The corner was not turned for the Stadium until 1934, when Arthur M. Wirtz swapped his Detroit Olympia to Jim Norris for controlling interest in the Madison Street arena.

Ever since, the Wirtz family has been on center stage in the Chicago sports panorama. The unlikely combination of hard-headed tycoon Wirtz and temperamental Norwegian Olympic ice-skating queen Sonja Henie brought crowds and prosperity flocking to the Stadium and other arenas across the country. The blend of Wirtz's business acumen and Henie's ambition struck gold.

Now that waiting out the Depression had proved profitable, Wirtz turned his attention to keeping the Stadium filled with a kaleidoscopic array of events. His promotions ranged from boxing, wrestling, college and pro basketball, ice shows, circuses and rodeos, track meets, and superstar concerts by Elvis Presley, Frank Sinatra, and others, to religious revivals and national political conventions.

The course of American history could have been changed by a Chicago machine payroller at the 1940 Democratic convention in the Stadium. The third-term nomination of President Franklin D. Roosevelt was meeting stubborn opposition when the voice of Chicago's sewer superintendent, Tom Garry, electrified the packed Stadium galleries: "Illinois wants Roosevelt! We all want Roosevelt!" An emotional tide stampeded FDR back to the top of the ticket and reelection. The Democrats returned here in 1944, with World War II assuring that Roosevelt would be tapped for an unprecedented fourth term.

Art Wirtz raked in millions and his reputation for squeezing the last dime from Stadium customers made him a favorite target of fan outrage. Bobby Hull and Stan Mikita led the Hawks to a 1961 Stanley Cup and sold-out hockey nights all through the decade. Refusing to meet Hull's modest demand for a $250,000 paycheck in 1972, Wirtz let the all-time Chicago hockey superstar get away, sending the Hawks and their fans into a prolonged tailspin.

The Bulls came along to steal fan loyalties in the mid-'70s, then took a 10-year vacation until Michael Jordon arrived to rescue the NBA franchise from terminal mopery. Since Paddy Harmon's demise, the parade of superstar individuals and events through Chicago Stadium has been constant.

With all its drawbacks, Paddy's palace has surpassed even his lofty expectations. Located in one of Chicago's toughest inner-city neighborhoods, the Stadium area can be a dangerous, even deadly, place. Jim Durham, the Bulls' play-by-play voice, got stuck up by an enterprising gunman inside the Stadium parking lot fence just minutes after a game ended, for example.

Although the Stadium is a dump that should have outlived its usefulness long ago, it has provided enough Chicago sports memories to last a lifetime.

Soldier Field: Lakefront White Elephant?

At least the facade of Soldier Field is inspiring. The rest of it probably was, too, when it opened in 1924. Now, almost 70 years and 70,000 Lake Shore Drive traffic jams later, the imposing pile of stone creates more problems than it solves.

Environmentalists don't like Soldier Field because it blocks their access to Lake Michigan. Fans are not crazy about a stadium that makes spectators in the front rows peer through all those people on the sidelines to see what's happening on the field. And the higher up they sit in the stands, the farther away the players get. In the rows just beneath the skyboxes, fans could use those TV sets the skybox swells check out between sips of Chablis and nibbles of Brie.

The Bears don't like it anymore, especially after an embarrassing spate of spats with Chicago politicians about clout precedence in a skybox. Both sides should have been shamed into grown-up behavior after reading stories of the "It's mine" dialogue that accompanied this ridiculous tug-of-war. Instead, the conflict hardened Bear boss Mike McCaskey's resolve to flee these peasants and find some taxpayers willing to build a stadium where he can throw out anybody he wants to.

The Chicago Park District, which owns and runs Soldier Field, is also unhappy because the Stadium has gobbled up millions of dollars for repairs and maintenance since 1978. That leaves Soldier Field sitting there in its prime lakefront location, Grecian colonnades towering over the neighboring Field Museum, Hayden Planetarium, and Meigs Field, the in-town airport. It's tough to be discarded while you're still being used. The best Soldier Field can hope for is a stay of execution until somebody figures out how to raise enough money to knock it down and haul away the rubble. Few tears of regret will be shed.

No Skin of His

The biggest disappointment for fanatic Bear fan Irv DuBoff of Skokie? His son, who now lives near Washington, D.C., has turned into a Redskin fan.

"I'm ready to disown him," said the man who has missed only one home game in 40 years, the 36-0 rout of Atlanta on November 24, 1985. DuBoff has been traveling to road games since 1976, and his auto license plate reads "Bears 1."

After a 1974 facelift, Soldier Field still looks noble on the outside, but dumpy as ever on the inside. The lakefront arena has endured, despite constant criticism over the years.

That's a sad final note for an ambitious project started in 1919 with talk of a mammoth stadium to honor the soldiers who had just returned from World War I. Construction began in 1923 with advanced engineering techniques devised to drive 10,000 foundation piles 60 feet down into the landfill that had carved Grant Park out of the lake.

The first event in the new, 45,000-seat Grant Park Municipal Stadium was Notre Dame's 13–6 victory over Northwestern on November 22, 1924. It couldn't have been nearly as entertaining as the official opening ceremony held on October 9, the anniversary of the Great Chicago Fire of 1871. Believe it or not, the main event was the on-field burning of a replica of Mrs. O'Leary's barn, where a cow allegedly kicked over a lamp to touch off the 1871 conflagration. Shades of Disco Demolition Night!

Another mind-boggling attraction that night included Colonel Robert R. McCormick, outspoken *Tribune* publisher, leading his polo team to victory in a hard-fought contest between two evenly matched teams. When Chicago's veterans wondered what had happened to their memorial, the stadium's name was changed to Soldier Field in 1925. The taxpayers approved a bond issue to enlarge capacity to 100,000, and while construction was going on, Northwestern chalked up a memorable 3–2 upset over unbeaten, untied, unscored-on Michigan, coached by Fielding H. (Hurry-Up) Yost.

Completion of the 1,000-foot-long, U-shaped structure called for one more dedication, so Vice President Charles G. Dawes did the honors on November 27, 1926. His remarks were forgettable, unlike the war waged on Soldier Field's turf that afternoon. A capacity crowd watched Army hold unbeaten Navy to a 21–21 tie in a classic chapter from their rivalry. The Bears also made their lake front debut in 1926, whitewashing the Chicago Cardinals 10–0.

The Golden Age of sports peaked in 1927 with Babe Ruth's 60 homers. Soldier Field contributed the "long count" Jack Dempsey–Gene Tunney bout, witnessed by 104,943 fans who forked over an all-time record gate of $2,658,660. Tunney was knocked down in the seventh round, but referee Dave Barry halted the count until Dempsey reached a neutral corner. That respite enabled Tunney to get up and lift Dempsey's heavyweight crown on a unanimous decision. In the same year, the all-time record football crowd of 123,000 turned out for Notre Dame's 7–6 squeeze past USC.

The high school spectacular of 1937 brought 120,000 to Soldier Field to see prep All-American Bill De Correvont run wild, leading Austin past Leo 26–0 for the city championship.

The *Tribune* promoted two of Soldier Field's long-running events, the annual Music Festival (1930–65) and the College All-Stars versa the pro champs, inaugurated by a 0–0 tie with the Bears on August 31, 1934. It was a good series at first, but the pro teams made things too one-sided in later years, running up a 31–9–2 edge. With insurance costs soaring and the NFL coaches screaming to get their All-Star rookies into training camp, the game had outlived its usefulness. The last chapter was written by a 1976 monsoon that inundated the field, mercifully erasing the final minutes of Pittsburgh's romp over the All-Stars.

The open end of the Soldier Field horseshoe was enclosed in 1935, and seating capacity was reduced to 65,793 when the stadium became a bowl in later renovations. The Bears moved in as permanent tenants in 1971, abandoning Wrigley Field because Cub owner P. K. Wrigley had cut the seating capacity. With crowds returning, a lot of work was essential to shore up Soldier Field's wooden grandstand underpinnings and avert a potential calamity.

The structure might have been permanently weakened by a dynamite blast to topple steel support towers for the Century of Progress exposition's Sky Ride cable cars. Emergency surgery begun in 1978 has been expensive. Maybe the best solution would be to abandon the place, let the stands collapse by themselves, and preserve the Grecian columns as a tourist attraction. The long-count memories will survive with or without them.

Mike Ditka (89) tore his jersey and ripped his guts to please Papa Bear George Halas in 1966. The coach's steely glare means Ditka didn't succeed this time, but he became the keeper of the Halas flame.

TEN

BULLS, BEARS, AND BUSTS

Chicago Franchises

S ome years ago the *Tribune* ran a series aptly titled "Chicago—City of Losers." It told each of our teams' tale of
woe in turn. But in the 1980s, some Chicago franchises have
had a taste of success. They couldn't handle it too well for
the most part, although the fans got high on just a few sips
of victory champagne.

Oddly enough, it was the Sting, still struggling for survival, that brought two soccer titles to Chicago in this decade. The Bears had their first Super Bowl triumph, and the
Cubs and White Sox each captured a divisional crown for
the first time. Michael Jordan has launched the Bulls back
into the NBA playoff picture, and the Hawks aim to rebound
under a new coach, Bob Murdoch. Overall, things look a lot
better than they once did on the Windy City sports scene.
Can it last? Next thing you know, they'll start calling it, "Chicago—City of Winners."

Bear Facts: It's a Frantic Franchise

There's been a lot of talk lately about "the fall of the House
of Halas" and similar exotic plots. Some fans fear their mon-

sters will turn into marshmallows, mirroring the yuppie image of the new management. Personally, I doubt it. Even forgetting the imposing presence of Mike Ditka, which isn't easy, almost 70 years of tradition will not vanish overnight without a trace. The same kernel of common sense that motivated Halas is still the majority viewpoint in Chicago: it's better to go right after what you want instead of sneaking up on it. Most of us are not as passionate in pursuit of our goals as Halas was in building the Bears from a starch company team to the pinnacle of pro football, or as Ditka is in restoring the Bears to that status. Chicago fans still understand and respect that kind of drive, determination and dedication. Great as he was, Gale Sayers is not regarded as *the* Bear running back. Neither is George McAfee, another explosive ballcarrier. They ran around tacklers, not over 'em. That's why Bronko Nagurski and Walter Payton share equal billing as the best Bear runners ever. It's also why Bill George, Dick Butkus, and Mike Singletary get Chicago's vote as the top Bear defensive players. And so on.

When Chicago fans got used to seeing Halas's teams run over the opposition, acceptance followed. They still grumble about letting Bobby Layne get away, because he could have been even better than Sid Luckman. There was a Detroit defensive back known as Night Train Lane. Well, this talented quarterback was Nightlife Layne. Maybe Halas figured he expended too much energy raising hell off the field. But then how long would Papa Bear have tolerated Jim McMahon's antics?

Except for Halas, most of the early Bears were normal guys, with an occasional eccentric such as center George Trafton. They had to be tough or they couldn't have played for him. After a while, most of his veterans learned to see through the crusty facade and appreciate the inner fires that drove this son of a Bohemian immigrant tailor to forge the NFL. "We have to be nice to George or he'll take his league back," NFL commissioner Pete Rozelle said in 1980 when the Bears were threatening to abandon Soldier Field.

Ditka is passing along the same intangibles to a player who may someday coach the Bears. In addition, the Halas way of life will survive because Mike McCaskey learned from his grandfather how to be tough, whether the fans or

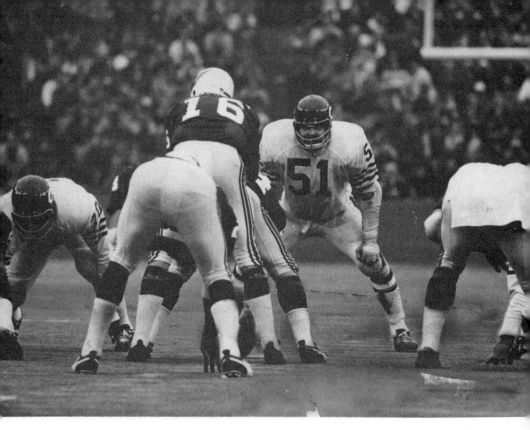

Dick Butkus prepares to pounce on Cards' quarterback Tim Van Galder. The Bears' ferocious middle linebacker was suspected of biting opponents or even devouring footballs.

anyone else like it or not. Halas did not set the Bears and the NFL up for survival with charm and personality.

Ditka understands that. He knows why Chicago, "City of the Big Shoulders," responds to the Bears' style and their power football tradition. The coach was careful to point out that being a Grabowski—his one-word summation of the Bear approach—was a state of mind, not an ethnic trait.

The explosive reaction of their fans to the Bears' reawakening under Ditka has been the best part of this astonishing story. It's obvious they had been waiting for years, with growing impatience, to see this team return to the methods that had paid off under Halas. If there's one trait Chicago fans have in abundance, it's patience. Ditka finally let them rake in the payoff for decades of perseverance.

So Bear football is back. It should stick around, even though Walter Payton, one of the strongest bridges to the Halas era, has played the last game of his brilliant career. By now, everybody knows why the Bears are lighting up Chicago. They have a fascinating cast of hitmen, from Steve (Mongo) McMichael to frustrated Olympic bobsledder Willie Gault, with one aim in life: to knock the jocks off their opponents.

Still, a Bear quarterback willing to take the same kind of punishment the Bear defense dishes out to others is essential. McMahon's kamikaze collisions with behemoths all over the NFL convinced his defensive unit that he must be as crazy as they are. For their kind of guy, they'll play with intensity bordering on mania.

The only problem is that McMahon's body takes the rap for his reckless spirit. The Bears need a McMahon II on the bench, ready to step in when the starter is carried off again. They might have him in Michigan's Jim Harbaugh. Big Ten football is a good training camp for Bear-style bashing, and Harbaugh has gotten up and walked away from enough crunching hits to impress Chicago fans with his toughness. Don't be fooled by the polite young man you see in TV interviews. Underneath, Harbaugh is a bigger, stronger McMahon.

Is he the Sid Luckman of the future?

Can the Cubs Win Again Before 2045?

Another fast Cub start and another midsummer flop. Another new phenom in the lineup—this time Andre Dawson—proves incapable of carrying the whole burden himself. Another season of high Cub hopes down the drain.

Sound familiar? It should. That's been the Cubs's theme for years. The team anthem changed from "Hey! Hey! Holy Mackerel!" to "Go Cubs Go" to a Beach Boys golden oldie: "Ivy on the wall/Sun up in the sky/Cubbies on a roll/We'll all be ridin' high," but the results have been the same.

Weary supporters would have preferred a recycled 1940s pennant to a recycled 1950s song. They got a tantalizing taste of it in 1984, only to come up one game short. The Cubs had played 5,865 regular-season games since their last National League flag in 1945 until their 1984 playoff against the San Diego Padres. The North Siders had lost 3,137 of those encounters, so the fans should not have been unprepared for what happened to them in that best-of-five series.

Discouraging as the playoff loss was, it pales in comparison with the historical burden the 1988 Cubs took into action: 31 losing campaigns in their last 42 tries. This star-crossed baseball team has hit the .500 level twice in that span (77–77 in 1952, 81–81 in 1977). They've been on the winning side of the ledger just nine times since the last World Series game was played in Wrigley Field, two months after the end of World War II. Keep in mind that six of those winning seasons were strung together in the prehistoric Leo Durocher era, from 1967 through 1972.

Since then, the beat goes on—one winner, one break-even year, one dozen losers. It's a record unmatched in baseball for futility. What's the solution? How do you bring a dead team back to life, especially when rigor mortis set in four decades ago? It used to be that the Cubs could kick away their yearly quota of 85 to 95 nontitanic tussles without creating too much dismay in the half-empty Wrigley bleachers. Now that Harry Caray and cable TV have combined to make half the nation's fans bleed Cubbie blue, their image as lovable losers no longer is a laughing matter.

The Cubs are big business now, with ratings, market share, and revenue per commercial minute riding on every wild pitch, dropped fly ball, or bases-loaded strikeout. All

The Cubs have been treading water for years, though seldom as much as in this 1987 dugout flood. Steve Trout, unaware that he'd soon be taking a boat ride to New York in a trade with the Yankees, splashes to the rescue of pitcher Frank DiPino.

those years of losing pretty in the sun-baked Friendly Confines need to be replaced by winning ugly, or any old way,
regardless of weather conditions. Where do they begin?

The first steps already have been taken. When the Cubs
stopped wasting money in pursuit of so-called superstars, it
was a turn in the right direction. Even if they only changed
their approach because the big-league owners got together
and agreed not to get mugged anymore by fast-talking
agents of slow-footed free agents, who cares? When a real
hitter like Andre Dawson has to pitch a tent in camp and
agree to any terms before the Cubs will sign him, you know
the fix is in.

What really matters is the live bodies being grown by the
Cubs down on their own farms. The most encouraging development in the peaks-and-valleys regime of Dallas Green
was player development. It doesn't matter if the level of major-league play goes down noticeably in the next decade or
so. Sooner or later, with the flow of big money for little effort
shut off, young prospects will prefer to consult with their
coaches instead of their accountants. For new Cub GM Jim
Frey, it's the doorway to remodeling the Cubs. He should
have learned that from watching high-salaried flops in his
stints as Cubs manager and radio spellbinder.

When that day arrives, if ever, the team with the best
scouting system and minor-league organization will prevail
over owners with huge bankrolls and tiny brains. Who
knows, the main topic in baseball clubhouse could even re-
vert to baseball.

The new faces of 1988 showed promise, even if most of
them need polishing in the minors. The main thing is to keep
the pump primed with a steady supply of promising kids like
Mark Grace, Jeff Hirsch, and Darrin Jackson. The Cubs
don't need a miracle. The loyalty of their fans through so
much famine, pestilence, despair, and defeat is among the
most miraculous phenomena in sports. All they really need
is ballplayers. Ex-Cub GM Green signed them, but he now
has a radio talk show in Philadelphia. Now its ex-radio talker
Frey's turn.

Go-Go White Sox? Sure, but Where?

The White Sox don't need to replay Abbott and Costello's classic comedy routine "Who's on First?" Their "who" is Greg Walker, a good first sacker, good hitter, and good guy. What they need to know most is where first base is going to be and when it will be there. More than anything else, the Sox could use some stability after years of upheaval on the field and in the front office.

With their new stadium situation hanging over co-owners Jerry Reinsdorf and Eddie Einhorn like the sword of Damocles, it's hard to make long-range decisions. Why plow millions into the farm system when political flip-flops could turn your team into the Ft. Lauderdale White Sox?

It's unfair to suggest that Sox decision makers Reinsdorf and Einhorn are too busy holding their limited partners at bay with a whip and chair to make decisions. Still, the team's nosedive since winning the American League West title in 1983 puts more pressure on them. The Sox struggle of 1987, following on the heels of the Hawk Harrelson fiasco of 1986, turned up the heat on Chairman Jerry and President Eddie.

Even worse, the crisis diverted attention away from the team and players, beaming the spotlight squarely on unrest in the executive suite. Sox fans got that queasy, here-we-go-again feeling when Reinsdorf admitted that the 13-man board of directors had narrowly defeated a proposal to move the team from Chicago if the new stadium deal didn't guarantee the owners a minimum 10 percent profit. That took a lot of loyalists back to the scary '70s, when the shaky Sox franchise seemed to be mounted on wheels, ready to roll toward the highest out-of-town bidder.

The Sox aren't getting rich at the turnstiles *or* in the AL standings. The investors' chief gripe is the total absence of dividends from their original gamble plus $8 million more chucked into the pot, half of it dug from the group's pockets and the rest in zero-coupon bonds, to be paid from scoreboard ads.

Einhorn pinned the financial problems on WGN-TV, which demanded a $1.3 million buyout of its 1981 contract to televise at least 60 Sox games. The rights fee per game was $6,000, the same amount paid for each Cub telecast. The

It's not easy to sum up as much White Sox history in volumes as this poignant picture does in three words—"Bill Veeck Drive." The block in front of Barnum Bill's ballpark was named in his honor.

Sox president said he had to settle the contract because the fee was far lower than the $5 million a season the Yankees got.

"The settlement kept us from using the money to buy players," Einhorn added. "We were close to being buried due to that and the losses we took in 1981 and 1982. We had to have a capital call [from the investors] of $6 million."

When the Sox were burning up the AL West in 1983, there was little criticism of Reinsdorf and Einhorn's authority to overrule the board of directors. When hard times followed, though, other investors who collectively had less than 10 percent of the actual ownership, suddenly seemed to hold 100 percent of the power.

Reinsdorf. "If 65 to 70 percent of the investors had strong feelings the team should be sold, I would have to deal with that."

General Manager Larry Hines is rebuilding the Sox. With all the new stadium hangups and the threat of Wrigley Field lights, will the new Sox emerge on the South Side in the Sunny South?

Blackhawk Blues: A Hot Tune on Ice

The Blackhawks thought they could mend their superstar
gap in 1976 by signing Bobby Orr to a $2 million contract.
Because of his battered knees, the former Boston Bruin stalwart put in next to no time in Chicago, scoring six goals in
26 games before he had to quit.

Then there was a futile attempt to bring back Bobby Hull,
the superstar they never should have allowed to go in the
first place. The era of coaching stability was ended by a
simple expedient of leaving a pink slip in Billy Reay's office
when he returned from a 1976 road game to spend Christmas with his family. Somehow, the Hawks usually found a
way to treat their own guys rougher than the opposition.

So Reay found himself out on the Stadium sidewalk after
13½ seasons at the Hawk helm, 1,012 games, 516 victories,
335 defeats, 161 ties, and a 58.9 winning percentage. All of
those totals are Blackhawk coaching records, but this never
was an organization noted for sloppy sentiment.

Bill White finished the dismal 1976–77 campaign behind
the Hawk bench, ringing in the era of musical coaches. Bob
Pulford took over next, followed in more or less rapid order
by Eddie Johnston, Keith Magnuson, Pulford again, Orval

Tessier Terrifies Heartless Hawks

Orval Tessier had a winning record just once in
three years as coach of the Blackhawks, but he left
behind a memorable one-liner. Tessier struck a nerve
for fed-up Hawk fans while the team was being
swept out of the 1983 NHL semifinals by Wayne
Gretzky and the Edmonton Oilers.

"These guys ought to stop off between games at
the Mayo Clinic and see about a heart transplant,"
Tessier fumed.

The fans loved it, but Tessier's abrasive style put
him in the doghouse with his players and the media.
The Hawks skidded to a 30–42–8 season and Tessier
got the ax in 1984, with another losing record assured.

Tessier, and Pulford one more time. That fell just two short of the Bulls' revolving-door policy, which chewed up nine coaches in a decade, but it was an impressive turnover by any standards.

Why do you suppose the fabled Gino Gasparini, hockey coach at the University of North Dakota, told the Hawks he preferred to keep wintering there instead of sampling the icy wind that blows off Lake Michigan? Maybe a glance at the 1987 season's 29–37–14 record and 17 percent power-play conversions (last in the National Hockey League) convinced him to tell owner Bill Wirtz to stick his coaching offer in the penalty box.

Almost by default the job went to Bob Murdoch, the last candidate still in line after Terry Crisp was hired by the Calgary Flames, where he and Murdoch had been assistants. That didn't seem to faze the 40-year-old Murdoch, who promptly promised improvement in the Hawks' power play. Since any display of power anywhere on the ice would boost the sagging morale of Hawk fans, rookie coach Murdoch was an improvement over the close-mouthed Pulford.

After the way things have fallen apart since the 3–0 playoff whitewash by Toronto in 1986, plenty of litter remains. When they sauntered away from the gate in the fall of '86 with nine wins in their first 32 games, Pulford knew it was time to stop coaching and concentrate on the general manager's post.

"Maybe it would help if I tried yelling at people the way Mike Ditka does," Pulford reflected. "That's just not my personality. I can't let it all hang out."

If Murdoch can convince the Hawks to stop hanging out downstairs in the Norris Division, Pully won't have to.

One Noble Bull, Fewer Bum Steers

The Bull franchise can be summed up in two words: Michael Jordan. They're better in all positions, except the most important one.

Ever since John (Red) Kerr had to decline a bid by Bull boss Dick Klein to be player-coach in 1966 because of his battered knees and back, the Bulls have been looking for one or two tall types who could play with their back to the

McKinney Makes the Grade

Billy McKinney, a new addition to the NBA executive ranks, was rewarded by the Bulls for being a good scout after his playing career ended. McKinney was named assistant to General Manager Jerry Krause, making all of the Bulls' 1987 draft picks after the third round.

"I have complete faith in Billy," Krause said. "The fact that he's black has nothing to do with his hiring."

basket while staying awake at the same time. The first words Kerr said when he ambled onto the practice floor and took one look at Nate (The Great) Bowman and Erwin Mueller were, "Boy, do we need a center." If the epitaph of the Bulls is ever chiseled on a tombstone, that will do nicely.

Here we are, more than a score of years later, and the Bulls still trying to find a center who can score. For each Tom Boerwinkle and Artis Gilmore to don Bulltogs, there's been a half-dozen of such imposters as Craig Spitzer, Reggie Harding, Dave Newmark, Paul Ruffner, Steve Patterson, Coby Dietrick, Jawann Oldham, and Mike Smrek.

By Boerwinkle's own admission, you couldn't slip a sheet of paper under his twinkling toes when he went up for a rebound. Yet, Long Tom still stands as the best center in Bulls' history, pulling down a team-record 5,745 rebounds in 10 years. The 6'11" Tennessee product nabbed 1,133 caroms, a snappy 13.8 average, in 1970–71 and collected 37 one busy Chicago Stadium evening against the Phoenix Suns on January 8, 1979. He got better than passing grades as a pinpoint passer in Dick Motta's ball-control offense, too.

It's been a new ball game for the Bulls since 1985, when Jerry Reinsdorf of the White Sox bought controlling interest near the end of Michael Jordan's rookie season. The North Carolina nonpareil went down with a broken foot early in his sophomore campaign, which probably made Reinsdorf wish he'd stuck to baseball.

But Air Jordan was off the runway for the 1986 playoffs—

With two Washington Bullets in front, Michael Jordan has to sneak up on the hoop. From any direction, Jordan is an unstoppable offensive force.

up, up, and away in a record-smashing 63-point bombard-
ment of the Celtics, in Boston Garden, yet. All that did was
give Reinsdorf and his new general manager, Jerry Krause,
an excuse to fire Coach Stan Albeck after the Celtics swept
the series.

Meyer Offer a Lot of Bull

Retired DePaul coach Ray Meyer became a Chicago institution in his 42 years at the Blue Demons'
helm. One incident that still rankles Ray is the phan-
tom offer he got to coach the Bulls in 1976.

"Jerry Krause denied it, but he made me a firm
offer to coach the Bulls for $50,000 a year," Meyer
said. "He told me, 'Ray, when you're tired of coaching, you can move right into the front office.' He
even talked about a press conference to announce
it."

Owner Arthur Wirtz of the Bulls fired Krause soon
after the story broke. Krause then worked as a
scout for the White Sox and got a second shot in
the Bulls' front office when Jerry Reinsdorf bought
the NBA team in 1985.

It also enabled the Bulls to gamble on Doug Collins, who
came up a natural on the first roll of the dice. Collins had no
coaching experience, but he'd been through one basketball
test after another, never flunking or backing away. From
high school in downstate Benton, Illinois to Will Robinson's
tyrannical coaching at Illinois State to the bloody, controversial 1972 Olympics to the spaced-out Philadelphia 76ers of
the NBA, Collins always had to battle for survival. He survived.

Good talent like Charles Oakley, Horace Grant, and Sam
Vincent offers hope. The joint jumps on game nights and the
payroll is down.

If this keeps up, they'll be able to afford a personality
coach for Krause.

Sting's Thing: Hollywood or Bust

There's no business like . . . soccer business? Well, there's been no business for the Chicago Sting, so show business is out and the franchise again is close to the brink. "Our post-game concert series was disastrous," Sting owner Lee Stern said. "We priced ourselves out of the soccer market with $25 (concert) tickets. I want to stay in Chicago but the Sting could be forced to move."

It's an uphill battle for the Sting, as usual. The North American Soccer League folded in 1984, just after the Sting won its second NASL title. Now the Major Indoor Soccer League is in trouble. Sting attendance in the Rosemont Horizon sank, despite the concerts, and the team is playing for its third coach in two years.

The Sting can't find an English language radio outlet in Chicago. The MISL can't get much TV exposure, either. Sounds like a tough spot for Stein, but he can handle it. Who has more experience in that sort of thing?

A South Side Team Is Not in the Cards

Just before last call, when the lights of a few thousand taverns try to penetrate the haze of smoke, don't be alarmed if you see ghostly figures flicker on the ceiling. Unless you've surpassed your quota of moose juice, they might be . . . they could be . . . they *are!* . . . the spirits of Chicago franchises past. More of these departed spooks return to their own haunts than you think. On the South Side, the one they recall when the evening grows later and the lager flows longer is the Chicago Cardinals.

The Cards were in Chicago in 1920, one year before the Decatur Staley AC moved into Wrigley Field and changed its name to the Bears. The Cards first met the Staleys in a 1920 Normal Park tussle and beat player-coach George Halas 7–6 to kick off a long, intense rivalry.

The Cards also did the Staleys a big favor that same year by whipping the Chicago Tigers 6–3 in a battle for survival. Owners Chris O'Brien of the Cards and Gil Falcon of the Tigers agreed the loser would give up his Chicago franchise to the winner.

This is where it all began, with a 1920 Decatur, Ill., company team called the Staley Starchmakers. George Halas took them to Chicago a year later, and started something big.

John (Paddy) Driscoll, the immortal dropkicker, ran 40 yards for the touchdown that forced the Tigers to clear out of Cubs Park (it was not redubbed "Wrigley Field" until 1926), making room for Halas to bring in his Staleys. The Cards and Bears played each other twice in 1922, once in '21 and '23, then began their celebrated home-and-home rivalry that ran uninterrupted from 1924 through 1952. Divisional alignments finally ended Chicago's twice-a-year family football feud.

Then the old foes met once a season until 1959, when the Bears won 31–7 in Soldier Field. The Cards moved to St. Louis in 1960 and didn't face the Bears in the regular season until 1965. The Bears also took that one 34–13, but it wasn't nearly as much fun. Something good had gone out of the Chicago sports scene, never to return. The crosstown rivals delighted in pulling upsets to dampen the other team's title hopes.

Perhaps the most memorable Card-Bear matchup was the 1929 Turkey Day affair in Comiskey Park, when Ernie Nevers carved up the Bears all by himself. The great back from Stanford ran for six touchdowns and booted four extra points, sparking the Cards' 40–6 romp. Coach Knute Rockne and his Notre Dame football team saw Nevers's personal 40-

point barrage, still the NFL's individual scoring record for one game.

The ranks of longtime South Side Sox fans are dwindling. When they get together, there's till a toast to "our Chicago Cards" and their Never-say-die spirit.

Other Chicago grid squads that failed were the Chicago Wind–Chicago Fire of the ill-fated World Football League in the mid-'70s and the Blitz, a United States Football League disaster area in 1983. The Blitz became the Arizona Wranglers the next year, but under any alias, even Coach George Allen couldn't turn these rejects into a football team.

The latest trial balloon is arena football, a scrambled, eight-man version of the real thing. The Chicago Bruisers played some experimental 1987 summer games in the Horizon, producing basketball scores and enough fans to try again.

In Chicago, Hoops Springs Eternal

Things were seldom hoopless around here, with George Halas backing the first pro entry, the Chicago Bruins. They started in 1925, joined the American Basketball League, and became another Depression casualty in 1931. Later, the Chicago American Gears gave college kids a chance to make some tuition and textbook money by playing under assumed names to protect their amateur status.

Right after World War II, arena owners from around the country formed the Basketball Association of America with the Chicago Stags as charter members. Max Zaslofsky was Chicago's box-office lure in the BAA's inaugural 1946–47 season, finishing fifth in league scoring with a 14.4 average. He sparked the Stags to a 39–22 record and into the championship playoff, where they were toppled by Joe Fulks and the Philadelphia Warriors in five games.

The Stags never got that far again in three more tries, folding after the BAA and National Basketball League merged in 1950 to become the National Basketball Association. There was a 12-year wait before Chicago insurance magnate Dave Trager bankrolled the Packers-Zephyrs for a two-year sojourn as Chicago's NBA entry. The Packers played in the Amphitheater in 1961–62 and the Zephyrs in

Rita Easterling looks for the hoop in a 1979 game against the Iowa Cornets. Easterling was the playmaker, floor leader and sparkplug of the Chicago Hustle.

the Coliseum in 1962–63. The 18–62 Packers and 25–55 Zephyrs were equally bad, so nobody minded when Trager shipped them to Baltimore in 1963.

Before the Bulls got a tenuous NBA foothold in 1966, Abe Saperstein tried to make the Chicago Majors and the American Basketball League sit up and take nourishment. He appointed the Majors to be second banana to his Harlem Globetrotters in Chicago Stadium doubleheaders, also trying the three-point basket, but even minors wouldn't go to see the Majors.

A special salute belongs to the Chicago Hustle, who created some excitement in DePaul's Alumni Hall from 1978 through 1981. It wasn't their fault that the Women's Basketball League folded, because the Hustle earned their nickname. They played a crowd-pleasing game, triggered by 5'6" playmaker Rita Easterling. Her quickness was a match for some NBA guards, but she couldn't lift the Hustle to a WBL championship.

After some internal strife that led to Doug Bruno replacing Bill Gleason as head coach, the Hustle built up a loyal following of 3,000 or more for home games. The league couldn't scrounge up enough backing to survive until it landed a TV contract, so the entertaining Chicago team vanished after just three seasons.

Another group of Chicago women who proved they had talent performed for the All-American Girls Baseball League in 1948. The league had been founded in 1943 by Cub owner P. K. Wrigley to provide some Midwest entertainment during World War II. It flourished briefly with teams like the Rockford, Illinois, Peaches and Grand Rapids, Michigan, Chicks, but never caught on in Chicago, despite a Wrigley Field showcase when the Cubs were on the road.

With the television age dawning and cars rolling off post-war assembly lines, Wrigley's women faced too much competition to last. In 1948 the league switched to overhand pitching from a distance of 52 feet. The players soon adjusted to the new challenge, but the All-American Girls League was down to five teams by 1954, and soon became only a fond memory.

The Cougars' Rosaire Paiement is up after beating Whalers' goalie Al Smith at the Amphitheater, but the Coogs couldn't stay afloat in the shoestring financial setup of the World Hockey Association. Eventually, they died of fan neglect and cash starvation.

Cougar Hockey More like Hookey

Last and deservedly least are the Chicago Cougars, a World Hockey Association entry in the mid-'70s. Even the purchase of the Coogs in 1974 by popular Hawk defenseman Pat (Whitey) Stapleton, along with Dave Dryden and Ralph Backstrom, couldn't save them from oblivion.

The only salvation might have been Bobby Hull's triumphal return to Chicago in a Cougar uniform. The Winnipeg Jets foiled that plan to enbarrass the Blackhawks, refusing to turn the Golden Jet loose while he was packing rinks all over Canada. The demise of the WHA caused severe pain in the wallet for both it and the NHL, but no pangs of nostalgia. Only long-underpaid hockey players won this war.